Acknowledgments First and foremost, deepest thanks to my husband
and partner in business and life, Klark Perez, for your incredible devotion and
strength in carrying the weight for both of us and our company, InVision
Digital and Media Arts, while I was writing. You juggled everything—from our
training around the world to my marathon writing schedule—without missing
a beat, and still found room to take on more with a smile.

Thanks to Patty Montesion for a career I adore as an Apple Certified Trainer
and the extraordinary opportunity to write this book. Your positive attitude,
energy, and enthusiasm for the program that you built from the ground up are
one of a kind. Also Jessica Steigerwald and Adam Green: What can I say? Your
guidance and support are invaluable.

Special thanks to Whitney Walker for your amazing leadership, patience, and
care with every element of this book. Thanks to Justine Withers for expertly
diving into the last lessons. Thanks also to Stephen Kanter for your insight
and notes, and Joanne Gosnell for your wonderful eye for grammatical detail.
Thanks to Serena Herr, Nancy Peterson, Laurie Stewart, Valerie Perry, and the
amazing Peachpit Press team for making this book a reality.

Thank you Alec Little for first introducing me to Soundtrack Pro and also thanks
to Apple's Soundtrack Pro team for revolutionizing audio postproduction.
A big thanks to my friends Byron Wijayawardena, Damian Allen, Adam Green,
Richard Harrington, Chris Bremer, David Hudacsko, and Camillo Brena for
helping me find and secure rights for the wonderful media used in this book.

Thanks to our friends at Universal Studios Florida for the opportunity to have
a production company and training center on the lot.

Extra special thanks to my family for their unconditional love throughout my
freelance career. Thanks "Meem," Lee, Dad, Ginny, Chris, Sessely, Jorin, Landon,
Kim, Guy, Emily, Chris, Jackson, Warren, Loretta, Chase, Bill, Paula, Peg, Jim,
Sergio, Virginia, Kent, Klark, and my dog Niki.

Contents at a Glance

Table of Contents

Working with Production Sound 240

Analyzing Files in the Waveform Editor 255

Working with Ambience 263

Lesson Review 274

Lesson 7   Recording Audio 277

Preparing the Project 278

Planning Your Recording Session 278

Exploring Both Recording Methods 281

Preparing the Project 292

Editing Recorded Files in the Timeline 293

Lesson Review 298

Lesson 8   Mixing Audio 301

Preparing the Project 302

Evaluating a Song 305

Understanding Basic Mixing 310

Balancing Volume Levels 311

Balancing Panning Levels 322

Automating Volume Level and Pan Envelopes 326

Recording Envelope Points in the Timeline and Mixer 337

Lesson Review 343

Lesson 9   Working with Audio Effects and
Finishing the Mix 347

Preparing the Project 348

Working with Realtime Effects 348

Working with Effects in the Mixer 359

Automating Effect Parameters 366

Working with Busses and Sends 371

Adding Effects to the Project 377

Setting the Overall Project Volume Level 379

Lesson Review 384

Getting Started

Welcome to the official training course for Soundtrack Pro, Apple's dynamic and powerful sound design and audio post-production software.

This book is a detailed guide to using Soundtrack Pro to create high-quality soundtracks for your music and video productions. It is based on the premise that a training book should go beyond a basic tour of the application by providing you with practical, professional techniques that you will use on a daily basis to add professional-quality sound design, music, and audio effects to your projects.

Whether you are a seasoned sound designer, or have never edited an audio project before, you will learn how to use Soundtrack Pro for a variety of real-world scenarios, including sound design for a suspense scene, audio effects editing for a film trailer, voiceover and dialog editing for a public service announcement, and mixing tracks for a professionally recorded pop song. You'll also record and save your own files, export projects as a mix, separate tracks, and use the companion Soundtrack Loop utility to tag and organize your files.

The Methodology

As part of the *Apple Pro Training Series,* this book emphasizes hands-on training. Each exercise is designed to help you learn the application inside and out, starting with the basic interface and moving on to editing and arranging audio clips in the Timeline using some of the 5000 files that come with the application. Then you'll move on to the Waveform Editor, where you'll modify sound effects and repair and enhance dialog. Finally, you'll learn to record and mix effects and output.

The book assumes a basic level of familiarity with the Apple OS X operating system. If you are new to Soundtrack Pro, it would be helpful for you to start at the beginning and progress through each lesson in order, since each builds on information learned in previous ones. If you are already familiar with Soundtrack Pro, you can start with any section and focus on that topic.

Course Structure

Video editors, audio hobbyists, and music producers switching to Soundtrack Pro from other audio or editing programs will have the most to gain by reading this book, which is designed to be an introduction to Soundtrack Pro and is not meant for those who have a lot of experience using this program. That doesn't mean that the book's lessons are basic in nature. Soundtrack Pro is sophisticated software, and the lessons are divided into seven sections to cover all aspects of sound design and audio post-production:

Lessons 1–2	Working with the interface
Lessons 3–4	Sound design and arrangement in the Timeline
Lessons 5–6	Working with the Waveform Editor
Lessons 7–9	Recording, mixing, and effects
Lesson 10	Exporting and managing files
Lesson 11	Advanced Soundtrack Pro techniques
Lesson 12	Using Soundtrack Pro with other Apple Pro applications

Working with the Interface

Lessons 1 and 2 lay the groundwork by introducing you to Soundtrack Pro, the interface, navigation, layout, the difference between time-based and beats-based projects, how to set the project properties, and some basic functions, such as searching for files and arranging them in the Timeline—techniques you'll use throughout the book.

Sound Design and Arrangement in the Timeline

In Lessons 3 and 4, you'll create the soundtrack for a suspense scene from scratch, including a full array of sound effects and music. You'll start by planning the scene's sound design and then add and sync reality sound effects to the picture. Next, you'll build additional tracks with foley sound effects and ambience. Finally you'll audition and select a musical part, double it, and transpose the score. Along the way, you'll also learn to create and save new window layout, and work with markers to help organize and sync the different audio clips.

Working with the Waveform Editor

Lessons 5 and 6 focus on the powerful Waveform Editor. First, you'll learn to open audio files from the Timeline into the Waveform Editor to amplify, stretch, edit, and customize the sound. Then you'll work with voiceover and dialog in the Waveform Editor to normalize, amplify, add ambience, silence, reduce noise, and analyze files to find and fix common problems like clicks and pops.

Recording, Mixing, and Effects

Lessons 7 through 9 step you through recording, mixing, and adding effects. First, in Lesson 7 you'll learn to set up your equipment and record and edit single and multitake recordings. Next, in Lesson 8 you'll mix a song, starting with balancing the volume and panning levels, then adding automation to the volume and pan envelopes to change the values over time. Once the basic mix is complete, in Lesson 9 you'll add effects to the tracks, group tracks together using a bus, and add effects to the entire project. Finally, you'll modify the output levels to prevent clipping.

Exporting and Managing Files

In Lesson 10, you'll work with the various export methods, including exporting a mix, selected tracks, busses, or outputs. You'll also learn to export with Compressor, reconnect media to a project, and save projects collected for archiving.

Advanced Soundtrack Pro Techniques

Lesson 11 is a collection of techniques ranging from scoring a marker to the playhead, to changing a clip's speed or offset. You'll also learn how to mix multiple outputs, and work with control surfaces so that you can use external mixing hardware with Soundtrack Pro.

Using Soundtrack Pro with other Apple Pro Applications

Lesson 12 illustrates the basics of integrating Soundtrack Pro with the other Final Cut Studio applications including Final Cut Pro, Motion, and DVD Studio Pro.

About the Footage

One of the most important things in a project-based book like this is the quality of the projects. I'm very fortunate to have so many talented friends and colleagues who contributed their work to this book. The wide range of real-world projects you'll work with originated in formats from DV, high-definition, and film. All of the projects were edited in Final Cut Pro.

Animated Clapboard Lessons 1, 2, 10, and 12. Created by Damian Allen for the book *Apple Pro Training Series: Motion,* Lesson 15.

Bloodlust Lessons 3, 4, and 10. The scene is from *Bloodlust,* a short film derived from *Bram Stoker's Dracula,* made by students at the ArtsEd School of Acting in London, 2002. Written and directed by Michael Ferguson, starring Margeret Sverris and Terje Naudeer, filmed and edited by Lisa James-Larson, production manager Rebecca Pearson, and original music by Jonnie Harrison. Shot using a Canon XL1 camera and edited on Final Cut Pro. Contact: drama@artsed.co.uk.

The Tangerine Dream Lessons 5 and 11. From acclaimed producers, Teton Gravity Research, comes a 16-mm ski and snowboard film that features some of the most progressive riding and remote locations ever caught on film.

Executive Producers/TGR Founders: Dirk Collins, Todd Jones, Corey Gavitt and Steve Jones; Supervising Producer: Josh Nielsen; Editor: Tate MacDowell; Graphics Editor: Jason Fish; Principal Cinematographers: Dirk Collins, Todd Jones, Corey Gavitt, Steve Jones, Dustin Handley, Pete O'brien, and Matt Herriger; Passengers: Sage Cattabriga-Alosa, Jeremy Jones, Chris Collins, Micah Black, Marc-Andre Belliveau, Victoria Jealouse, Jeremy Nobis, Peter Olenick, Michael Olenick, Ryan Oakden, Dana Flahr, Dylan Hood, Dash Longe, Erik Roner, Skogen Sprang, Travis Rice, Candide Thovex, Karina Hollekim, Will Burks, and more.

The Tangerine Dream is a film that represents 10 years of broken-down trucks, whiskey bottles, wanderlust, and the most down and dirty skiing and boarding that have ever been filmed. This vagabond tale takes you through the lifestyle of outlaw athletes whose skiing and passion continues to change the face of the sport. Filmed on location in India, Turkey, Switzerland, France, Alaska, Aspen, Utah, Montana, California, and Jackson Hole. *The Tangerine Dream* is currently playing on tour across the United States. Contact: www.tetongravity.com.

ADA Tour de Cure PSA Lessons 6 and 10. Part of a series of national PSA spots for the American Diabetes Association (ADA) in high-definition video produced by RHED Pixel. The PSA was created to help recruit more Tour de Cure participants, as well as raise more funds to support the ADA's mission.

RHED Pixel chose to shoot in HD so that the ADA's message could achieve greater impact by broadcasting on both standard and high-definition channels. The Tour de Cure is one of the ADA's key fund-raising events, and includes dramatic jib shots combined with first-person camera angles from a unique bike-mounted camera.

Extensive coverage was provided by DPs James Ball and Joe Di Gennaro during the ride. All post-production was handled in-house by RHED Pixel's staff, and the project was produced by RHED Pixel's Sara Evans and directed by Stephen Menick. RHED Pixel shot footage from the Napa Valley and Silicon Valley Tour de Cure events. The PSA will premiere in Spring 2006.

The footage was captured using the new Kona2 HD card, an uncompressed HDTV 10-bit QuickTime card for Mac OS X. With Kona's HD card, RHED Pixel is able to work with footage at a superior quality. Contact: www.RhedPixel.com

Something About You Lessons 7, 8, 9, and 10. Produced by Adam Green, Hector Rios (lead guitar), Thor Jeppesen (bass), Steve Purtic (drums), Jose Ortiz (lead vocals), and Gus Rios (rhythm guitar).

Guitar Riff Lesson 10. Performed and recorded by Camillo Brena.

West Coast Styles Lesson 11. West Coast Style—Freeride Fundamentals is the culmination of over 20 years of mountain bike training from world-class instructors Joan Jones and Daamiann Skelton of the West Coast School of Mountain Biking. Filmed on location in Vancouver, Canada, producer Chris Bremer and director Michael Maguire assembled a team of world champion riders, instructors, and video production professionals to create a comprehensive and easy to understand training video for beginning to advanced mountain bikers.

Freeride Fundamentals was photographed on Panasonic's DVX-100, using the 30p frame rate. Post-production took place over six months, in Orlando, Florida, and in Vancouver. Final Cut Pro project files were transferred remotely between the editor's workstations and instructor's Macs using iDisk. This allowed the instructors to maintain a close eye on the educational content, while being on the opposite side of the continent. DVD Studio Pro was used to author the DVD. More information is available at www.westcoaststyle.net.

Same Conversation Lesson 12. Same Conversation was written and directed by award-winning cinematographer Jon Fordham and produced by Melissa Drotar and Chris Bremer in Orlando, Florida. It was photographed on Sony's DSR-500WSPL/1 in PAL DVCAM by cinematographer Chris Wissinger. Chris Bremer edited on Final Cut Pro 5 using a Powerbook G4. Soundtrack Pro was used extensively in sound design and dialogue cleanup for the two actors, Mike Lane and Meg Wozniak. Same Conversation ©2005 Karmic Pictures.

System Requirements

Before beginning to use *Apple Pro Training Series: Soundtrack Pro,* you should have a working knowledge of your computer and its operating system. Make sure that you know how to use the mouse and standard menus and commands and also how to open, save, and close files. If you need to review these techniques, see the printed or online documentation included with your system.

▶ Macintosh computer with PowerPC G4 or G5 processor (450MHz or faster dual processors or 500MHz or faster single processor; 733MHz or faster recommended)

▶ Mac OS X v 10.3.9 or later

▶ QuickTime 7.0 or later

▶ 512MB RAM (1GB recommended)

▶ AGP or PCI Express graphics card

▶ Display with 1024-by-768 resolution or higher (1280-by-1024 resolution recommended)

▶ 500MB of available disk space for application installation; 8GB for installation of all Soundtrack Pro content (may be installed on separate disks)

Copying the Lesson Files

This book includes an *APTS_Soundtrack_Pro* DVD of all the necessary files you will need to complete the lessons. The Soundtrack Pro book files folder on the DVD includes numbered Projects&Media folders containing the applicable projects and media for each lesson. Some of the Projects&Media folders also contain additional files for non-Soundtrack media such as a DVD Studio Pro, Motion, or Final Cut Pro projects.

While installing these files on your computer, it's important to keep all of the numbered Projects&Media folders together inside the main Soundtrack Pro book files folder on your hard drive. If you copy the entire Soundtrack Pro book files folder directly from the DVD to your hard drive, you should not have to reconnect your project files to the media.

Installing the Lesson Files

1   Put the *APTS_Soundtrack_Pro* DVD into your computer's DVD drive.

2   Drag the Soundtrack Pro book files folder from the DVD to the desktop, or a location on the hard drive.

3   To begin each lesson, launch Soundtrack Pro, then follow the instructions at the beginning of the lesson to open the project files for that lesson.

Reconnecting Broken Media Links

In the process of copying the media from this book's DVD, you may break a link between the project file and the media file. If this happens, the next time you open a project file a window will appear saying that it can't find a file and asking you to reconnect the project files. Reconnecting the project files is a simple process. Just follow these steps:

1   If the Can't Find File window appears, click the Find File button.

2   Navigate to where the Soundtrack Pro book files folder resides on your hard drive, then go to the specific Projects&Media subfolder for the current lesson.

3   Select the media file you wish to reconnect from the File Browser.

4   Click the Use Selected Path to Reconnect Other Missing Files checkbox to make sure that it is selected (checked).

5   Click the Choose button to reconnect all the media for that project.

6   Repeat steps 2 and 3 until all project files have been reconnected.

About the Apple Pro Training Series

Apple Pro Training Series: Soundtrack Pro is part of the official training series for Apple Pro applications, developed by experts in the field and certified by Apple Computer. The series offers complete training in all Apple Pro products. The lessons are designed to let you learn at your own pace. Although each lesson provides step-by-step instructions for creating specific projects, there's room for exploration and experimentation. You can progress through the book from beginning to end, or dive right into the lessons that interest you most. Each lesson concludes with a review section summarizing what you've covered.

Apple Pro Certification Program

The Apple Pro Training and Certification Program is designed to keep you at the forefront of Apple's digital media technology while giving you a competitive edge in today's ever-changing job market. Whether you're an editor, graphic designer, sound designer, special effects artist, or teacher, these training tools are meant to help you expand your skills.

Upon completing the course material in this book, you can become a certified Apple Pro by taking the certification exam at an Apple Authorized Training Center. Certification is offered in Final Cut Pro, DVD Studio Pro, Shake, Motion, Logic, Aperture, and Soundtrack Pro. Successful certification as an Apple Pro gives you official recognition of your knowledge of Apple's professional applications while allowing you to market yourself to employers and clients as a skilled, pro-level user of Apple products.

For those who prefer to learn in an instructor-led setting, Apple also offers training courses at Apple Authorized Training Centers worldwide. These courses, which use the *Apple Pro Training Series* books as their curriculum, are taught by Apple Certified Trainers and balance concepts and lectures with hands-on labs and exercises. Apple Authorized Training Centers have been carefully selected and have met Apple's highest standards in all areas, including facilities, instructors, course delivery, and infrastructure. The goal of the program is to offer Apple customers, from beginners to the most seasoned professionals, the highest-quality training experience. To find an Authorized Training Center near you, go to www.apple.com/software/pro/training.

Resources

Apple Pro Training Series: Soundtrack Pro is not intended to be a comprehensive reference manual, nor does it replace the documentation that comes with the application. For more information about program features discussed in this book, refer to these resources:

▶   The Reference Guide. Accessed through the Soundtrack Pro Help menu, the Reference Guide contains a complete description of all features.

▶   Apple's website: www.apple.com.

1

Lesson Files	Soundtrack Pro book files > 01-02_Projects&Media > 1-1 Start, 1-2 Final
Time	This lesson takes approximately 60 minutes to complete.
Goals	Launch the Soundtrack Pro program
	Explore the Project window
	Navigate in the Timeline
	Explore the Media and Effects Manager
	Work with the Browser, Favorites, and Bin tabs
	Search for a file and add it to a project
	Extend and move files in the Timeline
	Reverse an audio file in the Waveform Editor
	Open and close the Mixer

Working with the Interface

Soundtrack Pro is powerful enough to arrange, edit, repair, and mix professional audio, yet simple enough that anyone can use it right out of the box.

Over the years, I've worked with many frustrated video and filmmakers who can shoot and edit the visual portion of their projects, but struggle to deal with the many audio issues that occur, including background and ambient noise, mixing, recording, and scoring.

That was before Soundtrack Pro. This software incorporates many of the same interface features as the other Final Cut Studio applications, including Final Cut Pro, DVD Studio Pro, and Motion. Best of all, you don't have to be a computer major or audio engineer to create professional quality soundtracks. If you can click a mouse, you can turn your Mac into an audio post-production studio—it's really that simple.

In this lesson, you'll work with the Soundtrack Pro interface and learn how to search for and preview files, use the transport controls, navigate in the Timeline, and open files in the Waveform Editor. Along the way, you'll also learn some useful keyboard shortcuts as you get to know the program.

Preparing the Project

Before you start, you need to install the Soundtrack Pro application onto your hard drive. You will also need to copy the lesson files from the DVD in the back of the book to your computer.

The instructions for loading the software and files are in the introduction of this book. Once those two steps are complete, you can move forward with this lesson.

Now that you have the Soundtrack Pro program and lesson files loaded onto your hard drive, you're ready to begin this lesson.

Launching Soundtrack Pro

As with any of the Apple Pro applications, there are three ways to launch Soundtrack Pro:

▶ Double-click the Soundtrack Pro icon in the Applications folder of your hard drive.

▶ Click the Soundtrack Pro icon in the Dock.

▶ Double-click any Soundtrack Pro project file.

For this exercise, you'll launch Soundtrack Pro by opening a project file.

1   Locate the Soundtrack Pro book files folder on your computer's desktop, then double-click the folder to open it.

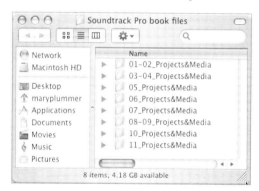

The folder opens, revealing the different lessons organized into Projects& Media folders that correspond with the lessons in the book.

2   Open the 01-02_Projects&Media folder to see all of the projects and media needed for Lessons 1 and 2.

The Introducing Soundtrack Pro folder contains all of the projects and media that you'll need to complete this tutorial.

3   Double-click the **1-1 Start** file to launch Soundtrack Pro and open the project.

When Soundtrack Pro opens, you will see three windows displaying the current project.

Utility window   Project window

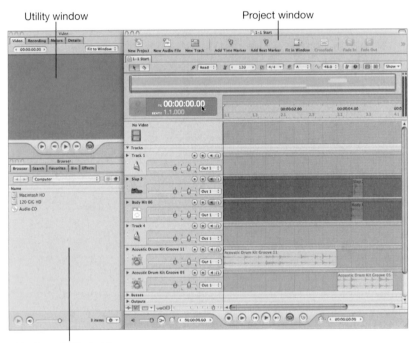

Media and Effects Manager

The largest window at the right is the Project window, which includes the Timeline. This is where you arrange audio files for your project. The two smaller windows at the left are the Utility window and Media and Effects Manager. You can use the Utility window to view a project's video, recording levels, master level meters, and details about individual clips within the project. In the Media and Effects Manager, you can browse, preview, and organize files, as well as add and modify effects.

Let's start with the Project window and play the current project.

Exploring the Project Window

In the Project window, you can create and edit your multitrack projects in the Timeline or edit audio files in the Waveform Editor. If you're familiar with the other Final Cut Studio applications, the Project window is similar to the Timeline window in Final Cut Pro and the Timing Pane in Motion. You'll find a customizable toolbar at the top of the window for easy access to common functions. At the bottom of the window you'll find handy Transport controls, as well as Timeline controls.

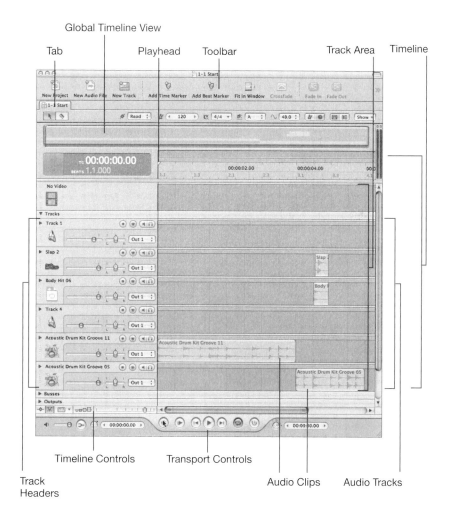

The green audio clips in the Timeline represent audio files that have been imported into the project from the Media and Effects Manager. You can arrange audio clips on tracks in the Soundtrack Timeline similar to the way that you arrange video clips on tracks in the Final Cut Pro Timeline.

The current project has six tracks, containing four different audio clips. These clips come from the Soundtrack Pro content of over 5000 royalty-free audio files included with the application. You can have a combined total of 128 tracks, buses, and outputs in a Soundtrack Pro Multitrack project.

You'll add additional audio clips to the empty tracks in a few minutes after you finish working with basic Timeline navigation.

> **NOTE ▶** If you've worked with the Soundtrack program, you're already familiar with the Timeline portion of the Project window. You can upgrade from Soundtrack to Soundtrack Pro, which will enable you to open your Soundtrack projects in the Soundtrack Pro Timeline.

Playing a Project in the Timeline

As with other Apple Professional applications, you can click the play button in the transport controls or simply press the spacebar to play the project.

1 Press the spacebar to play the project in the Timeline.

The playhead scrubs across the tracks as it moves forward in the Timeline and plays the project. Once the playhead reaches the end of the last clip in the Timeline, it automatically cycles back to play the song again from the beginning.

> **NOTE ▶** You can stop the playhead from cycling back by turning off the Cycle button in the Transport controls. But in general, it's a good idea to leave the Cycle button on unless you need to turn it off for a specific reason. That way whenever you play your project it will automatically repeat so that you can evaluate the sound more easily.

2   Press the spacebar again to stop playback.

The Return key always moves the playhead to the beginning of the project, while Shift-Return starts playback from the beginning of the project.

3   Press Shift-Return to start playback from the beginning of the Timeline.

4   Press the spacebar to stop playback at the current playhead position.

5   Press Return to move the playhead to the beginning of the project without starting playback.

Navigating in the Timeline

Now that you've played the project, you'll learn to navigate and zoom in and out of the Timeline. The current playhead position is displayed in both time-code (TC) and beats in the time display in the top-left corner of the Timeline. Timecode is generally used to reference video and is displayed as four pairs of numbers representing hours:minutes:seconds.frames. Beats represent musical time in measures.beats.fractions of a beat.

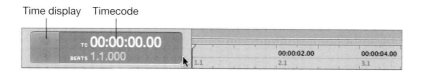

Time display   Timecode

NOTE ▶ The timecode will match any video clip imported into the project.

You can use several different methods to position the playhead in the Timeline: Click anywhere in the Timeline; drag the top of the playhead horizontally in the time ruler; or change the value in the playhead position slider.

1   Click the green triangle-shaped handle at the top of the playhead, and drag horizontally to the right in the Timeline.

You'll hear the sound of the clips as you drag the playhead. Dragging the playhead is called scrubbing because it scrubs the playhead across the clips in the Timeline.

2   Press the End key to move the playhead to the end of the song in the Timeline.

You can also navigate in the Timeline using gridlines.

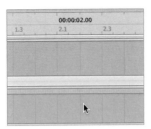

The left and right arrow keys move the playhead right or left one gridline at a time. Gridlines are the vertical gray lines within the tracks that keep beat-based loops in time with the music.

3   Press the left arrow key several times to move the playhead toward the left one gridline at a time.

Whether you drag the playhead or use the left and right arrow keys, the playhead snaps to the nearest gridline. You'll learn more about this feature in the next lesson. For now, you just need to understand basic playhead positioning in the Timeline.

4   Locate the Playhead Position value slider at the bottom-left of the Project Window.

This value slider is similar to the Current Frame value slider used in the Motion interface. Value sliders are unique because you can modify the value by clicking the incremental arrows, selecting the slider and typing a new number, or dragging over the slider with the mouse. Let's try it.

Your goal is to move the playhead to the timecode position 00:00:04.00 (four seconds, zero frames).

TIP In Final Cut Studio applications, you can enter timecode the same way that you enter time on a microwave oven. You don't need to put zero hours, zero minutes, then 30 seconds. Just type 30 seconds—and don't forget to add frames after seconds.

5   Click the Playhead Position value slider to select the timecode.

The timecode within the slider turns blue to indicate that it has been selected.

6   Type *4.00* (that's the number 4, followed by a period and two zeros), and press Return to change the current playhead position to 4 seconds.

The playhead jumps to exactly 4.00 in the Timeline.

Zooming in and out of the Timeline

Now that you can move the playhead around, it's a good time to learn how to zoom in and out of the Timeline.

To zoom in and out of the Timeline, you can use a zoom slider and keyboard shortcuts. The Zoom slider is located directly above the Playhead Position value slider at the bottom-left of the Project window. Since you're already in that neighborhood of the interface, let's take a moment to look at a few of the other Timeline controls.

The Zoom slider always zooms in and out of the playhead or selected clips. Since there are no clips selected, you will be zooming into the playhead position at four seconds in the Timeline.

1   Drag the Zoom slider to the left to zoom in to Timeline at the playhead position.

2   Drag the Zoom slider to the right to zoom out of the playhead position.

Notice that the dark gray scrollbar at the right of the Zoom slider changes size depending on the current zoom scale in the Timeline.

You can also drag the left and right edges of the horizontal Zoom slider to zoom in and out of the Timeline.

3   Drag the right edge of the scrollbar to change the scale in the Timeline.

Keep in mind that the scrollbar moves left and right to view different portions of the Timeline. If you happened to drag the entire scrollbar to the right, you may not see any of the clips in the Timeline.

Once you are zoomed in or out of the Timeline, you might want to condense or expand the entire project to fit in the Timeline window.

4   At the top of the Project window, click the Fit in Window button on the Toolbar.

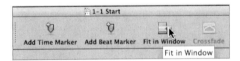

The Timeline scale changes to show the project from the beginning to the last clip at the end.

One of the easiest ways to zoom in and out is to use the up and down arrow keys. The up arrow zooms in, and the down arrow zooms out.

5   Press and hold the up arrow key to zoom all the way in to the Timeline.

Working with the Global Timeline View

When you're zoomed into the Timeline, or working with a large project with many tracks, you may need to use the Global Timeline View, located above the Time ruler, for navigation. The Global Timeline View shows a miniature version of the entire project.

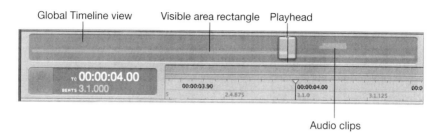

Global Timeline view   Visible area rectangle   Playhead

Audio clips

The visible area rectangle within the Global Timeline View represents the portion of the project that is currently visible in the Timeline window. Let's use the Global Timeline view to navigate to the beginning of the Sound Effects (SFX) clips on tracks 2 and 3.

Global Timeline View of SFX

1   In the Global Timeline View, drag the visible area rectangle to the right until you see the Slap and Body Hit sound effects appear in the Timeline.

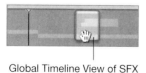

Global Timeline View of SFX

2 Press the down arrow key several times to zoom out of the Timeline until you can see the entire sound effects clips on tracks 2 and 3 in the Timeline.

The visible area rectangle in the Global Timeline view grows longer to reflect the zoom level change in the Timeline.

To fit the entire project in the Timeline, you can click the Fit in Window button again or use the handy shortcut.

3 Press Shift-Z to fit the project in the Timeline window.

The visible area rectangle in the Global Timeline view fits the entire global view, illustrating that you can currently see the entire project.

NOTE ▶ You can also use Final Cut Pro shortcuts to zoom in and out of the Soundtrack Pro Timeline. Press Cmd= (equal sign) to zoom in, and Cmd– (minus sign) to zoom out. Shift-Z also works to fit a project in the Timeline window in Final Cut Pro.

Now that you're familiar with the Project window, let's move on to the Media and Effects Manager.

Exploring the Media and Effects Manager

The Media and Effects Manager does exactly what its name suggests; it helps you manage your media and effects. In the next series of exercises, you'll work with several of the different tabs within this window as you add media files to the current project.

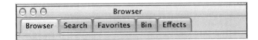

The Media and Effects Manager includes five different tabs. The Browser, Search, and Favorites tabs offer three different ways to locate your media files. The Bin tab displays all of the files in the current project, and the Effects tab can be used to add or modify effects.

Working with the Browser Tab

Like other Apple Pro Applications, the Browser allows you to access any compatible media file on your computer or network. For this exercise, you'll use the browser to locate the 01-02 Projects&Media folder in the Soundtrack Pro book files folder on your hard drive.

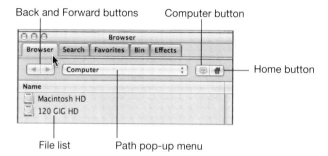

▶ *Back and Forward buttons:* Move through previously viewed levels of the hierarchy

▶ *Computer button:* Displays your computer's hard disk, internal drives, and other storage media currently connected to your computer

▶ *Home button:* Displays the contents of your computer's home directory

▶ *Path pop-up menu:* Displays the different levels of the file path to the current location, letting you view and move back to a previous level

▶ *File list:* Displays the files and folders at the current location

1 Click the Browser tab, if it is not already selected.

The title bar at the top of the Media and Effects manager reflects the name of the selected tab.

2 On the Browser tab, navigate to the 01-02_Projects&Media folder in the Soundtrack Pro book files folder.

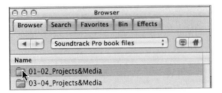

NOTE ► If you placed the Soundtrack Pro book files folder on the desktop of your computer, the path will be Home > Desktop > Soundtrack Pro book files > 01-02_Projects&Media.

3 Double-click the 01-02_Projects&Media folder to view the media contents of that folder in the Browser.

At the top of the list you'll see a file called **1_ClapBoard.mov**. This is a QuickTime movie file that you will add to the current project. First, it's a good idea to preview the file.

You can preview both audio and video files in the browser by selecting the file and pressing the play button in the bottom-left corner of the Media and Effects window.

4 Click the **1_ClapBoard.mov** file on the Browser to select the file.

5 Click the Play button at the bottom of the Media and Effects window to preview the file.

The Details tab in the Utility window becomes active and displays detailed information about the selected video file.

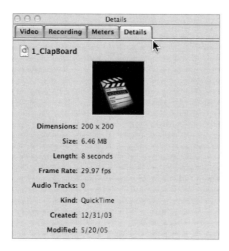

You can now preview a small thumbnail version of the **1_ClapBoard.mov** video file in the details tab.

NOTE ▶ You can preview audio files without using the Details tab. Previewing video clips requires the Details tab because there is no other way to see a video file without first importing it into the project.

The Details tab includes video file information such as the Dimensions of the clip, Size, Length, and Frame Rate. This clip is 8 seconds long, therefore the length of the finished project will also be 8 seconds.

Adding a Video File to a Project

Now that you've located the video file that you'll be scoring for this project, it's time to add it to the current project.

Keep in mind that Soundtrack Pro is an audio program. That means it can only be used to create and modify audio. Of course, you can add a video file to a project; you just can't modify the video file once it has been imported into the Timeline.

To add a video file, simply drag it to the video track at the top of the Timeline or drag it directly to the Video tab in the Utility window. Since you're already looking at the Details tab of the Utility window, you can just switch tabs and drag the file there.

1 In the Utility window, click the Video tab, or press Cmd-1.

The Video tab becomes active.

2 Drag the **1_ClapBoard.mov** file from the Browser tab to the empty space in the Video tab.

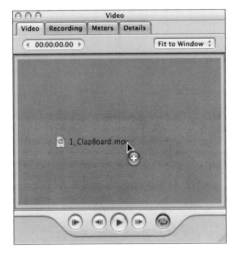

A small green circle with a plus sign (+) appears before you release the file to indicate that you'll be adding a file to the project.

Once you've added a video clip to a project, you can see it in the Video tab, and it also appears as a clip in the Video track at the top of the Timeline.

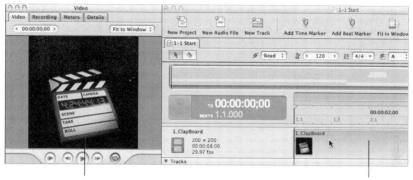

Video clip in Video tab   Video clip in Video track on Timeline

3   Click the Play/Pause button on the Video tab, or press the spacebar, to begin playback of the project.

Now you know why there are sound effects along with the drum loops in the project. The sound effects were added to accentuate the slap of the clapboard in the video.

You've probably also noticed by now that the drum clips need to be extended to last the entire length of the video clip. You also might have noticed that the project continually loops over and over from beginning to end until you stop it.

4   Pause playback, if you haven't already done so.

Time to add some more audio files to finish the project.

NOTE ▶ The **1_ClapBoard.mov** was created by Damian Allen, who is a professional commercial artist, Apple Certified Trainer, and author of *Apple Pro Training Series: Motion* (Peachpit Press).

Adding a File to Favorites

The Browser tab is used for locating files anywhere on your computer. Once you've located a file or folder, you can add it to the Favorites tab for easy access in the future.

While the Browser tab is still selected in the Media and Effects window, this is a perfect time to add a file to the Favorites tab using a shortcut menu. Like most of the Apple Pro Applications, Soundtrack Pro is loaded with handy shortcut menus, also known as contextual menus, which you can use to choose certain functions and features without going to the menus at the top of the interface.

You can access a shortcut menu by holding the Ctrl key and clicking the mouse, or clicking with the right mouse button if you have a two-button mouse.

1   On the Browser tab, Ctrl-click the **1_ClapBoard.mov** clip.

A shortcut menu appears with several choices pertaining to the selected file in the browser.

2   Choose Add to Favorites from the Shortcut menu.

Once you've completed a selection, the Shortcut menu disappears, and you've successfully added the **1_ClapBoard.mov** to your Favorites tab. How do you know? Just check the Favorites tab.

3   Click the Favorites tab on the Media and Effects Manager to view any files or folders that you've added to Favorites.

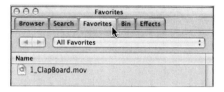

The **1_ClapBoard.mov** appears in the Favorites tab.

Files in the Favorites tab are easily accessible without additional navigation, and can be used in any of your Soundtrack Pro projects.

Using Files in the Bin Tab

To the right of the Favorites tab you'll find the Bin tab. The Bin tab contains a list of all the files used in the current project. The Favorites can be accessed from any project, including new projects, while the Bin tab only shows the files used in the current project. In this exercise you'll add a file to the project from the Bin tab.

1   Click the Bin tab to view the files used in the current project.

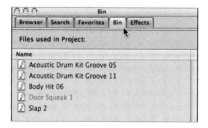

The Bin tab shows five different audio files, while the project clearly contains only four.

2   Click any of the audio files in the Bin tab to hear it.

NOTE ▶ If you accidentally double-click a file, you'll open an alert window regarding your Double-Click Preference. Click the Cancel button and try single-clicking on a different file.

3   Click the up or down arrow keys to select clips higher or lower in the list.

If you look closely, you'll see that four of the files are listed in black type, while the **Door Squeak 1** file is in lighter gray type. File names that appear in gray in the Bin tab have not been used, or are no longer in the current project, but can be added in the future. This is actually a very useful feature because if you change your mind and want to add a file that had previously been deleted, you don't have to go back and search for it again.

Sounds good, but actions speak louder than words. Let's add the **Door Squeak 1** file to Track 1 in the Timeline.

4   Drag the **Door Squeak 1** file from the Bin tab to Track 1 in the Timeline, and drop it around the middle of the track.

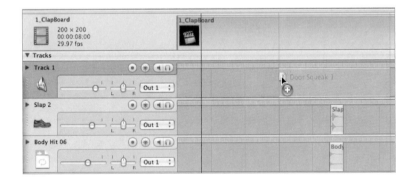

The green add symbol (circle with plus sign) appears to show that you are adding an audio file to the Timeline.

Now that the **Door Squeak 1** clip is in the Timeline, the file no longer appears gray in the Bin tab.

Also notice that the name of the track in the Timeline changed from Track 1 to Door Squeak 1. That's because empty tracks will assume the name of the first audio file added to that track.

5 Press Shift-Return to play the project from the beginning and hear the new sound effect with the rest of the clips.

6 Press the spacebar to pause playback.

Don't worry if you're Door Squeak sound effect doesn't match the video clip—you'll fix it shortly.

Searching for Audio Files

The Search tab is the last tab that you'll explore in the Media and Effects manager. The Search tab lets you easily access the 5000 audio files that come with Soundtrack Pro, along with any other audio files you add to your collection. The powerful search engine uses metadata (tags) within the audio files as search criteria. You'll learn more about tagging files with metadata in a later lesson. For now, you'll just familiarize yourself with the Search tab.

▶ *Button and Column view buttons:* Change the keyword view to either Button or Column view

▶ *Category pop-up menu:* Allows you to choose a particular category for the search

▶ *Setup button:* Opens the Search Setup dialog, so that you can add items to the Search database

▶ *Time Signature pop-up menu:* Allows you to limit search results to files with the selected time signature

▶ *File Type pop-up menu:* Allows you to choose whether to display all files, or only looping or non-looping files

▶ *Scale Type pop-up menu:* Limits your search results to audio files using the selected scale

▶ *Keyword buttons (Button view only):* Displays files matching the keyword in the Results list

▶ *Keywords list (Column view only):* Displays files matching the keyword in the Results list, and displays subcategories in the Matches list

▶ *Search Text Field:* Allows you to type text in the field to display matching files in the Search Results list

▶ *Nearby Keys button:* Limits search results to keys within two semitones above or below the current project key

▶ *Search Results list:* Shows the files matching the selected search criteria, in alphabetical order. Includes additional file information in columns displaying the tempo, key, and number of beats of each file

▶ *Preview controls:* Allows you to Play, Mute, or adjust the volume of selected items in the search list as you preview them using these controls

▶ *Media pop-up menu:* Allows you to choose menu items to add a Favorite, add a file to the Bin, open a file in the Waveform Editor, and perform other functions

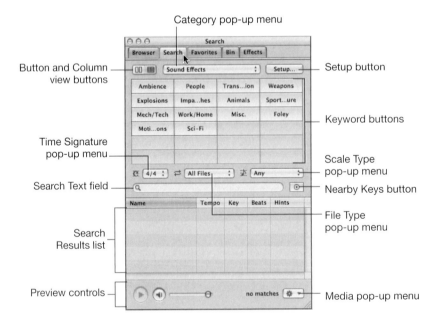

In this exercise, you'll use the Search tab to locate a specific guitar part for the current project, then add it to Track 4 in the Timeline.

1   Click the Search tab in the Media and Effects Manager.

The Search tab opens in either Column or Button view.

2   Click the Button view button to change the search keywords to buttons, if you are not already in button view.

3   Change the Category pop-up menu to Best Mix.

This button category includes a mix of common instruments, descriptors, and genres.

4   Click the Guitars keyword button.

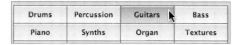

At the bottom-right corner of the Search tab, you'll see that the results include 514 items. You may see a different number if you have indexed additional files.

It could take a while to preview that many files. Instead, let's narrow the search further. Since you're looking for a guitar part with a nice delay effect already applied, you could try using the search text field.

5   Type *delay* in the search text field.

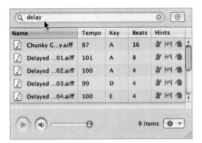

The search results narrow to 9 items—that's much more reasonable for this exercise.

If you can't read the filenames in the Name category, you can simply drag the right edge of the Name column header to extend it.

6   Drag the right edge of the Name column header toward the right until you can read the full names of the files in the list.

NOTE ▶ The Name column sorts the files alphabetically by name. If you clicked on the Name header while resizing it, you may have reversed the alphabetical sort. If so, click the Name column header again so that the **Chunky Guitar Delay.aiff** file is at the top of the results list.

7   Select the **Chunky Guitar Delay.aiff** file at the top of the list to preview (listen to) the file.

8   Press Cmd-I (I for Information), or click the Details tab in the Utility window to see details on the selected file.

By now you've noticed that the **Chunky Guitar Delay.aiff** file plays over and over. That is because it is a Looping file, designed as a musical part that can be repeated continually. Feel free to click the pause button at the bottom of the Media and Effects manager once you've heard the file loop a few times.

The Details tab includes information about the file, including the author's name, Sample Rate, Tempo, etc. If you look in the bottom-right corner of the Details tab, you'll see that it shows Looping file: Yes.

9   Drag the **Chunky Guitar Delay.aiff** file from the Search tab to the beginning of Track 4 in the Timeline to add the file to the project.

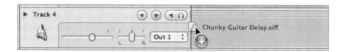

That's it. You're finished with the Search tab. Just one bit of housekeeping before moving on to the project in the Timeline. It's always a good idea to clear the search text field once you've completed a search so that your next search isn't limited to your previous search text.

10   Click the Reset button, which looks like an *X*, on the right side of the Search Text field.

11   Click the Video Tab, or press Cmd-1.

Now you're ready to finish the project in the Timeline.

Working with Files in the Timeline

Before you perform the last step for completing this project—extending or moving some of the files in the Timeline—you need to understand the difference between looping and non-looping files. (Soundtrack Pro supports both.) Most audio files, such as sound effects, are non-looping and do not change key or tempo as the project changes. But looping files, or loops, are designed and recorded to repeat and are usually used for musical parts. Loops are also tagged with information so that they will automatically adjust to match the project's key and tempo. You'll work more with the different file types, and changing project key and tempo in the next lesson.

First, you'll extend the looping drum files, and trim the end of the Door Squeak 1 file. Then, you'll move the Door Squeak 1 file into position so that it matches the action on the screen.

1   Click the Project window to make it active.

2   Press Shift-Z or Click the Fit in Window button on the Toolbar to fit the project to the window, if it is not already sized accordingly.

Extending Loops

The musical files on the lower three tracks are all loops. The Chunky Guitar Delay loop is already the same length as the video clip, so it does not need resizing. The Acoustic Drum Kit Groove 11 and 05 loops will need resizing. As you can see, all three loops in the project are different lengths. The length of the loop depends on the length of the original recording.

Rounded edges are just one of the features that distinguish looping files from non-looping files.

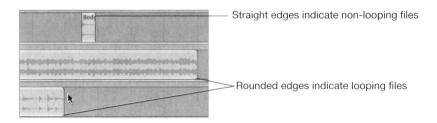

Straight edges indicate non-looping files

Rounded edges indicate looping files

1   Move the pointer over the right edge of the **Acoustic Drum Kit Groove 11** loop in the Timeline.

Selection Tool

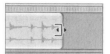

Resize Tool

The Selection arrow changes to a Resize tool.

2   With the Resize tool, drag the right edge of the **Acoustic Drum Kit Groove 11** loop toward the right to extend it one full loop segment.

Notches

The extended loop now repeats twice, with notches showing where the first looped segment ends and the second segment begins.

3   Extend the **Acoustic Drum Kit Groove 05** loop on Track 6 one full segment to the right.

The original **Acoustic Drum Kit Groove 05** loop was shorter in length, so the looped segments are also shorter than those in the track above.

4   Press Shift-Return to play the project; then pause playback.

Resizing Non-Looping Files

Next, you'll resize the Door Squeak 1 file to trim off the excess on the right edge of the clip in the Timeline. For this maneuver, you'll apply some of the skills that you learned earlier in the lesson, and learn a few new ones along the way.

1   Move the playhead over the middle of the Door Squeak 1 clip in the Timeline.

2 Press the up arrow key several times to zoom into the Timeline at the playhead position.

Now you have a pretty good view of the clip, but this would be a good time to make the tracks a little larger by clicking on the different track height buttons at the bottom of the Timeline. These buttons work the same in Final Cut Pro and Motion.

3 Click one of the larger Track Height buttons to resize the Timeline tracks.

4 On the Global Timeline View, drag the visible area rectangle up to view the top track in the Timeline, if you don't already see it.

When you make the tracks larger, the waveforms within each clip become larger as well. Now you can clearly see the waveform within the Door Squeak 1 clip. The waveform is the visual representation of the sound wave.

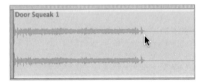

Waveform

Extending a non-looping file only reveals more of the waveform or empty space. In this case, you can already see the complete file, so extending it will only reveal empty space.

5 Extend the right edge of the Door Squeak 1 file to the right to demonstrate the empty clip space on a non-looping file.

Resizing files will always snap to the nearest gridline, unless the snapping feature is turned off. In this exercise, you'll work with snapping turned on.

Next you'll trim off the empty clip space to remove the portion of the clip without any audio. You can determine where the audio starts and stops by viewing the waveform within the clip.

6   Drag the right edge of the same file to the left as close as you can get to the end of the waveform without trimming any of the waveform off.

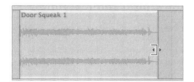

Now that you've trimmed the file, you'll need to move it so that the waveform ends right as the waveform for the Slap 2 file begins on the lower tracks.

To move a file rather than resize it, you simply select it from somewhere in the middle, away from the edge.

7   Select the Door Squeak 1 file and drag it to the left or right, depending on the starting position, until the end of the waveform ends near the beginning of the Slap 2 sound effect clip on the track below.

8   Play the project.

The Door Squeak 1 clip should now match the video, and end right as the clapboard slaps closed.

Saving a Project

You've added files and modified their lengths and position in the Timeline. This is a good time to save your work before moving on to the rest of this lesson. As a rule, you should save often to protect your work. For this exercise you'll choose Save As from the File menu, and create a new folder to save all of your Soundtrack Pro book projects.

There are different saving methods and details that you will learn throughout this book. At this time, you'll start with the basics.

1   Choose File > Save As to open the Save As dialog.

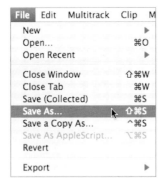

The Save As dialog opens.

Chances are, you are looking at a condensed dialog window. To expand the window, simply click the downward pointing triangle next to the Save As name field.

Condensed Save As dialog

2   Click the downward pointing triangle to expand the dialog window.

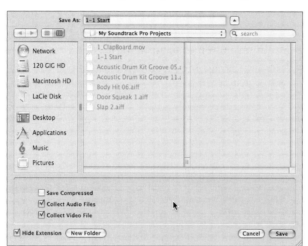

3   Click the Desktop icon on the Sidebar of the expanded Save As dialog.

You've now selected the Desktop as the location for the saved file.

4   Click the New Folder button in the lower-left area of the dialog to create a new folder on the desktop.

A New Folder window appears.

5   Type *My Soundtrack Pro projects* in the Name of new folder field of the New Folder window. Then click the Create button to create that folder.

The new folder has now been created and selected on the Desktop.

6   In the Save As dialog, deselect the Collect Audio Files checkbox at the lower left of the window.

Deselecting the Collect Audio Files checkbox means that you will save only the current project file rather than all of the files included in the project. The other checkbox option, Save Compressed, is used when you are finished with a project and need to save it with all the media files so that you can archive it or move it to another computer.

7 Click the Save button to save your 1-1 Start project into the new folder on the desktop.

Once you've initially saved the file, you can now save revisions by pressing Cmd-S.

Opening a File in the Waveform Editor

The project is fine as is, but why settle for fine when you can add some finesse and make it even better? Plus, as part of the overview in this lesson, it's time to take a quick look at the Waveform Editor. You'll be doing extensive work in the Waveform Editor later in the book, but at this time you can open it and modify one file as a sneak preview. Your goal in this exercise is to open the **Body Hit 06** clip in the Timeline into the Waveform Editor as an audio file project, and reverse the waveform.

There are many different ways to open a file in the Waveform Editor. You can open a file and edit the actual file, or open the file as an audio file project, which is a non-destructive way to modify a clip without changing the original file. That sounds like a wise choice for this lesson.

1 On the Timeline, double-click the **Body Hit 06** clip.

The Double-Click Preference dialog opens.

The dialog allows you to choose between destructive and non-destructive audio editing.

2   Make sure the first option to Create audio file project (edit non-destructively) is selected, then click OK.

A Create Audio Project window opens so you can save the project file. For
this exercise, you'll save the file in your My Soundtrack Pro Projects folder,
which should already be selected.

3   Change the name of the Audio Project to *Body Hit 06 Reversed,* in the Save
As field.

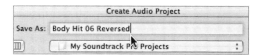

4   Choose the Desktop > My Soundtrack Pro Projects folder as the location,
if it is not already selected, then click the Save button.

The Project window changes to the Waveform Editor and displays the
Body Hit 06 Reversed audio project.

The Waveform Editor has similar features to those in the Timeline, except
that you only work on one file at a time, instead of multiple tracks and files.

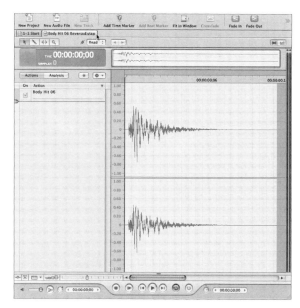

5   Press the spacebar to play the file in the Waveform Editor. Press it again to
pause playback.

For this exercise, you're going to apply a Reverse action from the Process
menu. You can combine many actions to a file within the Waveform
Editor, which you will work with more in Lesson 5, "Designing Sound in
the Waveform Editor."

6   Choose Process > Reverse to apply a Reverse action to the Audio File project.

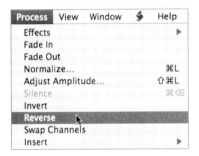

The waveform reverses.

7   Play the reversed waveform.

Reversing a waveform is a sound design technique to create a more dramatic or interesting sound effect.

8   Press Cmd-S to save the reversed Audio file project in the Waveform Editor.

9   Press Cmd-W to Close the Waveform Editor.

The audio file project that you created is now in the Timeline instead of the
original Body Hit 06 clip.

The reversed sound effect sounds good, but it needs to be earlier in the
Timeline.

Project Practice

Now's your chance to exercise your newfound skills. Your goal is to move the
Body Hit 06 Reversed file to a place earlier in the Timeline, so that it finishes
before the Slap 2 waveform begins. Be sure to zoom in to the Timeline as

needed, and adjust the track heights for a clear view. When you are finished, fit the Timeline in the window, and change the track heights back to a smaller size. Have fun!

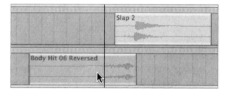

Opening the Mixer

There's one last window to look at in your tour-de-interface, and that's the Mixer window. You'll be working with the Mixer later in Lesson 8, "Creating a Basic Mix," but for now, it's good to know what it looks like. To open the Mixer window, you can use the Window menu, the Toolbar button, or a keyboard shortcut. For this exercise, you'll use the Window menu. While you're at it, though, be sure to notice the keyboard shortcut for opening the Mixer, which is Cmd-2. Shortcuts are always listed to the right of the menu choices.

1   Choose Window > Mixer to open the Mixer.

The Mixer window opens as a separate window and includes one channel strip for each track, plus an output strip.

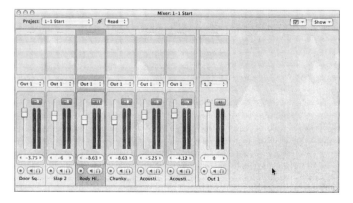

You can use the Mixer to adjust volume and pan levels for the different tracks, as well as record new files and add effects.

The Mixer can be used as a separate window or incorporated into the Interface below the Project window.

2   Press F2 to change the interface so the Mixer appears below the Project window.

> **NOTE** ▶ If you're working on a laptop computer, you may need to press the function key (Fn on the lower left of the keyboard) to use the function keys at the top of the keyboard.

This Layout condenses the size of the Mixer to accommodate the Project window.

3   Press F1 to hide the mixer and return to the standard layout.

4   Play the project once more for nostalgia.

5   Press Cmd-S to save the project.

6   Press Cmd-W to close the current project.

Congratulations! You've completed your tour and finished the first project.

Lesson Review

1.   What are the three primary interface windows when you open a multi-track project in Soundtrack Pro?

2.   A Soundtrack Pro multitrack project can include a combined total of how many tracks, buses and outputs?

3.   List three different ways that you can begin playback in the Timeline.

4.   What are the two ways that the current playhead position is displayed in the Timeline, and what is the difference between them?

5. What are two different ways that you can zoom in or out of the Timeline?

6. What are two ways that you can quickly fit an entire project in the Timeline window?

7. When would you use the Global Timeline View for navigation in the Timeline?

8. What is the difference between the Browser and Search tabs in the Media and Effects Manager?

9. Name two differences between looping and non-looping files.

10. You can preview audio files in the Browser, Search, Favorites, and Bin tabs. Which tab allows you to preview a video clip before adding it to a project?

Answers

1. The three primary interface windows for a multitrack project are the Project window, Utility window, and Media and Effects Manager.

2. A multitrack project can include a combined total of 128 tracks, buses, and outputs.

3. You can begin playback in the Timeline by clicking on the Play button in the transport controls, pressing the spacebar, or pressing Shift-Return to start playback from the beginning of the project.

4. The current playhead position is displayed as both timecode and beats in the time display in the top-left corner of the Timeline. Timecode is generally used to reference video and is displayed as four pairs of numbers representing hours, minutes, seconds, and frames. Beats represent musical time in measures, beats, and fractions of a beat.

5. You can zoom in or out of the Timeline using the Zoom slider or the up and down arrow keys.

6. You can click the Fit in Window button in the Toolbar or press Shift-Z to fit the project in the visible area of the Timeline.

7. When you are zoomed in to only part of the project, you can use the Global Timeline View to change the part of the project that is visible in the Timeline window.

8. The Browser allows you to access any file on your computer or external storage devices. The Search tab allows you to use metadata (tags) to search the indexed audio files in your collection, including the 5,000 files that come with Soundtrack Pro.

9. Looping files are recorded to repeat over and over, while non-looping files only play once. Also, loops include metadata that allow them to change to match the project tempo and key.

10. Video clips can be previewed in the Details tab before adding them to a project.

Keyboard Shortcuts

Navigation & Playback

Spacebar	starts playing or pauses the project
Return	moves the playhead to the beginning of the project
Shift-Return	starts playback from the beginning of the project
Right arrow	moves the playhead to the next gridline
Left arrow	moves the playhead to the previous gridline
Up arrow	zooms in to the Timeline
Down arrow	zooms out of the Timeline
Shift-Z	fits the project in the display size

Keyboard Shortcuts

Windows

Cmd-W	closes the active window
Cmd-I	opens the Details tab
Cmd-1	opens the Video tab
Cmd-2	opens the Mixer window
Cmd-4	opens the Browser tab
F1	displays the Standard window layout
F2	displays the Mixing window layout

2

Lesson Files	Soundtrack Pro book files > 01-02_Projects&Media > 2-1 Jazz Start, 2-2 Jazz Final
Time	This lesson takes approximately 1 hour and 15 minutes to complete.
Goals	Create a new project
	Explore the project properties
	Work with Tempo, Key, and Time Signature
	Change a project's time format
	Add, move, and remove tracks
	Change track formats
	Arrange musical parts in the Timeline
	View the Project Preferences window

Creating and Arranging a Multitrack Project

There are two types of projects that you can work on in Soundtrack Pro: multitrack projects in the Timeline, and audio file projects in the Waveform Editor. For this lesson, you'll focus on multitrack projects.

Understanding the different project properties, types of tracks, and multitrack projects is an important step in mastering Soundtrack Pro, yet often is overlooked by the casual user. In this lesson, you'll work with a variety of multitrack properties at the track level and at the project level. Then, you'll work with some arranging techniques to move and modify clips already in the Timeline to complete a project. Finally, you'll create a multitrack project from scratch and finish it using the skills you've learned so far.

Although this lesson is titled "Creating and Arranging a Multitrack Project," it goes a lot deeper than that. You'll be working with the different project properties, adding and removing tracks, changing a track's time format, arranging and modifying clips, and determining if the projects you create are time-based or beats-based. Along the way you'll also learn more Timeline maneuvers, techniques, and keyboard shortcuts. Once you're comfortable with the concepts in this lesson, you'll be ready for the more challenging real-world sound design projects in this book, which begin in Lesson 3, "Creating Suspense with Sound Design."

Preparing the Project

You will begin this lesson by opening a new project. If you have any other Soundtrack Pro projects open, you should close them at this time. If you just finished Lesson 1, "Working with the Interface," Soundtrack Pro should already be open and ready to begin.

1   Quit all open applications, except for Soundtrack Pro.

2   If Soundtrack Pro is not already open, Press Shift-Cmd-A from the Finder to go to the Applications folder on your computer. Then double-click the Soundtrack Pro icon to launch the program.

   Soundtrack Pro opens with a new Untitled project.

3   If Soundtrack Pro was already open, choose File > New Multitrack project, or press Cmd-N to open a new Multitrack project.

Working with a New Multitrack Project

Project properties include Tempo, Time Signature, Key, and Sample Rate. You can also determine whether a project is time-based or beats-based and what the initial number of tracks are.

New multitrack projects are created with the project properties set in the project Preferences. Once a project has been created, you can always modify its properties by using the Project controls located at the top of the Project window.

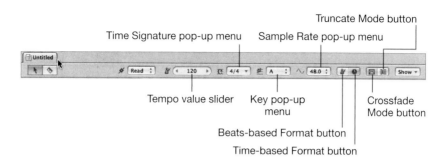

- *Tempo value slider:* Sets the tempo for current project in beats per minute (BPM). The range is 60 to 200 BPM.

- *Time Signature pop-up menu:* Sets the project time signature. The choices are 3/4, 4/4, 5/4, 6/8, 7/8, and Other.

- *Key pop-up menu:* Sets the current project's key. The range is any key in the chromatic scale from A to G#, or None.

- *Sample Rate pop-up menu:* Sets the project sample rate. The choices are 32 kHz, 44.1 kHz (CD-quality audio), 48 kHz (DVD-quality audio), 88.2 kHz, and 96 kHz.

- *Beats-based Format button:* Sets the project to a beats-based format.

- *Time-based Format button:* Sets the project to a time-based format.

- *Crossfade Mode button:* Sets the overlap mode to crossfade. The crossfade overlap mode creates a crossfade between two overlapping clips in the same track.

- *Truncate Mode button:* Sets the overlap mode to truncate (cut short) a clip when you drag another clip over it.

Any changes that you make to the current project properties will go unnoticed until you add clips and start to build your multitrack project.

Rather than start from scratch, you'll test some of the project properties on a finished project. First, though, let's take inventory on the current default settings of your Untitled project.

1   Count the number of empty tracks in the current project.

This is an easy task, since all new tracks are numbered sequentially. The default number of new tracks should be 8. If you changed your project properties in the Preferences window prior to this lesson, you may have a different default number.

Next, you'll look at some of the Project controls, starting with Tempo.

2   Check the Tempo value slider for the project's tempo; the default is 120.

3   Look at the Time Signature pop-up menu; the default is 4/4.

4   Notice the Key pop-up menu; the default key is A.

5   Examine the Sample Rate pop-up menu. The default setting is 48.0 kHz, which is also the default audio sample rate for video projects in Final Cut Pro and DVD Studio Pro.

6   Click the Beats-based Format button (metronome) to change the project time format to beats.

When the project time format is beats-based, the Time display and Time ruler display Beats above Timecode (TC).

7   Click the Time-based Format button (clock) to change the project format to time.

Now the project timecode is displayed above beats in both the Time ruler and the Time display.

What do all of those project controls mean? Good question, and you'll find out more in the next series of exercises.

8   Choose File > Close, or press Cmd-W to close the current project.

A Save dialog opens prompting you to save the project.

9   Click Don't Save to discard the project.

Opening a Project from Soundtrack Pro

In the previous lesson, you opened a project from the Finder and simultaneously launched Soundtrack Pro. This time, you'll open a project while Soundtrack Pro is already open. The projects that you'll be working with in this lesson are located in the 01-02 Projects&Media folder within the Soundtrack Pro book files folder.

1   Choose File > Open or press Cmd-O to bring up the Open window.

2   Navigate to the Soundtrack Pro book files folder in the Finder.

If your Soundtrack Pro book files folder is on the desktop, click the Desktop icon on the Sidebar of the Open window, then select the Soundtrack Pro book files folder.

3   Select the 01-02 Projects&Media folder to reveal the contents.

4   Double-click the **2-2 Jazz Final** project file, or select the **2-2 Jazz Final** project file and click the Open button to open the finished project.

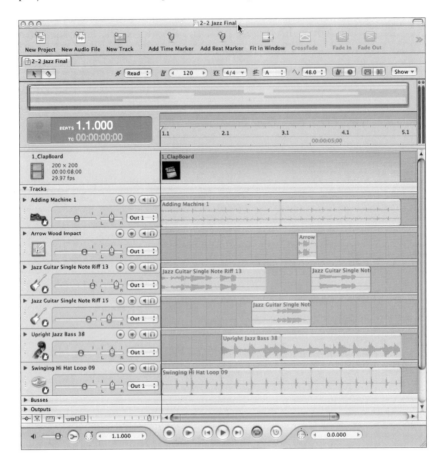

The **2-2 Jazz Final** project opens and is a variation of the project that you worked on in the previous lesson.

5   Press Shift-Z to fit the project in the Project window.

Exploring the Project Controls

It's much easier to experiment with the different project controls when you can actually see and hear the changes in the Timeline. Over the next series of exercises, you'll work with the project Time signature, Key, Time format, and Tempo controls to see and hear how they set the tone (literally) for your Soundtrack Pro projects.

> **NOTE ▶** Even if you're a video editor with little interest in music theory, don't let musical terms like *tempo, key,* and *time signature* send you flipping past this section of the book. It's important to understand these basics so that you'll be able to control the outcome of your projects.

Working with the Time Signature Control

Time signature is just a way of counting beats. The upper number indicates the number of beats per measure; the lower number is the basic beat value. The relationship between beats and measures is referred to as the time signature. The default time signature is 4/4, or four beats per measure. A waltz uses 3/4 time, one-two-three, one-two-three. A rock song, on the other hand, follows a faster, constant beat of 4/4 time.

1   Play the project in the Timeline once, then pause playback.

2   Press Return or the Home key to move the playhead back to the beginning of the project in the Timeline.

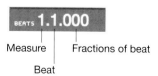

3   Play the project again, but this time watch the Beats counter in the Time display. The current time signature is 4/4 or four beats per measure. The first number is the measure, followed by the beats and then fractions of a beat.

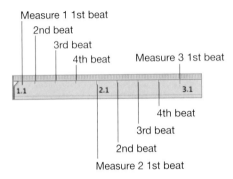

4   Continue playback again, and watch the Time ruler to see the relationship between beats and the tick marks between measures.

The hi-hat drum loop hits on each beat, which makes it easy to hear and feel the time signature of this piece.

5   Pause playback and press the End key to move the playhead to the end of the project.

The project ends around 5.1 which is the 1st beat of the 5th measure.

NOTE ▶ When you press the End key, the playhead moves to the end of the last clip in the Timeline. In this case, that's the video clip. Normally a musical piece would end on a beat at the end of a measure. However, the length of this piece is determined by the video clip, which is 8 seconds in length (timecode 00:00:08;00 NTSC 29.97 frames per second). The duration of the video clip is based on timecode, not musical time (beats).

6   Click the Time signature pop-up menu and choose 3/4 as the project time signature.

The Time ruler changes to the new time signature of 3 beats per measure.

7   Press Shift-Return to play the project from the beginning. While it plays, notice that the Beats change sequentially (1, 2, 3) in the Time display and there are only three tick marks for beats per measure in the Time Ruler.

The project sounds and looks the same in the Timeline.

8   Pause playback and press the End key.

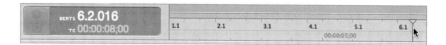

The project now ends around the 2nd beat of the 6th measure. There are only three tick marks in the Time ruler for each measure.

9   Press Return, and then change the Time signature back to 4/4 in the Time signature pop-up menu.

So what's the moral of this musical-time story? Basically, changing the time signature of a project will not change the way it sounds. It only changes the counting method used for keeping musical time in beats and measures.

Working with the Tempo Control

Tempo, the rate at which the beats occur in a piece of music, is measured in beats per minute (BPM). The faster the tempo, the more upbeat and energetic a piece of music sounds. The slower the tempo, the more relaxed a song sounds. The default tempo for a Soundtrack project is 120 BPM.

Changing the tempo of a project will make the files based on musical time play faster or slower. However, the video clip and all time-based files will remain unchanged. Actions speak louder than words, so let's try it. The Tempo value slider is located to the left of the Time signature pop-up menu.

Set the project tempo

1   Click and drag the middle of the Tempo value slider all the way to the left to set a tempo value of 60 BPM.

60 BPM is half of the original tempo of 120.

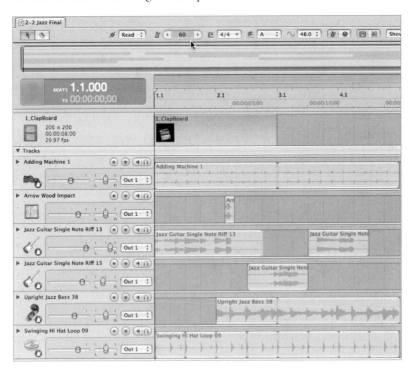

The video clip in the video track now appears to be half of the length of the overall project.

2   Play the project to hear it at the slowest tempo. While the project plays, notice that the music is painfully slow, yet the video does not appear slower in the video tab, and the sound effect on track 2 is still synchronized (in sync) with the video.

Now that you've seen and heard the effect of the slowest tempo, let's speed things up and try the fastest tempo. This time you'll type the new tempo into the value slider.

3   Click the Tempo value slider and type *200* (the fastest tempo); then press Return.

4   Press Shift-Z to see the full impact of the change in tempo in the Timeline.

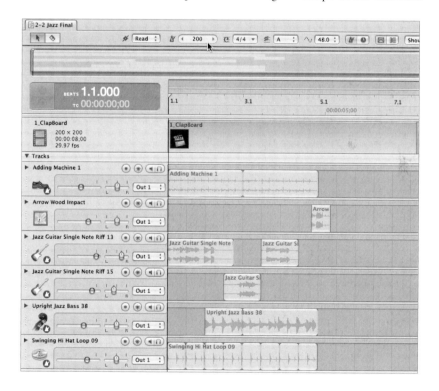

Now the video clip appears to be much longer than the musical clips.

5   Play the project at the current tempo.

That's the sound of jazz musicians after way too much coffee! What about the sound effect on track 2? The sound effect appears later than all the musical parts in the Timeline, yet it still maintains sync with the video. Why? Because the video and all time-based files remain unchanged. The music changed around them. In other words, changing the tempo of a project only changes the beats-based files, while the time-based files stay the same.

6   Pause playback if you haven't done so already.

7   Change the Tempo value slider back to 120 BPM, then press Shift-Z again to fit the project in the window.

Working with the Key Control

The default key for any project in Soundtrack Pro is the key of A. Every looping file you add to the Timeline will automatically adjust to match the key of the project. You can also change the key of the entire project at any time by changing the Key control, which is located at the right of the Time signature control.

1   Click the Key pop-up menu to change the key to A#.

2   Play the project.

The difference in key may not be very noticeable to the untrained ear. To make things more interesting, let's continue the key change experimentation with the project playing. Then you'll hear the changes in key with no ear training required.

3   With the project playing, choose the B key from the Key pop-up menu. Continue playback and try each different key to hear all variations of the project.

4   Change the key back to A.

Did you notice that the sound effect on track 2 was unaffected by the change in key? That's because the sound effect is a non-looping file. Non-looping files, such as sound effects, and dialog are not musically based so they are not recorded or tagged in a specific key.

Working with the Project Format Controls

Earlier in this lesson you clicked the Time-based and Beats-based format controls on an empty project. Now that you have a basic understanding of the Time Signature, Tempo, and Key controls, it's time to apply that knowledge to decide if the project should be beats-based or time-based.

The 2-2 Jazz Final project is currently beats-based, and for good reason—the project is primarily music, which is based on beats. If your Soundtrack Pro project is primarily dialog, sound effects, and non-looping parts, than the project should be time-based—based on timecode. If your project includes a mixture of the different types of files, you can always change the project's format as needed. However, a project's time format also determines which elements are resized visually in the Timeline during tempo changes.

1   Click the Time-based format button (clock) to change the project's format to time.

2   Click the Tempo value slider and drag the mouse right and left to raise and lower the tempo value.

As the tempo changes, the time-based elements (including the video clip and sound effect) remain fixed in the Timeline, while the beats-based elements grow longer and shorter to reflect the tempo changes.

3   Click the Beats-based format button (metronome) to change the project's format back to beats.

4   Drag the Tempo value slider again in both directions to see the changes to the files in the Timeline.

This time, the beats-based files remained fixed in the Timeline, while the video clip and sound effect extend or shorten to reflect the tempo changes. Keep in mind that a tempo change only affects beats-based files in the Timeline, regardless of the project's format. The video and time-based files don't actually change—only the way they are displayed in the Timeline relative to the beats-based files.

5   Change the project tempo back to 120.

Next, you'll put some of these skills to work as you add tracks, arrange clips, and complete the **2-1 Jazz Start** project.

Preparing the Project

At this time you'll need to open the start version of the project where you will arrange the clips to build the final version of the soundtrack.

1   Press Cmd-O or choose File > Open.

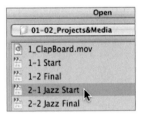

2   Select the **2-1 Jazz Start** project file and click Open.

3   The **2-1 Jazz Start** project opens in the Project window.

Moving Tabs in the Project Window

Each open project is represented by tabs, which are located in the top-left corner of the Project window. You currently have two different projects open, so you'll see two different project tabs.

1   Click the 2-2 Jazz Final tab to view the finished version of the project, then click the 2-1 Jazz Start tab to see the starting version.

You can keep the finished version of the project open as a reference while working on the starting version, so that you can switch back and forth between the two anytime.

The **2-1 Jazz Start** project is the primary project that you'll be working with for the remainder of the lesson, so perhaps you'd like to make it the first tab in the Project window.

2   Drag the 2-1 Jazz Start tab to the left and release it once it is positioned in front of the 2-2 Jazz Final tab.

Changing a tab's position does not change which tab is open. Only the project for the selected tab appears in the Project window.

Working with Tracks in the Timeline

The current project includes six tracks. The top two tracks are the Slap and reversed Body Hit sound effects that you worked with in Lesson 1. During the next series of exercises, you'll add and modify additional sound effects and then delete the original sound effects tracks. Once the sound effects are in place, you'll work on arranging the music to improve the overall piece.

Setting a Track's Format

You're already familiar with the different project formats, but did you know that you can also determine whether a track is time-based or beats-based? New tracks will be created in the same format as the project; however, they can always be changed once they are created.

What happens if a non-looping time-based sound effect is placed in a beats-based track? Nothing, unless you change the project's tempo. Changing tempo *will* effect some time-based clips if they are in a beats-based track. Whew! Just when you thought you understood the whole time-based vs. beats-based thing. Relax, it'll all make much more sense when you test it for yourself.

1   Take a close look at the top two tracks in the Timeline. These are time-based tracks and contain time-based non-looping files.

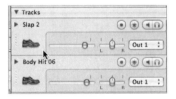

2   Now take a close look at the lower four tracks in the Timeline.

Notice anything different near the track icons?

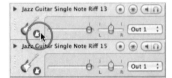

The small metronome symbol next to the track icon indicates that a track is beats-based instead of time-based. If there is no metronome symbol, then it's a time-based track.

You can change a track's time base in the Multitrack menu at the top of the interface or in a Shortcut menu. Let's try it the first way now.

3   Click inside the Slap 2 track (top track) in the Timeline to select the track.

The track becomes highlighted in blue to indicate that it has been selected.

4   Choose Multitrack > Track Time Base > Beats.

The beats-based metronome symbol appears next to the icon on the Slap 2 track.

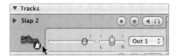

5   Play the project once to hear it without a tempo change.

The Slap sound effect is still in sync with the video, even though the track is beats-based.

6   Change the project tempo to 100.

The Slap sound effect moved according to the tempo change, while the video clip and Body Hit sound effects remained unchanged.

7   Play the project at the new tempo.

The musical parts are slower in tempo, and the slap is clearly out of sync with the video. Hence, it's a good idea to keep time-based clips in time-based tracks.

8   Change the project tempo back to 120.

The tracks all change accordingly.

9   Ctrl-click the metronome symbol on the Slap 2 track and choose Make-Time Based from the shortcut menu.

The first track is once again a time-based track. ———

10   Change the project tempo to 100 and play the project.

This time, only the beats-based tracks and musical parts change tempo. The sound effects remain in perfect time-based sync.

11   Change the project tempo back to 120.

That's it for the time-based vs. beats-based track experiment. Hopefully, it's not so confusing now that we've walked through it.

Saving the Project

This is a good time to save the project to your folder on the desktop.

1   Press Shift-Cmd-S to open the Save As window.

2   Choose the My Soundtrack Pro Projects folder on your desktop, if it is not already selected.

3   Uncheck the Collect Video and Collect Audio checkboxes, if they are selected, and click Save to save the project uncollected.

Adding Tracks in the Timeline

Your goal in this exercise is to create two new tracks that will contain non-looping, time-based sound effects that stay in sync with the video clip. What is the current project's time format? What time format do you want the new tracks to be? Remember, new tracks are created in the same time format as the project.

1 Click the Time-based format button (clock) to make the project time-based if that is not the current time format.

2 Press Cmd-T or choose Multitrack > Add Track to add a track to the Timeline.

A new time-based track titled Track 7 appears at the bottom of the Timeline. New tracks are always created in sequential numeric order below the lowest track in the Timeline.

Nice track. Although it would be even nicer if it was at the top of the Timeline with the other sound effect tracks.

Moving Tracks in the Timeline

Rearranging the order of tracks in the Timeline is as simple as grabbing them by the drag handle and moving them. The tricky part is finding the handle.

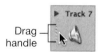

Drag handle

1 Look carefully at the left edge of Track 7. The dotted vertical line is the drag handle.

2 Click the drag handle on Track 7 and drag the track to the top of the Timeline.

A blue line (position indicator) shows the new position of the track before you release the mouse button.

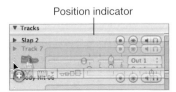

Track 7 should now appear at the top of the Timeline.

You can also add tracks to specific places in the Timeline by using a shortcut menu.

3 Ctrl-click the header of Track 7 and choose *Insert Track Before* from the shortcut menu.

A new track, titled Track 8, appears at the top of the Timeline.

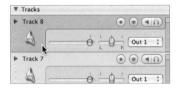

Okay, you've created two new time-based tracks in the Timeline; now all you need to do is add a few sound effects.

Searching for Sound Effects

Soundtrack Pro includes hundreds of professional quality sound effects that you can add to your projects. You'll be working extensively with sound effects in Lessons 3 and 4. For now, you'll just get acquainted with the Sound Effects file category in the Search tab. You're looking for one sound effect to replace the Slap and Body Hits effects when the clapboard closes and another to emulate the sound of the digital numbers changing on the slate itself.

1   Click the Search tab on the Media and Effects Manager.

2   Choose Sound Effects from the file category pop-up menu.

3   Click the Column view button to the left of the category pop-up menu to view the different Sound Effects Keywords.

There are over a dozen different Sound Effect Keywords, including Ambience, Animals, Explosions, Foley, Impacts & Crashes, Mech/Tech, Misc., Motions & Transportations, People, Sci-Fi, Sports & Leisure, Transportation, Weapons, and Work/Home.

The first sound effect you'll be looking for is something that sounds like the clapboard slamming closed.

4 Select the Impacts & Crashes Keyword on the Search tab.

The list of sound effects narrows to around 50.

5 Click once on the first sound effect in the results list, **Air Pressure Blast 1.aiff**, to preview (listen to) the effect.

Interesting, but not right for this project.

6 Press the down arrow key to preview the next file in the list **Arrow Body Impact.aiff**.

Great effect, the way you might imagine an arrow penetrating a body would sound. Not many people know what that actually sounds like, or would want to. Next.

7 Press the down arrow key again to hear the **Arrow Wood Impact.aiff** effect.

Perfect. It sounds like a variation on the effect you created in Lesson 1 when you combined a reversed Body Hit with a Slap sound effect. This one effect can be used to replace both of the previous effects.

8 Drag the **Arrow Wood Impact.aiff** file from the Search tab to Track 7 and release it near the middle of the track.

The track's name changes from Track 7 to Arrow Wood Impact to reflect the first file added to that track.

NOTE ▶ Don't worry about placement of the effect yet. First, you'll finish the search for the other sound effect.

9 On the Search tab, click the Mech/Tech category.

Mech/Tech stands for Mechanical and Technology sound effects.

10 Preview the first file in the list, Adding Machine 1.aiff.

This one is a little extreme, but might work really well for this animated slate. Let's try it.

11 Drag the Adding Machine 1.aiff file from the Search tab to the beginning of Track 8 (the top track) in the Timeline.

Your sound effects are in the Timeline, so now all you need to do is save.

12 Press Cmd-S to save your progress.

Moving Clips Manually

Since the new Arrow Wood Impact effect is like a combination of the Body Hit and Slap effects, you can use their waveforms guide for alignment. Once you align the new effect, you'll delete the old effects, track and all.

1 Move the playhead over the Slap 2 sound effect in the Timeline.

2 Press Cmd-8 to change the tracks to a Medium size, if they are not already that size.

NOTE ▶ The shortcuts for different track heights are: Cmd-6 Reduced (smallest), Cmd-7 Small, Cmd-8 Medium, and Cmd-9 Large.

3 Press the up arrow key to zoom in to the Timeline for a good view of the sound effect clips.

The waveforms in the Body Slap 2 clip show where the sound effect needs to begin, so just align the second part of the Arrow Wood Impact clip to the beginning of the Slap 2 waveform.

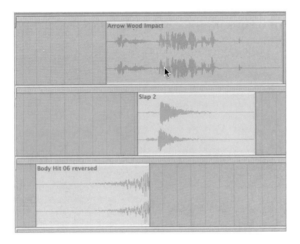

4   Move the Arrow Wood Impact clip left or right to align it with the other effects.

   TIP You can move the clip more freely without snapping to the nearest gridline by pressing N or de-selecting the Snapping button in the Timeline controls. Be sure to turn snapping on again when you're finished.

5   Play the project to hear the new combination of sound effects.

   Feel free to continue adjusting the effect until you're satisfied with its placement. Once you're finished, take a moment and return the Timeline to your normal settings.

6   Press Shift-Z to fit the project in the window, press Cmd-7 to change the track height to Small, and press Return to move the playhead to the beginning of the Timeline.

Removing Tracks

Now that you've added a new sound effects track, you can remove the Slap 2 and Body Hit 06 tracks in a few simple steps.

1   Click the drag handle on the Slap 2 track in the Timeline to select the track.

Next, you'll simultaneously select the Body Hit 06 track.

> **TIP** ▶ To select multiple tracks, hold the Command key and click the track headers rather than simply clicking the track within the Timeline. The easiest way to do this without accidentally changing one of the track controls is to click the drag handle on the left edge of the track.

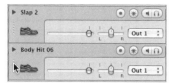

2   Cmd-click the drag handle on the Body Hit 06 track on the line above the volume slider to simultaneously select that track.

3   Choose Multitrack > Remove Tracks, or press Shift-Cmd-T to remove the selected tracks.

The Slap 2 and Body Hit tracks should no longer exist on your Timeline.

> **NOTE** ▶ If you accidentally deleted the wrong tracks, press Cmd-Z to undo the mistake and repeat steps 1 to 3 to delete the correct tracks.

4   Press Cmd-S to save your progress.

Changing a Clip's Playback Mode

So far, you've learned that projects can have either a time-based or beats-based format. You also know that individual tracks are either time-based or beats-based. Well, you also need to consider the looping or non-looping playback mode of the actual files within the tracks.

In Lesson 1, we worked with both looping and non-looping audio files. Loops are generally used to create repeating patterns, and often include musical phrases useful for creating music. Non-looping files are usually sound effects and non-musical sounds, such as dialogue.

When you add an audio file to the Timeline, it is added as a clip with the non-looping playback mode unless the audio file is tagged as a loop. Some files can be tagged to be either looping or non-looping files. Once you've added a clip to the Timeline, you can change the file's playback mode.

Why would you change a clip's playback mode? Suppose you have a sound effect, such as an Adding Machine, that you'd like to loop in the Timeline. The **Adding Machine 1** sound effect is a non-looping file, but you need to loop it so that it repeats to extend its duration. That's a good goal for this exercise, so first let's isolate (solo) the Adding Machine track to focus on that sound in the Timeline.

Soloing a Track

Each track includes Mute and Solo buttons so that you can either silence or isolate a track in the Timeline. The solo button looks like a pair of headphones and is located in the top-right corner of the track header.

1   Click the Solo button on the Adding Machine 1 track.

The Solo button darkens when it is on, and all of the other tracks turn darker gray to show that they have temporarily been muted.

2   Play the project to hear only the current Adding Machine 1 clip in the Timeline.

As you can hear, soloing a track can be very useful.

Converting a Clip to Looping

The Adding Machine 1 sound really works well with the digital numbers on the clapboard of the video clip. However, the sound doesn't last the duration of the project. Next, you'll extend the clip then convert the playback mode to looping.

1 Drag the right edge of the **Adding Machine 1** file to extend it the full eight seconds of the project.

Well, you've accomplished part of your goal. The clip is indeed longer. Unfortunately, because the file is non-looping, the extended portion of the clip contains empty space with no sound.

2 Ctrl-click the **Adding Machine 1** clip in the Timeline and choose Convert to Looping from the shortcut menu.

The **Adding Machine 1** clip in the Timeline converts to a looping file with two full looped segments in the Timeline.

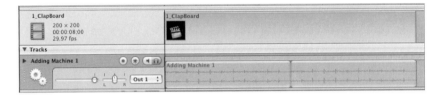

3   Play the project.

Amazing! Notice how well the looped sound effect goes with the video clip? Not only does it work, the change in sound between the loop segments actually matches the quick turn the clapboard makes onscreen. I wish I could take credit for that, but it's pure luck. Looping this particular effect might not work in some cases because of the change in sound between segments. However, in this case, it's perfect.

4   Click the Solo button again to unsolo the track.

Adjusting a Track's Volume

While you're focused on the Adding Machine 1 track header, let's turn the volume level of the track down a bit, so that it will be more subtle. The sound effect is just to enhance the piece, not overpower the percussion tracks.

Each track header also includes a handy Volume slider. You'll learn much more about working with volume levels in Lessons 8 and 9. For now, it's just important to know that you can raise and lower the volume level as needed for each track.

1   On the Adding Machine 1 track header, drag the Volume slider left to a level of around –12.

2   Play the project with volume lowered on the Adding Machine 1 track.

3   Press Cmd-S to save your project.

TIP ▶ Double-clicking the volume slider resets the track's volume to the default setting of 0.

Arranging Music in the Timeline

What's the difference between *recording* music and *arranging* music? Recording music usually requires recording equipment, musicians, instruments, a studio, and a lot of time. Arranging music, on the other hand, is the art of the music producer and involves carefully combining different instruments and music parts that sound good together to create a finished song.

For this lesson, the raw parts for this musical piece are already in the Timeline. All you'll need to do is change the arrangement a little to make the song even better.

Maintaining Musical Time

Before you start trimming and moving music clips around in the Timeline, you need to remember one really important thing.

Rule 1: Music loops are beats-based and depend on beats and snapping to stay in musical time.

Soundtrack Pro includes two foolproof features to keep your music loops in time and on beat: snapping and gridlines. Previously, you've moved sound effects around in the Timeline to match action in the video clip. You could move sound effects to any position on a track because they are time-based. Moving music clips involves a little more attention to musical timing.

What's the big deal about musical time (a.k.a. beats-based) format? Ever heard an orchestra tuning? Music time in a preschool class? Saturday afternoon at a music store with a dozen people testing out drum kits, guitars, and keyboards at the same time? The two things that can lead directly to musical chaos are parts that don't match the project key, or parts that are out of musical time. For now, you'll focus on musical time and beats-based loops, tracks, and projects.

1   Make sure the snapping feature is turned on. (It will appear darker gray.)

   TIP You can toggle snapping on and off by pressing the N key, clicking the Snapping button, or choosing View > Snap.

   That takes care of snapping. What about the gridlines? Well, you can't physically grab or move gridlines. However, zooming in to the Timeline displays more gridlines per measure, and zooming out displays fewer gridlines per measure. As you work with this lesson, feel free to zoom in or out as needed to control the number of gridlines per measure.

2   Notice how many gridlines you see in the first two measures of the project.

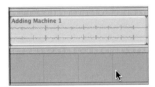

   The number of gridlines and their spacing depends on the current zoom scale, monitor resolution, and size of the project window.

3   Press the up arrow key to zoom in one level in the Timeline.

Now check how many gridlines you have. There should be more per measure than you had at the previous zoom level.

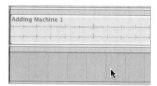

Since you'll be editing and arranging music, now is a good time to change the Project format back to Beats.

4   Click the Beats-based format button (metronome) in the Project controls to change the Time Ruler, and Time Display priority to Beats.

Trimming Musical Loops

The current musical piece isn't bad, but it isn't great either. It's somewhere in between. You don't have to be a musician to recognize when music works; it either does or it doesn't. You can also recognize mediocrity.

In the real world, most music starts with one or two instruments, then the other musicians or parts join in. Jazz is interesting in that some songs start with the bass to carry the rhythm, while in others, the bass joins in. How and when different instruments join the song is all part of the fine art of arrangement.

For this exercise, you'll use gridlines and snapping as a guide to trim and move the loops to make them sound more like actual musicians joining the song. Let's start by trimming the beginning of the Upright Jazz Bass part so it begins a little later in the song.

1   Press Return to move the playhead to the beginning of the project in the Timeline (Beat 1.1.000).

2   Press the right arrow key repeatedly if needed to move the playhead one gridline at a time toward the right until you reach the 1st beat of the 2nd measure (2.1.000).

3   Drag the left edge of the **Upright Jazz Bass 38** loop to the playhead (2.1.000) to trim the beginning of the bass part of the song.

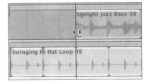

The bass part now starts at the beginning of the 2nd measure, also referred to in musical terms as Bar 2.

Next, you'll trim the empty space from the beginning of the **Jazz Guitar Single Note Riff 13** loop on the track with the same name. Trimming this loop and moving it to the left will kick the song off with the first guitar note.

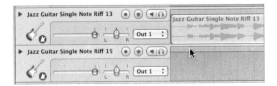

The pause at the beginning of the Jazz Guitar loop is only one beat, so trimming the pause will shorten the loop by one full beat.

NOTE ▶ There should be a gridline right before the first note begins within the loop. If not, you'll need to zoom in to add a gridline in that position.

4   Drag the left edge of the **Jazz Guitar Single Note Riff 13** loop one beat to the right.

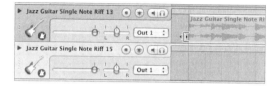

NOTE ▶ To trim or extend a loop, drag the left or right edge of the loop. To move a loop in the Timeline, drag from within the loop itself.

Now that you've trimmed the guitar clip, you can move it by dragging from within the loop itself.

5   Drag the trimmed guitar loop to the left and snap it to the beginning of the track in the Timeline (1.1.000).

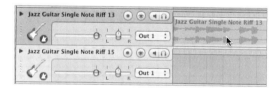

6   Play the revised song.

The beginning is good, but the end still has a bit of conflict between dueling guitar parts. To remedy this, you'll trim the **Jazz Guitar Single Note Riff 16** loop that is on the same track as the guitar loop you just trimmed.

7   Move the playhead to the 1st beat in the 4th measure (Bar 4 or 4.1.000).

8   Trim the left edge of the **Jazz Guitar Single Note Riff 16** loop to the playhead position.

When you move the pointer over the Timeline or drag a clip to a new position, you'll see blue vertical Position Indicators that you can use to help with alignment.

9   Drag the trimmed loop to the left until it starts on the 3rd beat of the 3rd measure (3.3.000).

Use the blue vertical Position Indicators (lines) in the Timeline to see the clip's position in the Time Ruler.

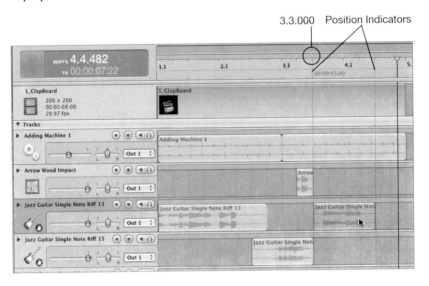

10   Press Cmd-S to save, then play the finished project in the Timeline.

Congratulations! You finished the project and learned about multitrack project properties and time formats along the way.

Setting Project Preferences

Now that you understand the basics of Time formats, Project controls, and Tracks, it's time to set the Project Preferences and create a new project. You'll learn different Soundtrack Pro preferences over the course of this book. For now, you'll focus on the Project Preferences, which determine the Project Properties for new projects that you create in Soundtrack Pro.

1 Choose Soundtrack Pro > Preferences, or press Cmd-, (comma) to open the Soundtrack Pro Preferences window.

2 Click the Project icon at the top of the Preferences window to view the Project Pane in the Preferences Window.

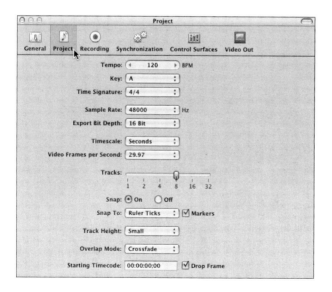

The Project properties listed in the Preferences window are self-explanatory, and similar to Project properties such as Tempo, Key, and Time Signature, which you worked with earlier in the Project window. The Timescale pop-up menu allows you to change the time format for the new project to either Seconds (time-based) or Beats (beats-based).

3   Click the Timescale pop-up menu and change the Timescale to Beats.

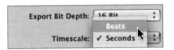

When you create a new project, the project and tracks will be beats-based. The other default settings should be fine.

NOTE ▶ If you changed any of the settings, make sure that they are set as follows before closing the Preferences window: Tempo 120, Key A, Time Signature 4/4, Sample Rate 48000, Export Bit Depth 16 Bit, Timescale Beats, Video Frames per Second 29.97, Tracks 8 (this sets the initial number of tracks in a new project), Snap On, Snap To: Ruler Ticks, Snap To Markers checkbox selected, Track Height Small, Overlap Mode Crossfade, Starting Timecode 00:00:00;00, and Drop Frame checkbox selected.

4   Click the Close (x) button at the upper left of the Preferences window or press Cmd-W to close the Preferences window.

5   Press Cmd-N to create a new multitrack project, then press Cmd-Shift-S and save the project as *Clapboard Score* in the My Soundtrack Pro Projects folder on your desktop.

Project Practice

It's your turn to create a simple score for the ClapBoard 1 video clip. You'll use all of the skills that you've learned so far in this book. First, you'll need to add the **ClapBoard 1.mov** clip, and then add some sound effects and music loops. The **ClapBoard 1.mov** clip should still be located in your Favorites tab. If not, you'll find it in the Browser in the 01-02 Projects&Media folder.

Once you're finished, save the final version of your project and press Shift-Cmd-W to close all open projects.

Give yourself a 15-minute time limit. Choose one or two sound effects and add several music loops and arrange a simple score. Feel free to adjust the project properties as needed. Have fun!

> **NOTE** ▶ In the real world, the numbers on a slate would move silently. Otherwise, the sound would interfere with the live sound recordings on the set. In this case you're working with an imaginary animated slate, and it can make whatever sound you want.

Lesson Review

1. What determines the project properties of a new multitrack project?

2. Which project property changes the pace or speed that looping beats-based clips play in the Timeline? What are the fastest and slowest settings?

3. What are the two time formats found in both Soundtrack Pro projects and tracks?

4. Most sound effects and non-musical clips are in which time format? Why?

5. Can non-looping time-based clips change to looping clips? If so, how?

6. Which button on the track header allows you to isolate the sound of that track?

7. What are the default settings for Tempo, Key, and Time Signature?

8. Will changing a project's time signature move clips out of sync or out of musical time?

9. What are the two features in Soundtrack Pro that can be used to keep musical beats-based loops in musical time?

10. How do you modify the number of gridlines per measure in the Timeline?

Answers

1. Project properties for new projects are determined in the Project pane of the Soundtrack Preferences window.

2. The Tempo value slider changes the pace or speed that looping beats-based clips play in the Timeline. The fastest tempo setting is 200 BPM; the slowest is 60 BPM.

3. Soundtrack Pro projects and tracks are either time-based or beats-based.

4. Sound effects and non-musical clips are usually time-based so that they will stay in sync with specific timecode in a video clip, rather than change position based on the beats-based tempo of the project.

5. Many non-looping time-based clips, such as the files that come with Soundtrack Pro, can change to looping clips by Ctrl-clicking the clip and choosing Convert to Looping from the shortcut menu.

6. You can isolate the sound of a track by turning on the Solo button (which looks like headphones) in the top-right corner of the track's header.

7. The default settings are Tempo 120, Key A, and Time Signature 4/4.

8. Changing a project's time signature only changes the number of beats per measure and the counting method used to keep musical time. Changing time signature will not move clips out of sync or musical time.

9. Snapping and gridlines are used to keep musical beats-based loops in musical time.

10. Zooming in and out of the Timeline will increase or decrease the number of gridlines.

Keyboard Shortcuts

Finder

Shift-Cmd-A	opens the Applications window

Windows

Cmd-W	closes the active window
Shift-Cmd-W	closes all active windows or open projects

Keyboard Shortcuts

Cmd-O	accesses the Open window
Cmd-N	creates a new multitrack project
Shift-Cmd-A	cpens the Save As window

Navigation and Timeline

Cmd-N	creates a new multitrack project
Cmd-T	adds a track to the Timeline
Shift-Cmd-T	removes selected tracks
Cmd-6	changes track height to Reduced (smallest)
Cmd-7	changes track height to Small
Cmd-8	changes track height to Medium
Cmd-9	changes track height to Large
N	toggles Snapping feature on and off
Click drag handle	selects track
Cmd-click drag handle	selects multiple tracks
Right or left arrow keys	moves playhead forward or back to the nearest gridline

Media and Effects Manager

Click once	to select and preview an audio file
Up and down arrow keys	preview the previous or next file in the list

3

Lesson Files Soundtrack Pro book files > 03-04_Projects&Media > 3-1 Start,
3-5 Final

Time This lesson takes approximately 1 hour to complete.

Goals Explore video clip details

Create a customized video layout

Store files in the Bin tab for easy access

Add markers to the Timeline

Work with a playback region

Add sound effects

Change a track's name and icon

Creating Suspense with Sound Design

Audio is often one the least appreciated crafts in filmmaking. If you have any doubt as to the importance of audio, try muting your television as you watch a commercial, television show, or movie. Not only would you miss out on the basic dialog, but sound design adds an extra level of reality, texture, emotion, and credibility to a scene.

In this lesson, you'll take the skills you've learned so far and apply them to the sound design of a suspense scene. First you'll watch the scene and determine a strategy for the sound. Then you'll add markers in the Timeline for specific sounds effects. Once the markers are in place, you'll work with sound effects to add reality, illusion of space, and mood to the scene. Along the way you'll also organize tracks, change track names and icons, and learn some new features and shortcuts.

Once you get the fundamental sound design in place, you'll be ready to move on to the next lesson where you'll add additional sound effects, music, and Timeline editing techniques to finish the soundtrack.

Preparing the Project

You will begin this lesson by opening the **3-1 Start** project file located in the 03-04_Projects&Media folder and playing the finished project. If you have any other Soundtrack Pro projects open, you should close them at this time. If you just finished Lesson 2, "Creating and Arranging a Multitrack Project," Soundtrack Pro should already be open.

1   Quit all open applications, except for Soundtrack Pro.

2   Open the Soundtrack Pro project **3-1 Start**.

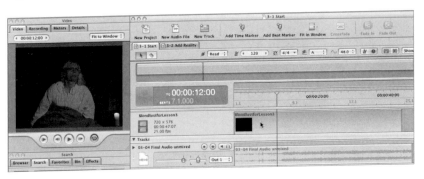

The project opens with a video clip already in the Timeline, and one audio clip on the top track. The **03-04 Final Audio unmixed** audio clip is an exported audio file of the project that you'll complete in Lesson 4, "Building Suspense with Editing Techniques."

3   Play the project to see the scene with unmixed audio.

> **NOTE ▶** This audio clip is unmixed because the final project tracks have not been through the mixing process where the track volume levels are adjusted and effects are applied. You'll learn more about mixing in Lesson 8, "Creating a Basic Mix."

Now that you know what you're aiming for in designing the sound for this scene, it's time to let it go. That's right. You're going to delete the audio clip from the project.

4   Select the 03-04 Final Audio unmixed track (top audio track) in the Timeline, then press Shift-Cmd-T to delete the entire track.

The track and its audio clip should no longer exist in the Timeline.

5   Press Shift-Cmd-S to open the Save As window.

6   Change the name of the project to Suspense Scene, making sure that the Collect Audio and Collect Video checkboxes are unselected, and then save it into the My Soundtrack Pro Projects folder on your desktop.

> **NOTE** ▶ It is important to save files uncollected while you build your project. Only save collected if you plan to archive or move the project to another computer. You'll learn more about archiving files and media management in Lesson 10, "Exporting, Managing Media, and Preferences."

You'll work on this Suspense Scene project for the duration of Lessons 3 and 4. If you don't complete an exercise, there are catch-up versions of the project that you can open at any time. You'll be prompted to save as you go along or open a catch-up version to continue with the lessons. Also, even though you deleted the **03-04 Final Audio unmixed** clip from the Timeline, it is still in the Bin tab if you'd like to hear it as a reference.

Working with Video in Soundtrack Pro

Importing a video clip into a Soundtrack Pro multitrack project is as simple as locating the file in the Media and Effects manager and dragging it to either the Video tab or the video track in the Timeline. You've already done that in Lessons 1 and 2.

There are several major differences between the computer-animated ClapBoard video clip you worked on in the previous lessons and the clip you'll be using now. This clip is significantly longer and involves live action, so the need to create an audible reality is much greater. Second, it was shot and edited in PAL rather than the NTSC video standard used for ClapBoard. Finally, this clip was exported into Soundtrack Pro from Final Cut Pro.

Soundtrack Pro will automatically change the project's video settings (Frame Rate and Frame Size) to match the imported video clip, but it's important to remember that you can only import a single clip. It can be long—up to four hours in length—but a Soundtrack Pro multitrack project can only include one video clip.

And it must be in a standard QuickTime-compatible file format supported by Soundtrack Pro, such as .mov, NTSC, PAL, and HD. You can even import MPEG-2 (m2v) files if you have installed the QuickTime MPEG-2 playback component.

How do you determine the frame rate or frame size of a video clip in Soundtrack Pro? All of these answers and more are in the details, which we will learn about next.

> **NOTE** ▸ NTSC (North America) is the broadcast standard, with 29.97 frames per second (fps) and a frame size of 720 × 486 for standard definition (SD) or 720 × 480 for digital video (DV). Europe and some parts of Asia use PAL, with 25 fps and a frame size of 720 × 576. Apple's Final Cut Studio applications support both NTSC and PAL clips in the QuickTime format.

Viewing Video Details

The Utility window's Details tab gives you easy access to information about the project's video and audio clips.

1   Select the **BloodlustforLesson3** clip in the video track of the Timeline.

The video clip turns blue once it has been selected.

> **NOTE** ▸ In all of Apple's Final Cut Studio applications, video files are represented as blue clips and audio files are green clips.

2   Press Cmd-I (for information) or click the Details tab on the Utility window to view the details for the selected clip.

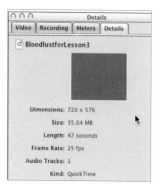

The Details tab displays the frame rate and frame size, as well as the duration of the clip (47 seconds). You can also see some of the details on the left edge of the video clip on the video track's header.

3   Press Cmd-1 or click the Video tab to bring it forward in the Utility window.

Resizing the Utility Window

The standard-sized Utility window is fine for previewing your video, but it's a bit small if you need to see intricate details within the frame. Fortunately you can resize it by dragging the Resize handle in the bottom-right corner of the window to create a much larger view.

1   Drag the diagonal lines of the Resize handle down and to the right to make the Utility window larger.

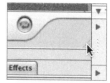

Let go of the mouse button when the Utility window is as big as you want it to be. You can even resize it while the clip is playing.

2   Press the spacebar, Shift-Return, or click the Play button to play the project.

3   While the project is playing, resize the Utility window again and then pause playback.

4   Press F1 to reset the interface to the Standard layout.

NOTE ▶ All of the primary windows within the interface have Resize handles for custom adjustments.

Another useful window feature, the Zoom button (+), will automatically change the Utility window's scale to fit the screen. It is the third button from the left in the top-left corner of the Utility window.

5   Click the Zoom button (+).

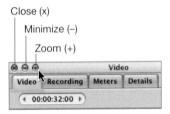

The Utility window will fill your computer screen.

6   Click the Zoom button again or press F1 to return to the Standard layout.

Moving and Resizing Tabs

You've already learned that you can rearrange the order of tabs in any window by dragging them to a different position. You can also drag a tab away from its default window so that it becomes a separate window. This feature allows you to customize the interface and view more than one tab from a window at a time. In this exercise, you'll remove and resize the Video tab. Then you'll learn how to save that window layout to use again later.

1 Drag the Video tab down and to the right to pull it away from the other tabs in the Utility window.

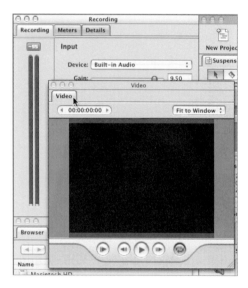

The Video tab becomes a separate window. You can move the new Video window just as you move any window in the interface, by dragging the title bar at the top of the window.

2 Move the Video window so that it is positioned over the Media and Effects manager. The top of the Video window should be even with the top of the Video track header in the Timeline.

   NOTE ▶ You won't be using the Media and Effects Manager for the next few exercises, so this layout helps you maximize your workspace and video image onscreen.

3   Drag the Resize handle in the bottom-right corner of the Video window until the window covers most of the Track headers in the Timeline.

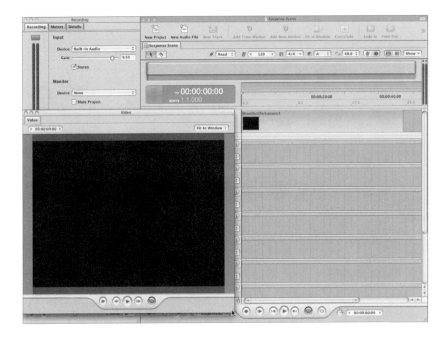

Make sure that you do not cover the actual Timeline tracks or the Time display at the top of the Timeline.

4   Play some of the video to see how it looks in the larger Video window.

Saving Window Layouts

Like other Apple Pro Applications, Soundtrack allows you to customize the different window layouts. You're already familiar with the Standard (F1) and Mixer (F2) layouts from Lesson 1, "Working with the Interface." There is also a third preset layout, Project Window Only (F3), which hides the other windows and fits the Project window to the screen. For this exercise, you'll save your current layout so that you can access it anytime that you're using Soundtrack Pro on your computer.

1   Choose Window > Save Layout to open the Save layout dialog.

2   Type *Big Video over M&E* in the dialog and click Save.

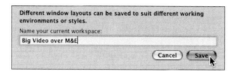

Now that you've saved the layout, you can access it under the Windows menu just as you would the other default layouts.

3   Press F1 to switch back to Standard layout.

4   Choose Widow > Layouts > Big Video over M&E to change the window to your newly saved layout.

Since the Project window and the Video window overlap, the active window will move to the front of the interface. Simply click the Video window to move it in front.

Voila! You can now create and save different layouts as needed.

TIP ▶ If you're working with two computer monitors, you can play a project's video externally using Digital Cinema Desktop. By connecting an Apple Cinema Display to your computer, you can play the video full-screen on one monitor and use the other monitor for editing. Soundtrack Pro also supports playback through an external video output device as long as you configure the Soundtrack Pro Video Out Preferences.

MORE INFO ▶ To learn more about using Digital Cinema Desktop or an external video output device, refer to the Soundtrack Pro documentation accessible through the Help menu.

Controlling Video Playback

Now that you have resized the Video window, this is a good time to master your video playback skills. You can control playback by clicking the Video transport controls or by using keyboard shortcuts. In this exercise, you'll refresh what you already know and add a few new shortcuts and buttons to your growing Soundtrack Pro skill set. Let's start with the transport control buttons, then move on to the keyboard shortcuts.

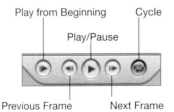

▶ *Play from Beginning:* Starts playback from the beginning of the video.

▶ *Previous Frame:* Moves the video back one frame earlier in timecode.

▶ *Play/Pause:* Plays or pauses the video from the current playhead position.

▶ *Next Frame:* Moves the video forward one frame later in timecode.

▶ *Cycle:* Plays the video as a continuous loop so that it repeats from the beginning each time the playhead reaches the end of the video.

1   Click the Play from Beginning button to start playing the video.

2   Click the Play/Pause button to pause playback and view the current time-code in the Time display.

3   Click the Previous Frame button to move the playhead one frame earlier.

   The timecode in the Time display changes by one frame.

4   Click the Next Frame button several times to move the playhead forward one frame at a time.

   You can also scrub through the video one frame at a time with the Previous Frame or Next Frame buttons.

5   Click and hold the Previous Frame button to play the video in reverse one frame at a time. Release the button to stop on a specific frame.

   Next, you'll repeat the exercise with keyboard shortcuts.

6   Press Shift-Return to start playing the video from the beginning.

7   Press the spacebar to pause playback.

8   Press Cmd–left arrow key to move the playhead one frame earlier.

9   Press Cmd–right key arrow several times to move the playhead forward one frame at a time.

10   Press and hold Cmd–left arrow key to scrub through the video one frame at a time. Release the keys to stop at a specific frame.

Project Practice

Time to practice your video playback skills. The more you work with the different buttons and keyboard shortcuts, the more efficient you'll become. Use the shortcuts or Video transport controls to find the specific frames listed below. Each of these frames are important visual cues for designing the sound for this scene.

▶   Play from the beginning and pause just before the woman sits up in her bed (00:00:05:11).

▶   Find the frame just before the latches on the door drop and the door swings open (00:00:07:16).

▶   Find the first frame where you see the Vampire (00:00:12:18).

> NOTE ▶ Sound effects are often placed on the first frame of a shot in the video clip or at the frame before a visual cue, such as the door latch moving.

Planning a Scene's Sound Design

And now for the moment you've all been waiting for—planning the sound design for your scene. Think of it like planning a party. First you come up with a theme, then you plan the decorations, food, and drinks. With sound design, first you come up with a theme or feel for the scene, then you plan sound effects and musical parts accordingly.

There are many layers to the art of sound design. Generally you start with the big picture, then work your way down to the details.

Imagining the Soundscape

What's a soundscape? It's the audible landscape of your scene that includes everything you would expect to hear in the contextual reality of the scene's location and time period. The overall soundscape includes ambient noise such as an air conditioner, street traffic, or the *walla* (that's sound designer jargon for murmur) of people talking in the distance, and sound effects such as a clock ticking, door slamming, or glass breaking as it falls to the floor. Let's start by taking inventory of your current "reality"-based soundscape, then apply the same technique to the scene.

1   Close your eyes for a minute and listen to all of the sounds around you.

What did you hear? Sometimes what you didn't hear is as important as what you did. For example, if a scene takes place in a bank near a busy street, you'd expect to hear computers, canned music, people, and cars. However, if the scene involves people locked in a soundproof bank vault, the lack of sound adds to the suspense.

2   Now, take a mental inventory of things in the room that might need sound effects, such as a computer printer, phone, pencil sharpener, alarm, door, or window. All of these elements are potentially part of the soundscape as well.

As a sound designer, you may also use sound effects to establish elements in the scene that aren't visible by the camera.

3   Imagine things that aren't visible, but might be in the room and could still be established audibly. These would be things like cell phones, pagers, a knock on the door, a dog barking outside, sirens passing, furniture being moved upstairs….

> **TIP** Using sound effects to establish sounds off camera is a great way to save money in the shooting budget as well. Hearing a car accident and then showing the aftermath is much cheaper to film than showing the actual accident. Also, working with animals and children can be expensive, but you can always hear a dog bark or a baby cry and perceive that they are there, even without seeing them.

Now turn your attention to the suspense scene in your project.

4   Watch the video clip and take a mental inventory of noises that you should hear, such as a door opening or footsteps.

5   Watch the video clip again and imagine story elements that you could establish with sound, such as crickets to show that it is nighttime or a barking dog to show that an intruder is lurking outside.

Organizing Sound Effects

Once you have decided on the overall theme or soundscape for the scene, it's a good idea to organize the sounds by audio priority. In other words, it's time for more planning. The sound elements of a scene can be organized into several categories, including reality, ambience, establishing, and mood. There are many different terms that can be used to describe sound effects and how they are used, but they still boil down to these general categories.

In the next series of exercises, you'll search for sound effects appropriate for this scene and place them in the Bin tab for easy access when you're ready to build the soundtrack. Choosing sound files and placing them in the Bin tab is like shopping for groceries before you cook a big meal. First you gather the ingredients, and then you start cooking. Otherwise, you're constantly running back and forth to the store. Or in Soundtrack Pro, you're constantly going back and forth to the Search tab to hunt for more files.

1   Press F1 to return to the Standard layout.

2   Click the Search tab to make it active.

3   Drag the Bin tab to the right edge of the Media and Effects Manager.

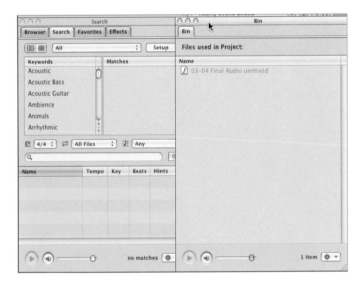

TIP ▶ Overlapping the Bin window over part of the Media and Effects Manager makes it easier to click the Bin window so that it moves to the front of the Timeline window.

4   Click the Timeline to make it active.

The Timeline covers most of the Bin window.

5   Click the left edge of the Bin window that is visible over the Media and Effects tab.

Nice customized layout. Why not take a moment and save it in case you decide to presort files to the Bin tab in a future project?

6   Choose Windows > Save Layout, and name the layout *Separate Bin*.

7   Click the Bin window if it is not already active and in front of the Timeline window.

NOTE ▶ Remember, the Bin window includes all of the audio files in the current project, even files that have previously been deleted. The **03-04 Final Audio unmixed** file is still in the Bin window, but it's been grayed out to show that it was removed from the Timeline.

Your Separate Bin layout is ready for files. Let's start with the reality sound effects needed for the scene.

Searching for Reality Sound Effects

Reality sound effects—a door opening, a glass breaking, a gun shooting—are used to make an action look realistic onscreen. However, in sound design, bigger is usually better and *reel* does not mean *real*. The sounds you choose for the scene must meet the expectations of the viewer rather than mimicking the sounds that would occur in the real world. For example, gunshots in the movies are loud and startling: Each shot explodes and resonates larger-than-life. People are so conditioned to movie gunshots that they would not believe the real, unaltered sound of gunshots if you chose to use that in your video instead. You'll often see witnesses on the news describing a shooting as "popping firecrackers" because they didn't recognize the sound of real gunshots.

The scene you are working on in this lesson needs at least two reality sound effects—a sound for the doorknob turning and a sound for the door opening. But the door can't just open silently—that would be real world, not reel world. In a suspenseful, dark, vampire-at-the-door scene, the viewer expects the door to squeak when it opens. Give in to audio clichés: Doors in scary places always squeak, horror films always have full moons and wolves howling in the distance, tires on getaway cars always squeal, and dogs always bark at bad people, to name a few. Sure, you could make it a well-oiled, perfectly maintained silent door if you like, but you'd be compromising the illusion of "reality" in the make-believe world of the scene.

Now that we've established the need for a squeaky door in your project, let's go find its voice.

1   Click the Column View button on the Search tab, if it is not already set to Column view, and choose Sound Effects from the Keywords pop-up menu, if that's not the current category.

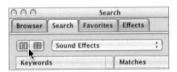

2   Click the Work/Home Keyword in the left column, then type *door squeak* in the search text field to narrow the search.

3   Preview each of the Door Squeak sound effects. Which sounds more eerie?

My vote is for **Door Squeak 2.**

4   Drag Door Squeak 2 from the Search results list to the Bin window and release it.

The filename will appear gray until you add the file to the Timeline. For now, the bin will be your audio shopping cart, containing just the files you might use in the multitrack project. You can always remove unused files from the bin once you've finished the soundtrack.

5 Click the Reset button (x) in the Search text field, and type *knob* to search for door knob sound effects.

> **TIP** ▸ When using the Search text field to narrow your search, it's a good idea to try a specific descriptor such as "knob" rather than something general like "door." Searching for "door" could result in dozens of files, including automobile doors, sliding doors, and slamming doors.

Soundtrack Pro includes three different Door Knob sound effects. Since you're just shopping around, why not take them all! You can decide which to use later.

6 Drag each Door Knob sound effect one at a time from the Search results list to the Bin window.

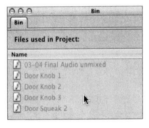

7 Reset the Search text field and save your project.

Your hunt for reality sound effects was a success. Now it's on to the next category—ambience.

Choosing Ambience to Add Presence

Ambience brings a room or location to life and can include anything from the beeping horns and rumbling motors of traffic on a busy street to the low rumble of a waterfall and chirping birds of a secluded forest. Ambient sound adds another layer of reality to a scene and fills the void of silence between dialog and action. It may be subtle, but if it's missing, the illusion of reality is broken and the scene comes across like a play performed on a make-believe set. True, many narrative scenes are filmed on a make-believe set, but it's your job as sound designer to color the scene with acoustic wallpaper.

The illusion of reality in this scene is that it is nighttime in a rural area, most likely somewhere near Transylvania. No problem, just add crickets and you have instant rural nighttime. If the scene is in the city, then you can exchange the crickets for light traffic with the occasional street cleaner and sirens.

1   Click the Ambience Keyword to focus the search to ambient sound effects.

Soundtrack Pro includes over 100 ambient effects.

2   Scroll down through the list to find the **Country Day**, **Country Night**, and **Crickets** files, and preview each effect.

The first two both evoke that feeling of country, so what's the difference between day and night? Crickets! There's also a lovely babbling brook and birds chirping throughout the Country Day file. At night, the birds are replaced by an Owl hoot, and the babbling brook has been muted to make room for crickets. Do natural water sources cease to make noise at night in the real world? Of course not, but this isn't real. You have to set audio priorities. Crickets trump just about any other nighttime sound.

For this exercise, the Country Night ambience is a little too busy and might distract from the rest of the scene. Let's just go with straight crickets.

3   Drag the **Crickets FX 01** and **Crickets FX 02** files to the Bin window, and reset the Search text field to prepare for the next search.

Next, you'll find an establishing sound effect.

Establishing a Story with Sound

Establishing sounds can be used to set the tone for a location or era, such as dinosaurs roaring during the Jurassic period or horse-drawn wagons and saloon music in Dodge City circa the early 1900s. Establishing sounds can also be used as part of the storytelling process to establish something that is not present in front of the camera but is still important to the character or story. In fact, it's quite easy to audibly establish rumbling thunder, exploding bombs, and crying babies without ever seeing them.

Your goal in this exercise is to find an establishing sound that will communicate that someone or something might be outside the character's bedroom window. When the scene opens, the woman is already awake. She doesn't seem alarmed, just awake. Why? Did she hear something? Perhaps a barking dog. Barking dogs don't always mean danger—maybe the dog wants to go inside, maybe a cat is walking along the fence, or maybe there's a vampire sneaking around the corner. The audience needs you to establish why the character is awake.

1   Click the Animals Keyword on the Search tab, and type *dog* in the Search text field.

There are lots of barking dog sounds to choose from, including small dogs, large dogs, and medium dogs. All are fine for different situations, but for this exercise you'll focus on the medium dogs.

2   Preview all three of the **Dog Bark Medium** files.

Listen for one that sounds like the dog is outside and is a combined bark and growl sound. **Dog Bark Medium 1** will work perfectly.

3   Drag it to the Bin window.

4   Reset the Search text field and save your progress.

Setting the Mood of the Scene

The final sound effect category that you'll be working with in this lesson is Mood. Sound effects and music can also be added to enhance the mood of a scene. Is the scene eerie, funny, happy, lonely, action-packed, or painfully boring? Sound can be a powerful tool for enhancing the overall mood of a scene. If the suspense scene that you're working on included funny cartoon sound effects, children laughing outside, birds chirping, and a happy ukulele tune, it would have an entirely different mood.

For this exercise, you'll be locating the sound effect for the vampire himself. Not the sound of him speaking, just the theme music that appears whenever he's around. A low sci-fi–type drone would add an ominous presence to the vampire scene.

1   Click the Sci-Fi Keyword on the Search tab, and type *drone* in the Search text field.

2   Preview all three drone sounds.

The **Drone Machine** will add a nice touch of mood to the scene without becoming distracting.

3   Drag the **Drone Machine** file to the Bin window and reset the Search text field.

Project Practice

What other sound effects might help set the mood? How about wolves howling in the distance? That would help establish the story line and enhance the eerie mood at the same time. So go to the Animals Keyword on the search tab. Find both of the **Wolves Howling** files and add them to the Bin window. The project could also use some wind ambience to go with the billowing fog outside. Find the **Wind 2** sound effect and add it to the bin as well.

Once you're finished adding files to the bin, change the interface to the Standard window layout and save your progress. Now that you've completed your initial sound effects search, you can mark where to place them in the Timeline.

Working with Markers

All of the Apple Pro Applications include markers that can be used to mark specific frames or points in time. In Soundtrack Pro, markers are very useful tools for making notes in the Timeline, as well as for marking specific points for music changes, sound effects, or dialog cues. You can mark a frame or beat, depending on the time format that you are using as a reference.

Soundtrack has four different types of markers that come in a unique color to make it easy to distinguish from the others. Time markers (green) mark a specific timecode frame and use timecode as a reference. Beat markers (purple) mark a specific beat and use the time in beats as a reference. Scoring makers (orange) are embedded in a video clip in Final Cut Pro and reference the video clip's timecode. You will work more with scoring markers in Lesson 5, "Designing Sound in the Waveform Editor." Finally, End of Song (red) markers can be added to the Timeline to mark the end of the project.

During the next series of exercises, you'll work with the Time, Beat, and End of Song markers to further organize your sound design ideas in the Timeline.

Adding Markers to the Timeline

To add a marker, all you have to do is move the playhead to the desired position and use one of the following methods:

▶ Choose Mark > Add Time Marker, Add Beat Marker, or Set End of Song.

▶ Press Option-B (for Beat marker) or -M (for Time marker).

▶ Click the Add Time Marker or Add Beat Marker button in the Toolbar.

> **NOTE** ▶ The toolbar buttons for adding markers will also make the Project window active. The Mark menu and keyboard shortcut methods for adding markers will only work if the Project window is active.

Let's use all three methods to set some markers that you'll need later on. This is also a good time to practice your Timeline navigation skills.

1   Click the Time-based format button, if the project is not already in that format.

2   Choose Window > Big Video over M&E to change the layout.

3   Play from the beginning and pause just before the woman sits up in her bed (00:00:05:11).

4   Click the Add Time Marker button on the toolbar.

A green time marker appears in the Timeline at the playhead position.

5   Find the frame just before the latches on the door drop and the door swings open (00:00:07:16). Click the Add Time Marker button on the toolbar to add the marker at the playhead position.

The remaining markers don't require the larger Video tab, so you can return to the Standard layout for the remaining markers.

6   Press F1 to change the window layout.

7   Find the first frame where you see the vampire (00:00:12:18) and press M to set a time marker.

Next, you'll mark the location for the music to start, so you'll use a beat marker.

8   Click the Beats-based format button to change the project's time format.

9   Move the playhead to the 3rd beat of the 8th measure (8.3.000), and click the Add Beat Marker button or press Option-B.

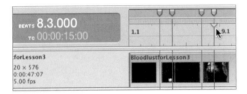

A purple beat marker appears at the playhead position. Since that is the only beat marker you'll be setting in this lesson, it's a good idea to change the project's time format back to time-based.

NOTE ▶ You do not have to change a project's time format in order to set a marker. You changed formats in this exercise as a reminder of the different time formats and to make it easier to navigate to that position.

Naming Markers

Once you've added a marker, you can open the Marker Edit dialog and name the marker or move its position on the Timeline. You can also move a marker by dragging it to a different point in time. In this exercise, you'll name the markers that you've added to the project so far.

1   Double-click the head of the purple beat marker.

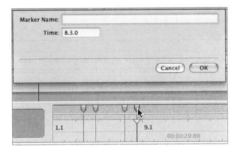

A dialog box opens with information about the marker. Notice that the Time field has the beats-based position of the marker (8.3.0).

2   Type *start music* in the Marker Name field and click OK.

The marker's name appears above the Time ruler.

3   Double-click the head of the first time marker (green) in the Timeline and name it *sits up*.

   NOTE ▶ You may need to Press the up arrow key several times to zoom in to the Timeline to see the names of markers.

4   Name the second time marker *door opens* and the third marker *vampire presence*.

5   Move the playhead to 50;00 in the Timeline.

   This is where you'll mark the end of the scene.

6   Choose Mark > Set End of Song.

   A red end of song marker appears in the Timeline.

Project Practice

It's your turn to add and edit the last marker in this exercise. Move to frame 16;15, set a time marker, and name the marker *breathe*.

Moving Between Markers

Now that you have set all six markers, you can easily move between them in the Timeline.

To move between markers, press Shift-M to move forward in the Timeline to the next marker and Option-M to move back to the previous marker. You can also go to the Mark menu and choose Go to Next Marker or Go to Previous Marker.

1   Press Return to move the playhead to the beginning.

2   Press Shift-M to move the playhead to the first marker in the Timeline.

3   Press Shift-M four times to move the playhead to the last time marker (breathe) in the Timeline.

4   Press Option-M to move the playhead back to the previous marker.

Moving between markers with Shift-M or Option-M does not include the red end of song marker.

5   Press the End key or click the Go to End button on the transport controls at the bottom of the Project window.

The playhead moves to the red end of song marker.

NOTE ▶ Moving between markers with Shift-M or Option-M also works in Final Cut Pro.

Catching Up

If you didn't complete all of the steps in the previous exercises for this lesson, feel free to close your current project and open the project **3-2 Add Reality** to catch up.

Building Sound Effects Tracks

Now that the first stages of planning the sound design are over, it's time to start building the tracks. That doesn't actually require heavy equipment or tools; it's just an expression for adding multiple audio files to a track or tracks. As the files accumulate in the Timeline, the sound builds to create the overall piece. Let's start with the first priority—the reality sound effects. You can use the markers that you've already set to snap the sound effects into position in the Timeline.

1   Click the Bin tab on the Media and Effects Manager.

All of the audio files that you've preselected should be in the list including: two crickets, three door knobs, one door squeak, a drone machine, wind, and two wolves howling. Sounds like the audible ingredients for a suspenseful vampire scene.

2   Press Return to set the playhead at the beginning of the Timeline.

3   Press Shift-M twice to move to the door opens marker. Zoom in as needed for a better view of the markers in the Timeline.

4   Check the snapping button to be sure that snapping is turned on.

5 Listen to the door knob sound effects to see which one fits the clip.

Door Knob 3 sounds like the heavy latches on the pair of doors that open in the video clip.

6 Drag the **Door Knob 3** file from the Bin tab to the Reality Sound Effects track (top track), and snap it to the door opens marker.

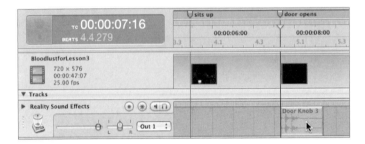

Snapping can also include markers, so you're able to snap to the desired frame without a gridline in that position.

7 Play the clip in the Timeline to see how it works with the video.

Sounds real doesn't it? Now all you need to do is add a little squeak for an extra dose of reality.

8 Drag the **Door Squeak 2** file from the Bin tab and snap it to the right edge of the **Door Knob 3** clip.

9 Play the clips in the Timeline.

Amazing! The combination of two simple sound effects can add life and "reality" to a scene. Before you move on to the other effects, this is a good time to learn how to create a playback region.

Creating and Removing Playback Regions

Sometimes you want to play just part of the Timeline. In this case, you want to play only the reality sound effects on the top track. Creating a playback region is an easy way to isolate a particular portion of the Timeline. Playback regions are created by clicking and dragging the bottom half of the Time ruler. Your goal in this exercise is to create a playback region that isolates the two sound effects clips in the Timeline.

1 Click the bottom half of the Time ruler at the door opens marker and drag it to the right just beyond the end of the **Door Squeak 2** clip in the Timeline.

 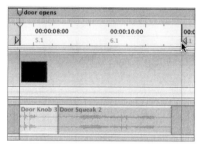

The Time ruler is marked with a lighter section with blue In and Out points. This is the playback region.

2 Press the spacebar to start the playback loop.

Notice that when the playhead reaches the end of the playback region, it repeats the section seamlessly.

3 Press the spacebar again to stop the playback.

4 Press the Home key to go to the beginning of the playback region, or press the End key to move to the end of the playback region.

NOTE ▶ If the playhead is already within the playback region, the Home and End keys move it to the beginning or end. If the playhead is outside of the playback region, the Home and End keys move it to the beginning or end of the project in the Timeline. Return also takes the playhead to the beginning of the playback region, while Shift-Return always starts playback from the beginning of the Timeline.

You can resize a playback region by dragging its In or Out points.

5 Click the playback region Out point and drag it to the right to the vampire presence marker.

It's even easier to remove a playback region.

6 Click the bottom half of the Time ruler outside of the playback region.

The region disappears.

7 Press Shift-Z and then save.

The next time you want to focus the playback in the Timeline to one isolated section, you can simply create a playback region.

NOTE ▶ If you didn't complete the previous steps, feel free to open the **3-3 Add Illusion & Mood** project to catch up.

Project Practice

It's your turn to add the remaining sound effects to their designated tracks and markers. Don't worry about the length of the clips and volume levels of the tracks—you'll edit them in Lesson 4. Follow the bullet points below for instructions, and don't forget to save once you've completed the exercise.

▶ Listen to both Crickets sound effects in the Bin tab. The second one is more subtle and less distraction, so add **Crickets FX 02** to the beginning of the second track in the Timeline.

▶ Add the **Wind 2** clip to the third track from the top, and align it to the door opens marker (07;18).

▶ Add the **Dog Bark Medium 1** clip to the beginning of the Establishing
track.

▶ Listen to both of the Wolves Howling sound effects in the Bin tab. The
first one sounds like scared wolves, which may work well at the end of the
piece. The second one sounds more like wolves announcing their presence,
or perhaps the presence of their kin, the vamipire. Add **Wolves Howling 2**
to the upper Mood track and start it around 2;16 in the Timeline. (The
wolves howling clip is about half the length of the barking dogs clip, so
it should start after the dogs barking and end before the dog barking
clip ends.)

▶ Add the **Drone Machine** clip to the lower Mood track so that it begins at
the vampire presence marker.

▶ Play the project to hear the preliminary sound design.

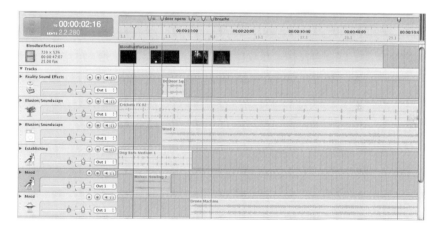

Did you notice how easy it was to build the project? That's because you had
a plan, gathered the effects you wanted to work with, and set markers in the
Timeline for easy alignment. Nice work.

> **NOTE** ▶ If you didn't complete the previous steps, feel free to open the
> **3-4 SFX Added** project to catch up.

Changing Track Names and Icons

Each track header includes an icon that represents the Keyword category of the track's contents. The icon and track name match the first clip placed in an untitled track. If the tracks were prenamed before adding clips, as they were in this project, the tracks maintain the names they were originally given.

You can change a track's name to better represent the contents of that track. For example, you may have several different reality sound effects in one track. Rather than keep the name of the first clip, you could call the entire track *Vampire SFX* or *Suspenseful Ambience*.

Naming Tracks

To change a track name, all you have to do is click in the Track Name field on the track header and type a new name.

1   Click inside the mood track name field on the lowest track.

2   Type *Vampire Drone* in the name field to rename the track.

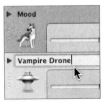

Changing Track Icons

Soundtrack offers many track icons to choose from, and it's easy to change them. Why? To better represent the contents of the track so you'll be able to distinguish it from the other tracks. Notice that most of the lower Illusion/Soundscape tracks have icons that represent the Keyword category of the contents; however, the **Wind 2** clip has an icon that looks like an audio file. Since the track contains the ambient sound of wind, let's also change the icon to match.

1   Click the track icon on the lower Illusion/Soundscape track.

A window with all of the different icons appears onscreen. You can choose from any of the icons in the menu. There aren't any wind or weather icons, so you'll need to try something else.

2   Select the icon that looks like a tree, since wind is an outdoor ambient sound.

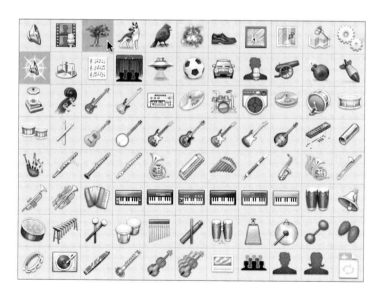

The track now has a new icon.

3 Press Cmd-S to save your project.

Congratulations! You completed the lesson and the preliminary sound design for this project. In the next lesson, you'll add additional effects and learn some editing techniques to fine-tune the arrangement in the Timeline and finish the soundtrack.

Lesson Review

1. What video file format is supported by Soundtrack Pro?
2. How do you navigate from frame to frame in the Timeline or Video tab?
3. Where do you find information about a video clip in the Timeline?
4. How can you resize the Utility window or Video tab to fit the entire screen?
5. Under which Soundtrack Pro menu can you choose preset layouts and save customized layouts?
6. Which tab can be used to store preselected files that you'd like to use in a multitrack project?
7. What are the three types of markers that can be added to the Timeline in Soundtrack Pro? What are the keyboard shortcuts to add these markers?

8. What are the navigation shortcuts to move between markers in the Timeline?

9. What is a playback region and how do you create one in the Timeline?

10. How do you change a track's name and icon?

Answers

1. Soundtrack Pro supports standard QuickTime-compatible file formats.

2. You can navigate from frame to frame by clicking the Next Frame or Previous Frame buttons on the Video tab's transport controls, or use the keyboard shortcuts Cmd–right arrow or Cmd–left arrow.

3. You can find information about a video clip in the Details tab or on the Video track header.

4. You can resize the Utility window or Video tab to fit the entire screen by clicking the Zoom button (+) in the top-left corner of the window or by dragging the Resize handle in the bottom-right corner of the window.

5. You can choose preset layouts and save customized layouts in the Window menu.

6. You can store preselected files for a multitrack project in the Bin tab.

7. You can add time markers (green), beat markers (purple), or an end of song marker (red). There are also scoring markers (orange), which can only be added in Final Cut Pro. The shortcuts are M to set a time marker and Option-B to set a beat marker. There is no shortcut to set an end of song marker.

8. Shift-M moves to the next marker, and Option-M moves to the previous marker.

9. A playback region is an isolated portion of the Timeline with In and Out points that allows you to playback on that region. You can create a play-back region by clicking and dragging the bottom half of the Time ruler.

10. You can change a track's name by clicking the name text field in the track header and typing a new name. To change a track's icon, you simply click the icon on the track header and choose a different icon from the icon menu.

Keyboard Shortcuts

Opening and Saving

Shift-Cmd-S	opens the Save As window

Markers

M	sets a time marker
Option-B	sets a beat marker
Shift-M	moves to the next marker
Option-M	moves to the previous marker

Playback Region

Return or Home	moves the playhead to the playback region In point
End	moves the playhead to the playback region Out point

Utility Window

Cmd-I	shows the Details tab
Cmd-1	shows the Video tab

Keyboard Shortcuts

Layouts

F1	displays Standard layout
F2	displays Mixer layout
F3	displays Project Window Only layout

4

Lesson Files	Soundtrack Pro book files > 03-04_Projects&Media > 4-1 Start
Time	This lesson takes approximately 60 minutes.
Goals	Adjust track volume levels
	Split audio clips in the Timeline
	Duplicate clips
	Move clips with precision
	Edit clips with the Razor tool
	Transpose music clips
	Crossfade and truncate overlapping audio clips
	Select a project timeslice to delete excess media

Lesson 4

Building Suspense with Editing Techniques

In Lesson 3, "Creating Suspense with Sound Design," you created the initial sound design for the vampire scene. Now you'll use editing techniques to take your sound design to the next level and finish building the tracks. Your goal here is not only to learn these editing techniques, but also to apply them to your soundtrack and craft the audible elements of suspense within the scene. Along the way you'll also learn some shortcuts and tricks of the trade that you'll be able to use on your own projects in the future.

Preparing the Project

You will begin this lesson with the Suspense Scene project that you created in the previous lesson. If you did not complete the steps from Lesson 3, you can open the 4-1 Start project file.

1   Quit all open applications, except for Soundtrack Pro.

2   Open your Suspense Scene project from Lesson 3, or open the 4-1 Start project file located in the 03-04_Projects&Media folder.

3   Play the project once and listen to the sound effects as you watch the video.

Adjusting Track Levels

As you just watched the project, your inner sound editor was probably wondering, "What's the deal with the crickets and wind effects dominating the soundscape?" The ambient sounds are overpowering the other tracks, but don't worry—you just need to adjust the volume levels. Normally, you'd save that until the mixing process, unless the levels are too distracting to be ignored. This is one of those instances. So your goal in this exercise is to place the wind, crickets, and howling wolves in the background where they belong.

The default level for audio tracks is 0 (zero), which is a relative number assigned to all audio tracks in Soundtrack Pro. Since most audio clips are at a normal volume level when imported, they don't need to be amplified much louder and you can only raise the audio level by a maximum of six decibels (6 dB). However, you can lower it by as much as 96 decibels (–96 dB), which silences the track completely.

You'll learn much more about the specifics of mixing levels in Lesson 8, "Creating a Basic Mix." For now, you'll just make some general adjustments to make the overall sound more natural for the scene. Let's start with the track containing Crickets FX 02.

1   Drag the Volume slider on the first Illusion/Soundscape track to the left to set a level of about –10 dB.

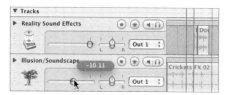

A small numeric display appears to show you the current level as you drag the slider.

NOTE ▶ The Volume slider allows you to set approximate levels, so don't worry if it's not exactly 10 dB. When you get to Lessons 8 and 9, you'll learn to set more specific volume levels in the Mixer and work with track volume envelopes.

2   Drag the Volume slider on the second Illusion/Soundscape track to about –10 dB to lower the volume of the **Wind 2** clip.

3   Play the project to hear the lowered Illusion/Soundscape tracks.

Good—now they feel more like background sounds rather than CRICKETS and WIND! Next you'll adjust the Mood track so the wolves will sound like they're somewhere in the distance, rather than in the same room.

4   Lower the volume level of the Mood track to about –12.

5   Play the beginning of the project to hear the more distant sound of the **Wolves Howling 2** clip.

That's much better, but there's one thing that's still not quite right. The crickets should sound louder when the door opens to the outside.

Splitting a Clip in the Timeline

Part of the job of a sound editor is to make sure that sounds change along with the action on the screen. The more acoustically aware you are of the way sound works in the real world, the better you'll be at editing sound effects and re-creating reality for the world onscreen.

The **Crickets FX 02** clip also makes a fine example for this exercise. Up to this point, you have dragged the edges of a clip to extend or shorten it. You can use the new Split feature to split a clip at the playhead position, creating two separate clips. Once a clip has been split, you can move, delete, copy, paste, and extend each section independently.

First you'll split the **Crickets FX 02** clip when the door opens. Then you'll create another track and move the first part of the clip to the new track. Finally, you'll lower the volume level on the new track so the crickets are much quieter before the door opens. Sounds easy, right? It is!

1   Select the **Crickets FX 02** clip in the Timeline.

2   Move the playhead where you want to make the split, in this case to the door opens marker (07;16).

3   Choose Edit > Split or press S to split the clip at the playhead position.

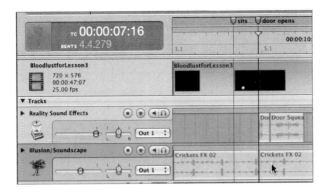

There are now two separate **Crickets FX 02** clips in the first Illusion/Soundscape track.

4   Ctrl-click the drag handle (left edge) of the first Illusion/Soundscape track and choose Insert Track After from the shortcut menu.

A new track appears.

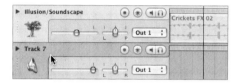

5   Click the name field on the new track, and type *Crickets* to change the name; then click the track's icon and choose a tree icon instead, to match the other Illusion/Soundscape track icons.

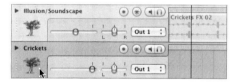

6   Drag the first **Crickets FX 02** clip down to the beginning of the new Crickets track.

7   Lower the volume level of the Crickets track to around –20.

8 Play the project from the beginning to hear the changes.

Mission accomplished.

9 Don't forget to save! If you're working with the **4-1 Start** project, choose File > Save As and name the project *Suspense Scene* in the My Soundtrack Pro projects folder on your desktop. If you're already working with the Suspense Scene from the previous lesson, simply press Cmd-S.

NOTE ▶ If you missed any steps up to this point in the lesson, feel free to open the **4-2 Add Knobs** project file to catch up.

Adjusting Clips with Precision in the Timeline

The preliminary sound is in place, and the basic elements of reality, mood, and ambience are working together to create the overall soundscape. But suspense is all about constantly upping the story ante. At the moment, we hear a dog bark and see the character sit up in bed. But would a barking dog be enough to make you bolt upright from a deep sleep? Probably not, especially since we don't know what spooked the dog. We need some frightening proof that there is a stranger lurking about. Audiences are very susceptible to audible manipulation. That may sound devious, but it's part of the craft of sound editing and design. So let's startle the character (not to mention the dog and the audience) by rattling the doorknob a little. That would certainly make me sit up and take notice.

You already know how to drag clips in the Timeline, but you can also adjust clips with precision using the Edit menu or a handy set of keyboard shortcuts. In the next series of exercises, you'll add two additional Door Knob sound effects to the Reality track to enhance the suspense and give the character incentive to sit up. Once you've added the clips to the track, you can shift or nudge them into position.

Building Suspense with Sound Effects

It just so happens you have a set of three different Door Knob sound effects in the Bin tab that you selected in the previous lesson. That's lucky, because with just one effect, it would be difficult to repeat it without it sounding like the same thing twice. For this exercise, you'll choose one of the Door Knob effects and place it on the Reality track. Technically, it will be used to establish something we don't actually see onscreen, but you'll place it on the Reality track because grouping similar sound effects together will simplify the mixing process later on.

1   Click the Bin tab to view the clips that you added in the previous lesson, along with the clips currently in the project.

2   Preview the **Door Knob 1** and **Door Knob 2** files in the Bin tab.

Door Knob 1 sounds like someone trying to open the door. Context is everything in sound design. This sound effect might be hilarious in a Keystone Cops–type scenario, with a bumbling fool locked in an out-house. In this case, the same sound effect could be quite frightening because it implies that someone or something is trying to get into the bedroom from outside.

3   Drag the **Door Knob 1** file from the Bin tab to the beginning of the
Reality track.

The clip is a bit too long for this scene. A little sound effect can go a long
way in establishing a potential intruder. You'll need to find the part of the
track that you want to work with, then split the track and discard the parts
that you don't want. That will be easier if you zoom in on the clip, and
there's a perfect shortcut for just that.

4   Select the **Door Knob 1** clip, if it's not already selected, and press Option-Z.

Now that you're zoomed in, you can also use Shift-Cmd-+ (plus) or
Shift-Cmd-– (minus) to view the track with a larger or smaller height.

5   Press Shift-Cmd-+ to see a larger track height.

6   Select the **Door Knob 1** clip, if it's not already selected.

7   Play the clip from the beginning and stop the playhead after you hear
3 jiggles of the knob (approximately 01:09).

8   Press S, or choose Edit > Split to split the clip at the playhead position.

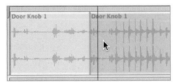

9   Select the second **Door Knob 1** clip (the section after the split) and press Delete.

The excess **Door Knob 1** sound effect is deleted from the Timeline.

NOTE ▶ Deleting a selection means you get rid of it without the intention of using it again. If you want to cut and paste a selection instead, you'd use the Cut command or Cmd-X, which works like a combination of deleting and copying. Similar to the Delete function, Cut deletes a selected item from its current location; but then it copies the item into temporary memory so that it can be pasted in a new location. Each time you Copy or Cut, you replace the old item in temporary memory with the new selection.

Fixing Mistakes with Undo and Redo

Wait! What if you accidentally deleted a section and you want it back? Or perhaps you undid something and changed your mind yet again. No problem. Like most great software, Soundtrack Pro comes fully loaded with fix-it tools.

Undo and Redo are exactly what they sound like: commands that let you move back or forward a step. In fact, you can undo or redo many steps, not just the most recent one. Undo and Redo work with cutting, copying, and pasting—basically anything you add, subtract, or move. Remember the shortcuts for easy access: Cmd-Z to undo, and Shift-Cmd-Z to redo.

NOTE ▶ Undo and Redo will not change the overall window and track layouts. So if you zoom into the Timeline, move the playhead, or change the window layout, you'll need to change them back the old-fashioned way.

Shifting a Clip in the Timeline

Now that you've trimmed the **Door Knob 1** clip in the Reality track, you can shift it into position so that it acts as a catalyst to make the character sit up in bed. Shifting clips moves a selected clip to the nearest gridline. The more you are zoomed in to the Timeline, the more gridlines and thus the more refined the shifted movement. Fortunately, you planned the project well in the previous lesson, so you already have a marker in the Timeline that you can use as a guide.

1   Press the down arrow key to zoom out of the track until the sits up marker (the first marker in the project) is visible in the Timeline.

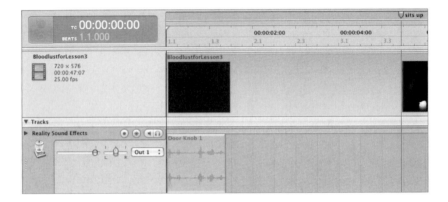

2   Select the **Door Knob 1** clip on the top track, if it is not already selected.

3   Choose Edit > Adjust > Shift Right or use the shortcut and press Shift-Option–right arrow to shift the clip one gridline to the right. Continue pressing Shift-Option–right arrow until the clip is about halfway over the sits up marker.

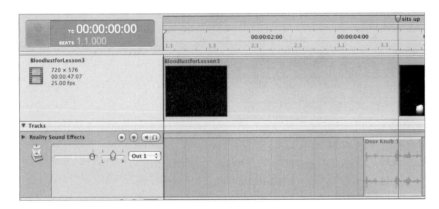

As you might guess, to shift a clip to the left you would first select it and then choose Edit > Adjust > Shift left or press Shift-Option–left arrow. You can also simply drag the clip into position, but this technique of using keyboard shortcuts to shift the clip is more precise.

4   Play the beginning of the project to see how the timing works with the **Door Knob 1** clip and the action in the scene.

Perfect! I just got chills watching the scene.

Nudging a Clip within a Track

You've demonstrated that you can shift a clip one gridline at a time within its track in the Timeline. To move it by an even smaller increment, you can also nudge a clip one frame at a time, overriding gridlines and snapping. For this exercise, you'll add another Door Knob sound right before the door opens to enhance the suspense further. Then, you'll nudge it left or right to fine-tune its position in the Reality track. First, let's create a playback region around the sits up and door opens markers.

1   Drag the bottom half of the Time ruler from around 4;00 to 8;00 to create a playback region that includes the **Door Knob 1** clip (knob rattling sound) and the **Door Knob 3** clip (door opening sound).

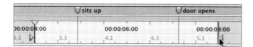

2   Click the Solo button on the Reality track to isolate the sound of that track.

3   Drag the **Door Knob 2** clip from the Bin tab to the Reality track and place it in the empty space between the other two door knob clips.

4   Press Return to move the playhead to the beginning of the playback region and then play the project.

You can nudge a clip while the playhead is moving or paused.

5   Pause playback and select the **Door Knob 2** clip, if it's not already selected.

6   Play the project again and, while it's playing, nudge the clip to the left by pressing Option–left arrow or to the right by pressing Option–right arrow. Continue nudging the clip until you're satisfied with its position.

The sound effect will work virtually anywhere in that space between the other clips, so adjust to your own liking.

Personally, I find there's something unnatural about the **Door Knob 2** clip, no matter where I place it. If you feel the same, you can fix it in the next exercise.

TIP ▶ Nudging works really well for sound effects, dialog, and other non-musical clips. However, you shouldn't use the nudge feature on musical beats-based loops because it will nudge them out of time with the other musical clips in the Timeline.

Project Practice

You just know when sound works. If you're not sure, it isn't right. When it works, you don't have to give it another thought. Why doesn't it work? As an editor, I can't help but notice the pause between the new **Door Knob 2** sound and the **Door Knob 3** clip that is the sound of the door actually opening. The hesitation steals the urgency from the scene and feels like an inept intruder, rather than a determined one. But guess what? It's your job to fix it. You have the skills, so now put them to work.

First, turn off snapping and then trim the empty space at the end of the **Door Knob 2** clip. (The empty space is the part without any waveform showing.) You can either drag the right edge to trim, or use the new Split feature and then delete the excess. Next, move the clip close to the door opens marker so that it sounds like someone rattling the knob just before the door opens. Play the project and nudge the clip until you're happy with the result.

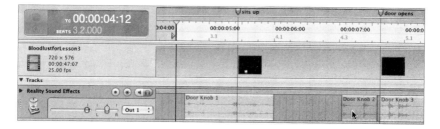

Once you're finished placing the clip, you'll need to do a little housekeeping. Remove the Playback region, turn snapping back on, and unsolo the track to hear the modified Reality track with the rest of the project. When you're finished, save your progress.

> **NOTE ▶** If you didn't complete the previous steps, feel free to open the **4-3 Add Foley** project to catch up.

Adding Foley Sound Effects

When a scene is filmed, the sound mixer records production sound, which includes dialog and whatever sound happens to be picked up by the micro-phones as the actors perform the actions in the scene. The primary focus of production sound is good clean dialog. The other sounds are usually replaced by more dramatic re-enactments referred to as foley sound. Foley sound is named after Jack Foley, who was a stand-in and screenwriter during the silent era of film and later helped Universal make the transition to sound. Just as actors record the voices of animated characters in an animated film, foley artists re-enact the audible actions of real actors onscreen, including every-thing from footsteps to door slams, body hits to clothes wrinkling.

What this scene needs next is some foley sounds to bring the actress's move-ments to life. Chances are you probably don't have a foley recording stage, foley actors, and a full assortment of recording equipment to record the sounds. In lieu of the real foley experience, Soundtrack Pro includes an assortment of foley sound effects.

> **NOTE** ▶ Though they can never be as spot-on accurate to the video as foley sounds recorded for the scene by trained foley artists, pre-recorded foley sounds will work fine for many scenes, including this one.

Building Foley Tracks

In the next series of exercises, you'll search for specific foley sound effects and then add them to the Timeline. First you'll create three new tracks below the Reality track.

1 Ctrl-click the Reality track header and choose Insert Track After from the shortcut menu.

2 Repeat step one twice until you have a total of three new tracks.

3 Rename the new tracks (from top to bottom) *Foley*, *Clothes*, and *Exposition/Character*.

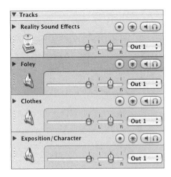

4 Watch the scene and look for any actions that the actress takes onscreen that should create sound.

I notice three things that need sound: footsteps, breathing, and the movement of the bedspread when she climbs out of bed. If you didn't pick up
on all three, watch the scene again and look for those cues.

Auditioning Foley Sound Effects

Now that you know which sounds you're looking for, it's just a matter of searching for the right sound for each action onscreen. Let's start with the footsteps.
You can search for foley sound effects in either the column or button view,
whichever you prefer. Once you find effects you think will work, you can
audition them with the rest of the project to see how they work *before* you
add them to the Timeline. To audition a file in the Media and Effects Manager,
simply preview the file while the project is playing. It'll be easier to audition the
file with the project if you create a playback region. While you're at it, this might
be a good time to set a marker for when the actress climbs out of bed.

1 Play the project and pause when the actress pulls back the bedspread to
climb out of bed (around 23;00).

2 Press M to set a time marker at the playhead position. Then, double click
the head of the marker and name the marker *out of bed*.

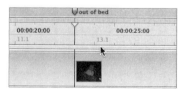

3 Press the right arrow key to move the playhead one second to the right. Continue pressing the right arrow key until the playhead is at 30 seconds in the Timeline.

> **NOTE ▶** You may need to zoom in or out of the Timeline so that the right and left arrow keys move the playhead one second at a time.

4 Create a playback region from the playhead position (30;00) to the out of bed marker (23;00).

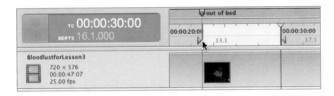

5 Click the Search tab, then change the search category to Sound Effects.

6 Click the Foley keyword in the Sound Effects category and type *footsteps* in the search text field.

There are 63 different footstep files. Foley artists record footsteps to match the screen by wearing different shoes and walking on surfaces that match those in the scene. For this scene the actress has bare feet and isn't moving very fast, so you can focus on the footstep files at the top of the list that include the word *bare* in the file name.

NOTE ▶ Foley sound effects have very literal names to make it easier to identify the type of file that you are searching for.

7 Press the spacebar to begin playing the playback region in the Timeline.

When you audition a foley sound with the project, the audio you're pre-viewing may not match up exactly with the picture, but you'll have a good idea if it will work or not.

8 Select the first file in the list **Footsteps Bare Down 1** to preview it along with the project.

Not even close. Next!

9 Press the down arrow key to move to the next file in the list. Continue pressing the down arrow key until you've previewed all of the bare footstep files.

Did you find one that worked? The **Footsteps Bare Scuff** file seems to work really well with the picture. Let's try it.

10 Drag the **Footsteps Bare Scuff** file from the Search tab to the foley track so that it starts at the out of bed marker.

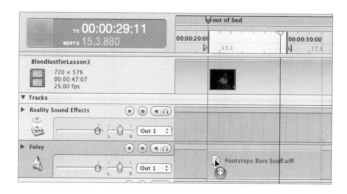

Project Practice

The first foley sound effect is in the Timeline. Now all you need to do is move it into position so that it matches better with her feet hitting the floor and her first steps. Play the project, and shift or nudge the clip until it works with the video. It doesn't have to be perfect as long as it sounds like it goes with her movements onscreen. If you have trouble finding a position that you like, try starting the clip at 24;00. When you're finished, save your progress.

Duplicating a Clip in the Timeline

Another handy feature in most applications (including Soundtrack Pro) is the duplicate feature, which automatically duplicates the selected clip and places the duplicate to the right of the original clip in the Timeline. This can be very useful when you are working with non-looping files and want them to repeat, such as the footsteps clip.

There are three standard ways to duplicate a selected clip in the Timeline:

▶ Choose Edit > Duplicate.

▶ Press Cmd-D.

▶ Ctrl-click the clip and choose Duplicate from the shortcut menu.

In this exercise, you'll duplicate the Footsteps Bare Scuff clip using the keyboard shortcut. First, listen to the project without the playback region to see if you actually need more footsteps.

1   Clear the current playback region and play the project.

    The footstep sound definitely ends prematurely, hence the need to duplicate the clip.

2   Select the Footsteps Bare Scuff clip in the Foley Track.

3   Press Cmd-D.

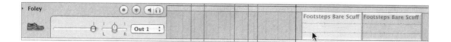

A duplicate **Footsteps Bare Scuff** clip appears on the Foley track at the right of the original clip.

Putting It All Together

Time to put together the skills that you've learned so far to add a foley sound effect for the bedspread moving as the actress gets out of bed.

1   Create a playback region around the out of bed marker that includes all of the movement of the bedspread (approximately 21;12 to 23;06).

2   On the Search tab, type *Clothes* in the search text field.

3   Audition each of the five different foley clothes effects to find a good choice for the scene.

Personally, I like **Clothes 2**, but feel free to use a different file if you prefer.

4   Drag your choice to the play range area of the Clothes track.

5   Play the project and shift or nudge the clothes clip until the beginning fits with the movement of the bedspread (about 22;00).

6   Remove the playback region.

7   Select and play the clothes clip; pause playback when the bedspread stops moving in the video, around 23;12.

> **NOTE ▶** You may not actually see the bedspread moving in 23;12, but if you follow the action of the scene, it would stop around then.

8   Press S to split the selected clip at the playhead position.

9   Delete the section of the clip after the split.

Nice work! You're ready to add another effect on your own.

Project Practice

There are still a few sounds missing to make the character's fear more audible. The obvious choice would be a scream, except her mouth doesn't open and she's hypnotized by the vampire, so screaming isn't an option. Instead, loud breathing and a pounding heartbeat can express fear or tension. You'll find these types of sound effects in the People category of sound effects.

Your goal is to add a sound effect to the breathe marker on the Exposition/Character Track. You'll find two Breath Female sounds to choose from. Select the best one for the scene and add it to the track. **Breath Female 2** is probably best because it sounds more like quick, fearful breathing, instead of the long, heavy breathing in **Breath Female 1.** Then trim the sound effect so that it only occurs during her close-up shot when you see her breathing. Trim and nudge the clip as needed for the desired result. Then add a heartbeat sound effect that begins at 24;00, after she gets out of bed. (There is only one heartbeat sound effect and you'll find it under the People category.) Finally, lower the volume level on the Clothes track to around –5 and the Exposition/Character track to around –8. When you're finished, save your progress.

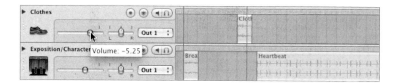

NOTE ▶ If you didn't complete the previous steps, feel free to open the **4-4 Add Music** project to catch up.

Crafting Suspense with Music

There are two things to consider when building the soundtrack for a scene. Is the scene going to be sound-effects based or music-based? Of course, the scene can include both types of elements, but generally one is more dominant. For example, a car chase scene could be driven literally by a heavy music track that keeps the pace and feel moving forward at full throttle with every musical phrase. There are still sound effects when needed, but the music is without question the dominant element. The alternative is a car chase sequence with heavy sound effects—horns honking, tires squealing, people screaming, engines revving at ribcage rattling levels—while the music is merely a light, adrenaline-enhancing highlight. Both scenarios can result in very effective and exciting chase scenes.

Music can completely change the feel of a scene and can turn nearly any performance into a three-hanky tearjerker or goose-bump–inducing thriller. For this scene, the sound design you're working on is sound-effects based, with a subtle music track. In the next series of exercises, you'll add several music loops to the soundtrack to build suspense, and take the emotion of the scene to the next level.

Auditioning Music Loops

Soundtrack Pro includes over 4000 royalty-free musical loops to choose from. Rather than searching aimlessly through that musical haystack of files, you'll narrow the search to the Designer Synth loops. Still, there are over twenty different Designer Synth loops, so let's focus on the first six.

To make the auditioning process easier, you'll start by creating a playback. Then you'll audition the first six Designer Synth loops with the project to see which one works best with the scene. How will you know when you find the right one? Trust your instincts. You'll never appreciate how good a music part works until you hear a few that don't. Here's your chance. One of the first six Designer Synth loops works really well with the video; the others vary, but definitely lack the same impact.

1   Create a playback region from the purple Start Music marker to the red End of Song marker.

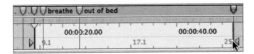

This is the portion of the Timeline where you'll add the music.

2   Click the Search tab on the Media and Effects Manager, change the keyword pop-up menu to Instruments, and type *Designer Synth* in the search text field.

3   Play the project in the Timeline and select the **Designer Synth 01.aiff** file to audition it with the scene.

Nope. Too heavy on the synth. Might work for a sci-fi scene about dancing alien fireflies, but not *this* scene.

4   Press the down arrow key to audition the next file. Continue auditioning files until you reach **Designer Synth 06.aiff.**

Wow. The haunting piano sounds like it was written for this scene.

NOTE ▶ Music is incredibly subjective, so you might like one of the other loops better. For this exercise, you'll work with the **Designer Synth 06** file, but you can always replace it with a different part after this lesson.

Adding Music Tracks

You've located the music loop to enhance the scene, now all you need to do is add it to the music tracks. First, you'll need to create the music tracks, then you can add the music.

1   Press Cmd-T twice to create two new tracks at the bottom of the Timeline.

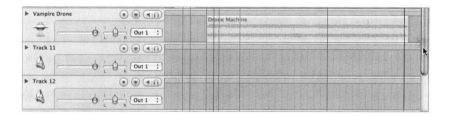

2   Drag the vertical scrollbar on the right edge of the Timeline down to view the new tracks, if they're not already showing.

You'll add the music loop to the Timeline so that it begins at the start music marker in the Timeline (15;00).

3 Drag the **Designer Synth 06.aiff** file from the Search tab to the start music marker on the lowest track in the Timeline.

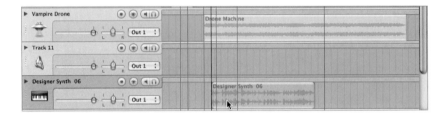

The track's name changes to Designer Synth 06 to reflect the clip that you just added to it.

4 Play the project to hear the music with the other tracks in the Timeline.

Doubling a Musical Part

One way to really "fatten" a track is to double a part. That's musicspeak for having twice the number of instruments play the same part at the same time, making the piece louder and fuller.

The easiest way to double a part in Soundtrack Pro is to create a new track above or below the part you want to double. Then, copy the original and paste a duplicate in the second track.

1 Select the **Designer Synth 06** clip on the lowest track of the Timeline, if it is not already selected.

2 Press Cmd-C or choose Edit > Copy.

3 Select the empty track above the Designer Synth 06 track.

4 Move the playhead to the purple start music marker, then press Cmd-V to paste the clip into the selected track.

> **NOTE ▶** If you accidentally pasted the clip to the wrong track, press Cmd-Z to undo, and try again. The pasted clip will always go to the playhead position on the selected track.

You've successfully doubled the track, but doubling also combines the levels of the two clips which raises the volume of the doubled part in the project. Let's take a moment to lower the volume level of both Designer Synth 06 tracks.

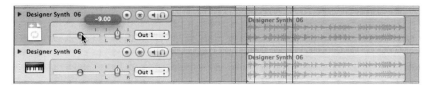

5   Lower the volume level of each Designer Synth 06 track to −9 dB.

6   Play the project to hear the doubled music tracks.

7   Save your progress.

Editing with the Razor Tool

As you can see, doubling music clips is easy and effective. However, it would be even better if you trim away some of the doubled clip so that it's only doubled for key moments of the music.

Previously, you have trimmed clips in the Timeline by dragging the edges or splitting the clip. In this exercise, you'll edit the upper **Designer Synth 06** clip using the Razor tool. The Razor tool works the same as the Blade tool in Final Cut Pro—they even have the same shortcut, B for blade. You can also click the Razor tool in the top-left corner of the Project window.

1   Click the Beats-based format button to change the project's time format.

This exercise requires a beats-based time format so that the gridlines and snapping will be in musical time. Feel free to zoom in or out of the Timeline or change the track size as needed so that you can cut the top clip at the 1st beat of the 12th measure.

2   Move the playhead to 12.1.000 in the Timeline.

3   Click the Razor tool in the top left-corner of the window, or press B.

The pointer changes from an arrow to a razor blade.

4   Click the upper Designer Synth 06 clip at the playhead position with the Razor tool.

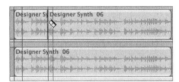

The clip splits into two sections on either side of the razor cut.

5   Press A to switch back to the Selection (arrow) tool.

6   Select the section before the cut and press Delete to remove it from the project.

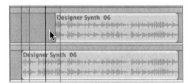

TIP ▶ To quickly move the playhead to an exact location, double-click the current playhead position in the Time display and type a new destination. For example, for the 1st beat of the 12th measure, type 12.1.000 (that's the number 12 plus a period followed by 1 and another period; the zeros at the end are optional).

7   Move the playhead to 16.3.000, press B to select the Razor tool, and click the first **Designer Synth 06** clip at the playhead position.

8   Cut the clip again at 21.4.000.

9   Press A to switch back to the Selection tool.

10 Click the section of the edited clip between 16.4.000 and 21.4.000, and press delete to remove it.

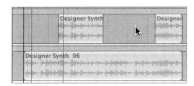

11 Play the project and save your progress.

If you're wondering why we just went through all of that trouble to create a doubling effect that isn't very dramatic, hang in there. You're about to learn a very powerful music editing trick.

NOTE ▶ The Razor tool can split a clip no matter where it is in the Timeline, but only one clip at a time. The Split feature (S) allows you to split all selected clips, but only at the playhead position.

Transposing Audio Clips

Transposing is a musical term for changing the key of a piece of music. Soundtrack automatically transposes every tagged music loop that you bring into the Timeline to match the key of the project. If the natural key for a clip already matches the project key, no change will take place.

1 Ctrl-click the first section of doubled clip on the upper **Designer Synth 06** track.

A shortcut menu appears with editing options for that clip.

2 Select Transpose.

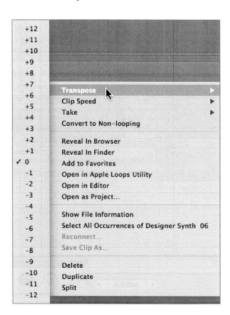

Notice the vertical list of numbers from +12 to −12. These represent semitones, which measure the distance the clip is transposed. This clip is currently set to 0, which is equal to the key of the current project (A). If you want to know the original key of an audio file, you can find it in the Details tab in the Utility window.

3   Select –12 in the submenu.

A small –12 appears on the clip to show that it has been transposed by –12 semitones.

4   Press Return to move the playhead to the beginning of the playback region, and then play the transposed clip.

This sounds great. Let's analyze what you did.

There are seven different musical notes, A to G. Each note can be performed by different instruments and can be distinguished by its own sound or pitch. If you ever saw *The Sound of Music*, you'll remember that the musical nanny taught the children the notes by singing each one: "Do-re-mi-fa-so-la-ti-do." Each sound represents a note, one step at a time, until the whole thing repeats an octave higher. You can also go the other direction, an octave lower.

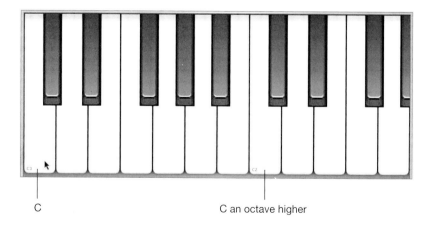

C   C an octave higher

A piano keyboard has white and black keys. The white keys are the notes A to G, and the black keys are sharp and flat variations of the notes, or half steps between. If you pick any piano note or key and count the keys (black and white) until the note repeats, you will count 12 keys. So, if you take any clip in the Timeline and transpose it by +/– 12 (as you did in the last exercise), it will play the exact same notes an entire octave higher or lower.

You can also transpose clips by only a few semitones to alter the key and build a chord. You have to be careful when doing this. If you hit the wrong key, you and everyone else will know it.

Transposing loops by +/– 2 semitones will sound good. If you are going for a happier feel, +/– 3 semitones corresponds with the major chords.

> **TIP** ▶ Doubling a track and transposing it by +/– 12 is an excellent way to enhance the sound of a particular part. Not only does the doubling make the sound louder, but transposing makes it richer with harmony.

Project Practice

Now that you've heard how the doubled part sounds when it's transposed one octave lower, it's your turn to try a different variation. Transpose both of the edited **Designer Synth 06** clips by –9. Play the project to hear the doubled-and-transposed parts. What a difference three semitones make! The new version has an eerily melodic sound, which works well in the context of the scene.

Adding a Stinger for Effect

One of the most powerful musical elements in crafting suspense is the stinger. You know, that subtle string sound that creeps into the scene and stings you emotionally without warning. For example, imagine a scene that involves a character walking down the hall toward his apartment door. He hasn't a care in the world. He might be talking on a cell phone, and the only music is the light thump of a neighbor's stereo. But a musical stinger begins as he approaches the door and fumbles for his keys, so tension is starting to mount for the audience even before the character notices that his door is already ajar.

What makes stingers so effective is that they slowly creep into the soundtrack, and by the time the audience notices, their adrenaline is already pumping. Stingers are used for instant suspense. Let's demonstrate.

1 On the Search tab, select the **Designer Synth 07.aiff** file.

That's a stinger. It causes an almost Pavlovian response of fear for both the character and the audience. You'll add the stinger to the Mood track.

2 Drag the **Designer Synth 07** file to the out of bed marker on the Mood track (12.3.000).

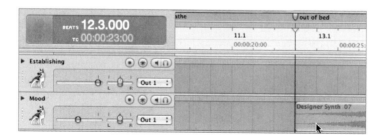

3   Clear the playback region, play the full scene with the finished music tracks, and save your progress.

Did you notice the power of the stinger mixed with the other music? My goosebumps just got goosebumps.

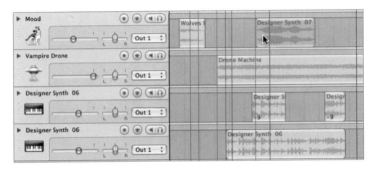

NOTE ▶ If you didn't complete the previous steps, feel free to open the project **4-5 Add Overlap** to catch up.

Overlapping Clips in the Timeline

You've created a suspenseful soundtrack from scratch that flows well with the scene, adds reality, and enhances the emotion, actions, and mood. Overall it works and you're nearly done, but it could use a little more mood enhancement after the stinger ends. Onscreen, the young woman turns toward the camera and the vampire slowly moves in front of the camera, essentially fading out the scene. This seems to be the perfect opportunity to reintroduce the sound of howling wolves. Better yet, let's overlap the end of the stinger clip with the beginning of a howling wolves clip to create a crossfade.

When you overlap clips in the Timeline, you can create either a crossfade or truncate the overlapping clips, depending on the overlap mode of your project. The default overlap mode is crossfade.

Creating Crossfades Between Audio Clips

When a project is in crossfade mode, a crossfade is created automatically for the overlapped part of two audio files. Crossfades let you create smooth transitions between one audio clip and the next, avoiding abrupt changes in volume that can result from placing audio files back-to-back.

Let's duplicate the **Wolves Howling 2** clip at the beginning of the Mood track and overlap the duplicate with the end of the **Designer Synth 07** file. You've already learned that you can duplicate a clip with Cmd-D, or copy and paste clips in the Timeline. In this exercise, you'll learn a new time-saving duplicating trick called option-dragging, which works in all Final Cut Studio applications.

1   Click the Crossfade Mode button located above the Global Timeline view in the upper-right corner of the Project window.

2   Press N to turn off snapping, if it is on, so you'll have more freedom of movement with the duplicate clip.

3   Select the **Wolves Howling 2** clip at the beginning of the Mood track.

4   Press and hold the Option key (which makes a duplicate) and drag the duplicate clip to the right; then release it so that it partially overlaps the end of the **Designer Synth 07** clip.

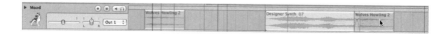

5   Solo the Mood track and listen to the crossfade between the clips.

Extending a Crossfade

Crossfades are created for the overlapped part of the two audio files. You can drag the boundaries of the crossfade to adjust its length or simply overlap more of the clips to create a longer crossfade.

1 Zoom in to the Timeline for a better view of the crossfade.

2 Move your pointer over the crossfade in the Timeline.

There are three different ways to use the mouse pointer to modify the crossfade in the Timeline. If your pointer is over the lower middle of the crossfade, the Selection tool becomes a Hand tool that you can use to move the actual crossfade to a different point on the clip without changing its length. If you move the pointer to the right or left edges of the crossfade boundary, you can extend or collapse the crossfade. Or, if you select the crossfade from the center where the two lines intersect and drag left or right, you can overlap the clips further, thus extending the crossfade.

For this exercise you'll drag the crossfade from the center where the lines intersect to move more of the **Wolves Howling 2** clip over the stinger clip, extending the crossfade in the process.

3   Drag the intersecting lines (center) of the crossfade to the left the distance of one gridline or so, to extend the crossfade and the amount of overlap between audio clips.

4   Press the down arrow key several times to zoom out of the Timeline until you can see the entire Mood track up to the end of song marker.

Next you'll add the **Wolves Howling 1** clip from the Bin tab and overlap it with the end of the **Wolves Howling 2** clip. If you recall, you didn't use the **Wolves Howling 1** clip in Lesson 3 because the wolves sounded more scared and submissive. If the vampire is dominant over them, it only makes sense that they sound submissive at the end of the scene when he is present. Also, their sound substitutes a voice for the young woman who has no voice of her own because she's been hypnotized by the vampire.

5   Drag **Wolves Howling 1** to the end of the Mood track and overlap the end of **Wolves Howling 2.**

Adjust the crossfade as needed until you're satisfied with the sound of the overlapping clips.

6   Unsolo the Mood track and listen to the project in the Timeline.

Truncating Overlapping Audio Clips

Instead of crossfading overlapping clips, you can truncate them by changing the project's overlap mode. In this exercise, you'll truncate the **Footsteps Bare Scuff** clips, since the footsteps sounds continue in the track even after the woman stops moving onscreen. Your goal is to move the right footsteps clip to the left to start it sooner in the track. That will overlap the previous footsteps clip and cut it short. Let's try it.

1   Solo the Foley track and zoom in for a good view of both **Footsteps Bare Scuff** clips.

2   Click the Truncate Mode button to change the project overlap mode.

3   Click the Time-based format button to change the project's time format.

4   Move the playhead to 43 seconds in the Timeline (43;00), which is where you want the second clip to end.

5   Drag the second **Footsteps Bare Scuff** clip on the Foley track to the left and align the end of the clip with the playhead.

Notice that in truncate mode, the clip on the right overlaps the clip on the left without creating a crossfade.

6   Unsolo the track and save your progress.

7   Press Shift-Z to fit the entire project in the window so that you can admire your audio masterpiece.

Creating a Master Timeslice

Now that you've finished the sound editing, you can take a moment to clean up the end of the project. The red end of song marker works as a period on the soundtrack, so that the playhead knows where to stop playback. Right now you have quite a few clips that extend beyond the red marker. Not that there's anything *wrong* with that, but if you want to ensure that everything ends at that moment, you can trim every clip in the Timeline at the same time with a timeslice.

What's a timeslice? It's exactly what it sounds like, a slice of the Timeline. You can create timeslices within a track or timeslices that include the entire project. For this exercise you'll create a timeslice selection that starts at the red end of

song marker and extends to include everything beyond the marker (50;00).
Once you've selected a slice of the Timeline, you can cut, copy, or delete the
selection. You can use the Selection Length value slider located in the bottom-
right corner of the interface to determine the length of the master timeslice.

1   Press the End key to move the playhead to the end of song marker.

2   Press Cmd-Shift-– (minus) to zoom out vertically until the tracks are the
smallest (minimized) size.

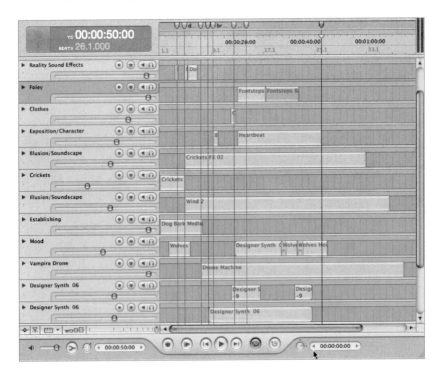

The Selection Length value slider works very much the same as the Playhead Position value slider located at the left of the transport controls. Both value sliders can be modified by typing a new value, clicking the incremental arrows, or click-dragging over the slider's value. The difference is that the Playhead Position value slider lets you view or change the current playhead position, while the Selection Length value slider creates a Master timeslice (selection) starting at the playhead position.

3 Click-drag the Selection Length value slider to the right until the ends of clips extending beyond the red marker are within the blue selection (28;00 in the Selection Length value slider).

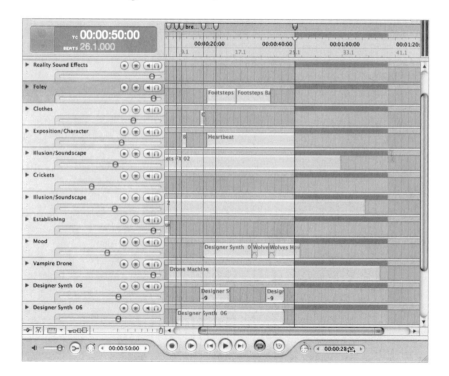

The blue area in the Timeline shows the selected master timeslice.

4 Press Delete to remove the elements contained within the timeslice.

5 Click anywhere in the Timeline to deselect the timeslice selection.

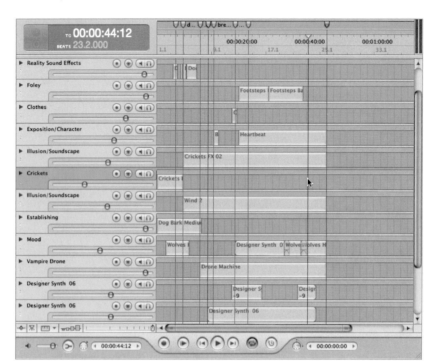

6 Save your progress and play the finished piece. Feel free to click the Zoom button (+) on the Utility window to fit the Video to the screen and play the project again.

Very impressive. You planned and executed the total sound design and editing for this scene from scratch! Now that you've finished, just imagine the possibilities for your own projects using Soundtrack Pro.

Lesson Review

1. What are the highest and lowest volume levels that you can set for each track? What is the default volume level?

2. How do you split a clip using the Split feature?

3. What is the difference between the Split feature and the Razor tool?

4. What are the two methods for moving selected clips in the Timeline without dragging them? What are the shortcuts for each method?

5. What nickname is given sound effects that re-enact the actions of the characters onscreen, such as footsteps and rustling sheets?

6. What are three of the four ways that you can duplicate a clip in the Timeline?

7. When you add a tagged music loop to the Timeline, will the loop maintain its native key or change to the project key? Where can you see a clip's native key?

8. How can you change the key of a tagged loop in the Timeline, and what is the maximum amount that it can be changed?

9. What are the two overlap modes in the Timeline?

10. What is a master timeslice, and how can it be used in Soundtrack Pro?

Answers

1. The highest volume level that you can set for each track is 6 dB, and the lowest is –96 dB. The default volume level for each track is 0 dB.

2. To split a clip using the Split feature, you must first select the clip, then move the playhead to the position where you'd like to split the clip, and choose Edit > Split or press S.

3. The Split feature allows you to split all selected clips, but only at the playhead position. The Razor tool can split a clip no matter where it is in the Timeline, but can only split one clip at a time.

4. The two methods for moving clips without dragging them are *shifting* and *nudging*. Shifting a clip moves it left or right one gridline at a time; the shortcut is Shift-Option–right or left arrow. Nudging a clip overrides snapping and moves a clip by the smallest increment; the shortcut is Option–right or left arrow.

5. Sound effects that re-enact the actions of characters are referred to as foley effects, named after actor Jack Foley.

6. You can duplicate a clip in the Timeline by selecting the clip and pressing Cmd-D, Option-dragging it, choosing Edit > Duplicate, or Ctrl-clicking the clip and choosing duplicate from the shortcut menu.

7. When you add a tagged music loop to the Timeline, the loop always changes to the project's key. You can view a loop's native key in the Details tab.

8. Transposing a clip allows you to change the key of a tagged clip by up to 12 semitones (one full octave) higher or lower.

9. The two overlap modes are crossfade and truncate.

10. A master timeslice is a selection of the Timeline that includes all tracks and their media. You can use a master timeslice to cut, copy, paste, and delete selected areas of the Timeline.

Keyboard Shortcuts

Editing

S	Split a clip
Cmd-D	Duplicate
Cmd-C	Copy
Cmd-V	Paste
Cmd-X	Cut
Cmd-Z	Undo previous step
Shift-Cmd-Z	Redo previous step

Keyboard Shortcuts

Tools

B   Razor tool

A   Selection tool

Zooming

Option Z   Zooms in to the selected clip(s)

Shift-Cmd-+   Zooms vertically to a larger track height

Shift-Cmd--   Zooms vertically to a smaller track height

Moving Clips

**Shift-Option–left
or right arrow**   Shifts clip left or right one gridline at a time

**Option–left or
right arrow**   Nudges clip left or right by smallest increment

Tracks

Cmd-T   Creates a new track

5

Lesson Files   Soundtrack Pro book files > 05_Projects&Media > 5-1 TD
Start, 5-5 TD Final

Time   This lesson takes approximately 90 minutes to complete.

Goals   Open a clip in the Waveform Editor

Explore the Waveform Editor interface

Apply Fade In and Fade Out actions to a file

Work with the audio Stretching tool

Copy, paste and silence parts of a Waveform

Create a customized sound effect

Designing Sound in the Waveform Editor

If you've enjoyed the lessons up to this point, this one ought to make your inner sound designer very happy. It's not just a tour of Soundtrack Pro's powerful Waveform Editor. It's more like an off-road safari where you'll discover wild sound design features and arm yourself with a host of new graphical editing tools to stretch, process, alter, and customize sound effects.

Your assignment, should you choose to accept it, is to enhance the soundtrack of a real-world trailer for Teton Gravity Research's exciting new film, *Tangerine Dream.* Not only will you modify existing sound files, but you'll also combine audio files to create new effects. Along the way you'll also learn to navigate the Waveform Editor's interface while picking up more sound design tricks and shortcuts.

After this lesson, you'll never *see* sound the same way again. And you'll never have to settle for a conservative-sounding, all-natural audio file when your project demands something special. So here you go—and by all means *do* try this at home.

Preparing the Project

You'll begin this lesson by opening and playing the **5-5 TD Final** project located in the 05 Projects&Media folder. Once you've seen and heard the final version, you'll open the **5-1 TD Start** project and save it in the My Soundtrack Pro projects folder on your desktop.

1   Quit all open applications, except for Soundtrack Pro.

2   Close any open Soundtrack Pro projects, except for the project **5-5 TD Final.**

3   Open the multitrack project **5-5 TD Final,** if it's not already open.

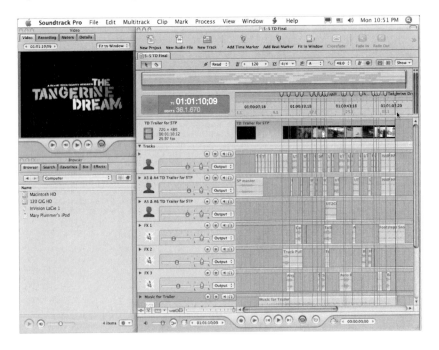

The TD (Tangerine Dream) project was sent to Soundtrack Pro from Final Cut Pro and includes one video clip, all of the dialog clips, plus 16 orange scoring markers. Scoring markers are created in Final Cut Pro and cannot be deleted, edited, or moved in Soundtrack Pro. These scoring markers were added during the video editing process to mark specific places that needed sound effects. The music file at the bottom of the Timeline was created in a separate Soundtrack Pro project and mixed before importing it into this project as a single stereo file.

NOTE ▶ If you'd like to see the actual Soundtrack Pro project for the music track, you can open the **1 Trailer Music** project in the Music for Trailer folder located in the 05_Projects&Media folder.

4   Click the Zoom button on the Utility window to fit the Video tab in the screen. Watch the video once with the finished sound design.

Fun stuff! The challenge with a project like this is to make the sound design as exciting as the X-treme footage in the trailer, without making it distracting.

5   Press F1 to return to the Standard layout.

6   Mute the Music for Trailer track at the bottom of the Timeline and play the project again.

This time, watch the playhead as it scrubs across the different effects on the FX 1, FX 2, and FX 3 tracks.

All of the raw sound effects came from the Soundtrack Pro content. However, many of them have been modified in the Waveform Editor to make them fit better with the images onscreen.

Now that you know what you're aiming for, let's open the Start version of the project and get this sound design safari under way.

7   Press Cmd-W to close the current project.

8   Press Cmd-O and open the **5-1 TD Start** project located in the 05_Projects&Media folder.

9 Save the project uncollected in the My Soundtrack Pro projects folder on your desktop.

NOTE ▶ If you check the Details tab or look at the video track header, you'll see that the video for this project is in the NTSC broadcast standard with a frame size of 720 × 480, 29.97 fps, and a length 00:01:10;12.

Creating an Audio File Project

In Lesson 1, "Working with the Interface," you briefly opened a file in the Waveform Editor and reversed the audio. This time, you'll get a chance to pause and explore the interface before editing the actual files. First, you'll need to create an audio file project that will open in the Waveform Editor.

1 Press Return to move the playhead to the beginning of the project in the Timeline.

2 Press Shift-M to move to the first marker (20;08).

3 Press the up arrow key to zoom in until you can read the names of the first three scoring markers.

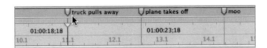

Each of the scoring markers is named for the effect that should occur around that frame in the Timeline.

Some of the effects need to be placed more exactly than others. For example, the sound of a truck moving doesn't need to sync specifically to an exact frame, nor does the sound of a plane taking off or a cow mooing. However, the sound of a skier falling and bouncing off a rock before plummeting over a snowy bank should match the action. (When you get to that part of the trailer, you'll create a specialized sound effect.) For now, let's focus on opening the **Truck Pull Away** file as an audio file project in the Waveform Editor.

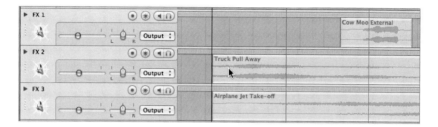

Understanding Audio File Projects

As you know, there are two types of projects in Soundtrack Pro. There are *multitrack projects*, which you've been working with since the first lesson, and *audio file projects*. The difference between them is fairly self-explanatory. Multitrack projects include multiple tracks of audio that you edit, arrange, and mix in the Timeline. Audio file projects contain one audio file and are modified in the Waveform Editor.

There are two ways to open an audio file in the Waveform Editor. First, you can open it as a file, which saves the changes to the actual audio file. This method is referred to as destructive editing because once you change the original audio file, you can't go back. The other option is to open the file as an audio file project, which is non-destructive and allows you to make changes to the audio while leaving the original file intact.

All of the sound effects you'll be working with in this lesson come from the Soundtrack Pro content. Rather than destructively edit the actual audio files, you'll create audio file projects that work in the Waveform Editor.

Opening and Saving an Audio File Project

Soundtrack Pro supports a variety of file formats that can be opened in the Waveform Editor including: Audio file project, AIFF, WAV, MP3, AAC (except protected AAC files), Sound Designer II, NeXT sound files, and QuickTime movie files. In this book, you'll be working with AIFF files, which can also be used in Final Cut Pro.

For this exercise, you will open the **Truck Pull Away** file in the Waveform Editor and modify the waveform. Then you'll save the changed audio file. The Truck Pull Away file is on the FX 2 track and starts at the truck pulls away marker.

There are three ways to open a clip as an Audio File Project in the Timeline:

▶   Select the clip and choose Clip > Open as Project…

▶   Ctrl-click and choose Open as Project from the shortcut menu

▶   Double-click the clip in the Timeline and select the Create audio file project (edit non-destructively) option from the Double-Click Preference dialog

Let's go with the third option and double-click.

1   Double-click the Truck Pull Away clip in the Timeline.

The Double-Click Preferences dialog opens.

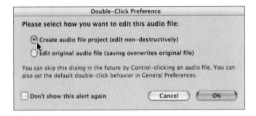

2   Make sure the Create audio file project (edit non-destructively) radio button is selected and then click OK.

NOTE ▶ The default double-click preference in Soundtrack Pro is to create an audio file project. You can change the double-click behavior in General Preferences.

A Create Audio Project window opens.

This window allows you to name the audio file project and save it to a specific location. For this exercise, you'll save the project as Truck Pull Away TD (for Tangerine Dream) to distinguish it from the original file. You'll also save it in the same location as your multitrack project.

3   Type *TD* after the name Truck Pull Away in the Save As field.

The audio file project you create will now be called Truck Pull Away TD.

4   Choose the My Soundtrack Pro projects folder from the Where pop-up menu.

This pop-up menu sets the designation of the saved audio file project.

NOTE ▶ If you need to navigate beyond the condensed view in the Create Audio Project window, you can click the downward pointing triangle button on the right side of the Save As field to expand the window view. You can also condense the view anytime by clicking the upward pointing triangle button once the window has been expanded.

5   Click Save to save the audio file project and open it in the Waveform Editor.

Exploring the Waveform Editor

The Waveform Editor has many of the same features as the Timeline, such as a playhead, ruler, track controls, transport controls, and Time display. In the next series of exercises, you'll explore some of the features unique to the Waveform Editor, as well as some familiar features that work the same as the Timeline.

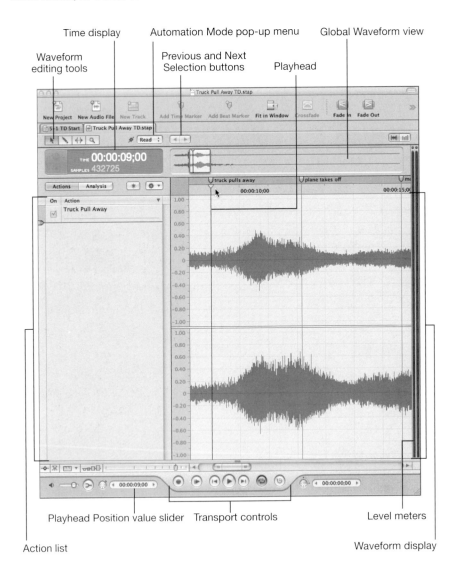

▶ *Waveform editing tools:* Includes the Selection, Sample Edit, Audio Stretching, and Zoom tools for graphically editing audio files.

▶ *Automation Mode pop-up menu:* Allows you to choose the automation mode for recording automation to the file. You'll learn more about recording automation in Lesson 8, "Mixing Audio Tracks in Soundtrack Pro."

▶ *Previous and Next Selection buttons:* Allow you to move backward and forward through selections you've made in the Waveform display.

▶ *Time display:* Shows the current position of the playhead, just as the Time display in the Timeline does.

▶ *Global Waveform view:* Shows you a miniature view of the entire waveform and the playhead position, so that you can move quickly to different parts of an audio file.

▶ *Waveform display* (and editing area): Allows you to see and select parts of the waveform of the audio file (or its frequency spectrum, in Spectrum view).

▶ *Level meters:* Show the levels of the audio file as it plays.

▶ *Transport controls:* Contains transport buttons to control playback and the position of the playhead, and turn recording on or off. These are the same transport controls that are in the Timeline.

▶ *Playhead:* Shows the part of the audio file currently playing.

▶ *Actions and Analysis buttons:* Shows either the Action list and related controls or the Analysis Type, Parameter, and Analysis Results lists and related controls.

There are two audio waveforms showing in the Waveform display area because the file you are working with is a stereo audio file. All stereo files are the combination of the left and right channels of audio. If you open a mono audio file you'll see only one audio waveform.

Navigating with Markers

Before you dive in to the interface and start zooming and navigating around, it's a really good idea to know where you are so that you don't get lost. Sure, the audio file project only contains one audio file, but it's a biggie, over 100 seconds long, and you're only working with around 10 seconds of it in the Timeline.

When you open an audio file project, it references the *whole* audio file, not just the part that you use in the Timeline. Gray markers, indicating the beginning and end of the clip in the Timeline, only appear if there is not already a scoring marker at the first or last frame of the clip.

> **TIP** ▶ To see a file's length and other properties, you can click the Details tab in the Utility window or simply press Cmd-I. On the Details tab, click the File button to view the file's details, including Length in seconds.

Fortunately, the audio file project opens with the playhead on the truck pulls away scoring marker at the beginning of the clip in the Timeline. Also, the portion of the audio visible in the Timeline fits within the Waveform display area of the Waveform Editor. Orange scoring markers from the Timeline also appear in the Waveform Editor as a reference. In this case, the clip starts at a scoring marker, so let's use that marker to identify the beginning of the audio file showing in the Timeline.

1   Press Cmd-– (minus) to zoom out of the Waveform display one level.

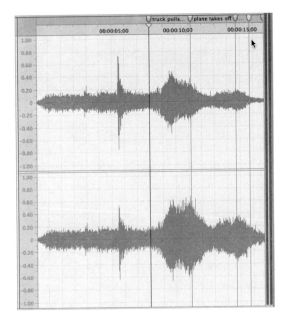

The playhead is still on the truck pulls away marker, and now you can clearly see the gray marker that indicates the end of the clip in the Timeline.

NOTE ▶ The image visible in the Waveform display will vary slightly depending on the resolution of the screen. So your display may not look exactly like this screenshot.

2   Press Shift-M three times to move the playhead three markers forward (to the gray marker).

3   Press Shift-Z or click Fit in Window on the toolbar.

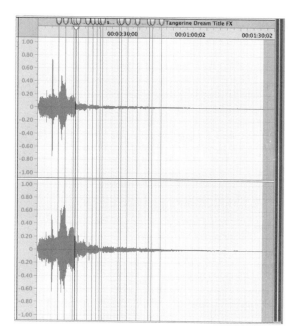

Whoa. There is a lot of waveform with markers showing when you zoom all the way out.. If not for the gray marker, you might not have any idea where you are in reference to the clip in the Timeline that you set out to modify.

4 Press the up arrow key several times to zoom back into the playhead position (gray marker).

   NOTE ▶ If you accidentally pressed Cmd-+ on the numeric keypad to zoom into the Timeline, you actually zoomed into the waveform instead. Press Shift-Cmd-– (minus/underscore key) to zoom back out of the waveform. You'll work more with these zoom features shortly.

5 Press Option-M three times to move the playhead left to the truck pulls away marker.

   Now you should be able to clearly see both the truck pulls away marker, and the gray marker revealing the end of the clip.

   NOTE ▶ There can only be one marker on a frame in either the Timeline or the Waveform Editor. Gray markers are only visible in the display area of the Waveform Editor to mark the beginning and end of the clip in the Timeline.

So, you've just learned hands-on that zooming in and out with the up and down arrow keys and navigating with markers work the same in the Waveform Editor. You also know how to orient yourself, even within a really large audio file. Now, you can move on with the other interface features.

Playing Audio Files in the Waveform Editor
You can play an audio file in the Waveform Editor by clicking the Play/Pause button in the transport controls or simply pressing the spacebar. As the waveform plays, you'll see the corresponding video clip playing in the Video tab. Since the clip was originally opened in the Timeline, it references the multi-track project's video.

1 Press the spacebar to play the audio file in the Waveform Editor and pause after the playhead passes the gray marker.

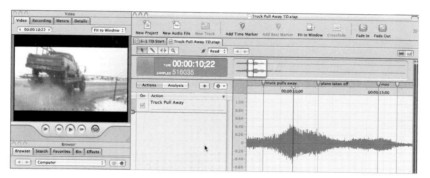

Notice that the truck sound works well with the tow truck pulling away in the video clip.

2 Move the playhead back to the truck pulls away marker.

3 Look at the Time display in the top-right corner of the Project window to see that the current playhead position is 9;00.

4 Press the right arrow key to move the playhead one second forward to the right.

The right or left arrow moves the playhead one second to the right or left at this zoom level. If you zoom in further, it will move one frame left or right, or zoom out fully to move multiple seconds at a time. You can also move the playhead using the Playhead Position value slider in the bottom-left corner of the window.

5 Click the Playhead location slider and type *16.22* (16 period 22), then press Return to move the playhead to that frame, which also happens to be the gray marker.

There you have it. Playing and navigating the playhead is easy enough, and should feel a lot like working in the Timeline.

Using the Global Waveform View

Another terrific navigational tool in the Waveform Editor is the Global View because it gives you the overall map of the waveform and shows which portion you are currently looking at in the Waveform display area. The Visible Area rectangle is located near the beginning of the audio file and includes only what you can currently see below.

1 Drag the Visible Area rectangle to the right to change your view of the waveform.

2 Press Shift-Z to fit the waveform horizontally to the display area.

The Visible Area rectangle expands to show the entire waveform, as does the Waveform display.

3 Press the up arrow key twice to zoom in to the playhead in both the Global view and the Waveform display area.

4 Drag the Visible Area rectangle to the left until you can clearly see both the truck pulls away marker and the gray marker in the Waveform display area. It should look just like it did when you started this exercise.

TIP Make a habit of glancing at the Global view whenever you first
open a file in the Waveform Editor. It's like looking at the "you are here"
spot on a map of the waveform. That way you have an idea of where you
started and which portion of the waveform you're actually working on in
case you lose your position somewhere along the way.

Setting Ruler Units in the Waveform Display

There are four different units of measure that can be used in the Waveform
Editor. Whether you measure yourself in inches or centimeters, you're still the
same height—what changes is simply the way it's being recorded. The same
goes for measuring the waveform in the Waveform Editor. Most of the time
waveforms are measured by a Normalized scale, with 0 (zero) in the center of
the waveform, 10 as the highest amount, and –10 as the lowest amount. Soundtrack Pro also offers Sample Value, Percent, and Decibels units for measuring
with the Sample ruler.

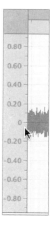

Unlike the horizontal Time ruler at the top of the window, the Sample ruler is
vertical and is located on the left side of the Waveform display area. Since this
is a stereo file, there are separate rulers for the left channel (top) and right
channel (bottom).

1   Look at the current Sample ruler which is set to the default Normalized scale.

2   Press Ctrl–down arrow several times to zoom all the way out so that you can see the full Normalized scale with 10 at the top and –10 at the bottom.

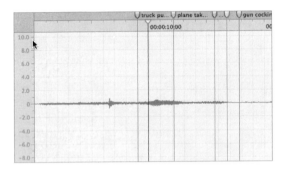

The waveform looks significantly smaller. Does that also mean it is quieter if you play it?

3   Press Option-M three times to move the playhead back to the truck pulls away marker.

4   Press the spacebar and play a few seconds of the audio file to test the volume.

It should sound exactly the same as it did before. The waveform only appears to be smaller because you are zoomed out away from it. It's like watching a football game from the blimp.

5   Press Ctrl–up arrow several times to zoom in on the most detailed increments (.10 to –.10) in the Sample ruler.

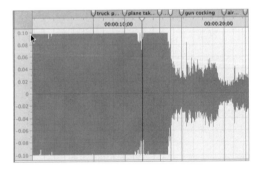

6   Press Ctrl–down arrow to zoom out until the highest and lowest peaks in the waveform are visible in the display area.

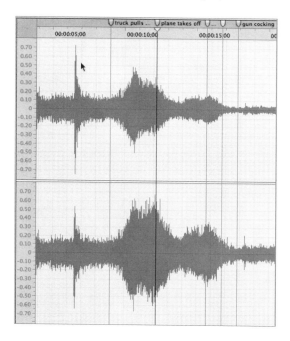

Next you'll change the unit of measure on the ruler to Sample Value, Percent, and Decibels see the different ruler choices.

7   Choose View > Sample Ruler Units > Sample Value, or Ctrl-click the Sample ruler and choose Sample Value from the shortcut menu.

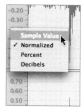

The waveform doesn't change, but Sample ruler units change to Sample Values.

8   Change the Sample ruler units to Percent and then to Decibels.

9   Change the ruler one last time back to Normalized.

> **NOTE** ▶ Remember the up and down arrows zoom in and out horizontally, Ctrl–up or down arrows zoom in and out vertically. Neither zoom mode ever changes the volume of the actual waveform, only the scale at which you see it.

Viewing a Frequency Spectrum

You can also view an audio file's frequency spectrum rather than its waveform. To change the display area from waveform view to frequency spectrum view, simply click the Spectrum view button.

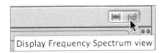

1   Click the Display Frequency Spectrum view button in the top-right corner of the Waveform Editor to display the frequency spectrum view.

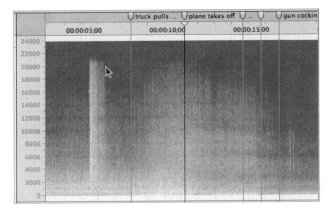

The display area changes to the frequency spectrum. The vertical ruler now shows the different frequencies from highest to lowest.

NOTE ▶ The human ear can hear a range of frequencies between roughly 20 Hertz (Hz) to –20 kilohertz (kHz). The higher the frequency's number, the higher the frequency; the lower the number, the lower the frequency.

2   Click the Waveform view button to return the display area to the waveform view.

3   Move the playhead to the truck pulls away marker and zoom horizontally until you can see both the truck pulls away marker and the gray marker above the Time ruler.

Feel free to use the Zoom slider at the bottom of the window to adjust the horizontal zoom scale, or use the up and down arrow keys. You can also use the Global view if needed.

Okay, you're comfortable with the basic interface and can find your way back to the starting zoom levels and marker positions. That means you've made it through the Waveform Editor readiness preparedness section of the lesson and you're ready for the more exciting stuff, actually editing waveforms.

Processing Audio Files in the Waveform Editor

In the previous lesson you edited clips in the Timeline by resizing them, splitting them, or slicing them with the Razor tool. Those editing techniques change the length of the clip in the Timeline, but they do not affect the audio file's waveform itself. The Waveform Editor differs because it is designed to do exactly what its name suggests, edit waveforms. This type of editing is referred to as *processing* audio files. The individual changes that you make to the file are recorded as actions in the Action list. In the next series of exercises you'll learn how the Waveform Editor works as you process a series of sound effects with progressively more challenging techniques.

Selecting Part of an Audio File

The first step in editing a waveform is selecting the part of the file that you'd like to edit. It's simple enough once you get the hang of it.

1   Move the pointer over the Waveform display anywhere in the middle between the upper and lower waveforms.

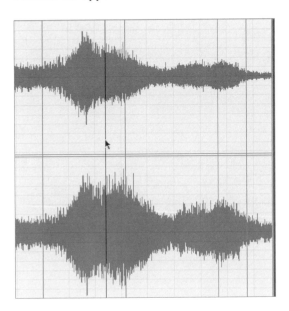

2 Click-drag the middle of the display to select a section of the waveform.

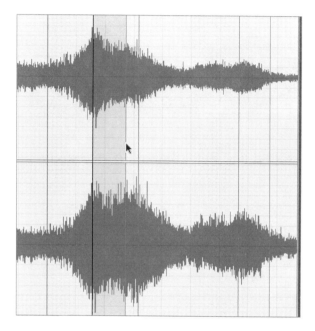

The selected area is highlighted blue. Notice that the selection includes the upper and lower waveforms. That is because you selected from the middle between the waveforms.

3 Press the spacebar to play the selection.

The playhead cycles over and over within the selection, similar to the playback region in the Timeline.

4 Click anywhere on the display to clear the selection.

5 Move the pointer toward the top of the Waveform display, above the upper waveform until you see a small *L* appear next to the pointer.

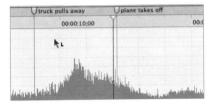

The upper waveform is the left audio channel, so the *L* indicates that you are selecting only the left channel. The bottom of the display selects only the right channel and shows an *R* near the pointer.

6 Click-drag the playhead near the top and select a section of the left channel waveform only.

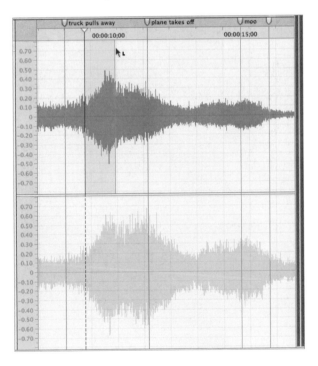

NOTE ▶ You do not need to clear the selection before choosing another. However, you can only have one section of the Timeline selected at a time.

7   Click-drag the playhead near the bottom of the display to select the right channel waveform only.

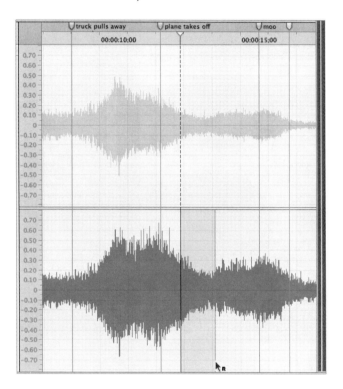

8   Click again anywhere in the display area to clear the selection.

NOTE ▶ For this lesson you will always select both the left and right channels of the waveform, so when prompted to select the waveform, select from the middle of the display.

Using Other Selection Techniques

Besides click-dragging the display area, you can also select between markers, one frame or second at a time, or the entire file. Let's start with selecting between markers.

1 Double-click the middle of the display between the truck pulls away and plane takes off markers.

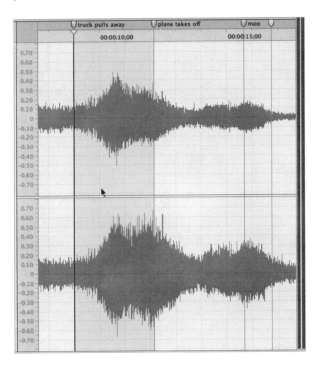

The selection includes only the waveform between the markers.

NOTE ▶ If there are no scoring, beat, or timing markers, double-clicking the middle of the Waveform display will select the entire audio file.

2 Press Cmd-A to select the whole waveform.

3   Click the head of the truck pulls away marker to clear the selection without moving the playhead.

The playhead should still be at the marker position (09;00). Suppose you want to select exactly one second starting at the truck pulls away marker? You could drag, but the easiest way is to press Shift–right arrow, which automatically begins the selection at the playhead position and extends it one gridline to the right. At the current zoom level, one gridline is one second.

4   Press Shift–right arrow.

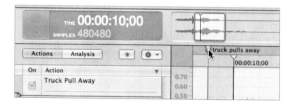

The playhead moves one second to the right (10;00) and selects the wave-form between the starting position and the ending position one second later. Don't clear the selection. You'll use it in the next exercise.

5   Look at the Selection Length value slider in the bottom-right corner of the window.

It shows that the selection is 29 frames in length, which is one second in NTSC Drop-frame timecode (29.97 fps).

Applying Actions to Fade In and Fade Out

Once you've selected part of the waveform, you can apply many types of actions, ranging from fades to professional effects. In this exercise, your goal is to apply both a Fade In and a Fade Out to the waveform. You can do so by clicking the Fade In and Fade Out buttons on the Toolbar at the top of the window or by choosing Process > Fade In or Fade Out. Next you'll use one method to apply the Fade In and the other to apply the Fade Out.

1   Click the Fade In button in the top-left corner of the toolbar.

The selected part of the waveform now shows that the beginning of the selection starts at 0 (zero) and tapers as the amplitude (height of the wave) gets higher until the end of the selection is at the original level. You can actually *see* the audio Fade In on the waveform. You'll also notice a Fade In action in the Action list.

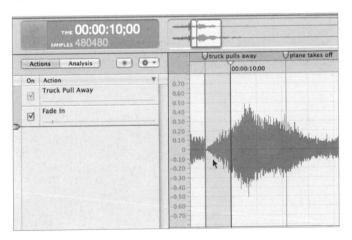

2   Press the spacebar to play the selection and hear the Fade In.

Next you'll add a Fade Out that ends at the gray marker.

3   Press Shift-M several times to move the playhead to the gray marker.

The Shift–left arrow shortcut won't work here to select one second earlier because the gray marker isn't recognized as a snapping point for selections or clips. Instead, you'll drag the playhead left while watching the Selection Length value slider until you reach your goal.

4   Click-drag the pointer from the gray marker to the left until the Selection Length value slider shows 29 frames.

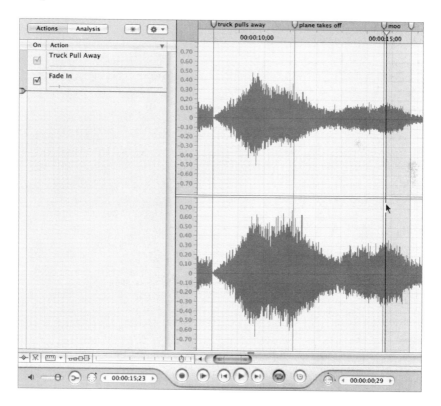

5   Choose Process > Fade Out to apply the action.

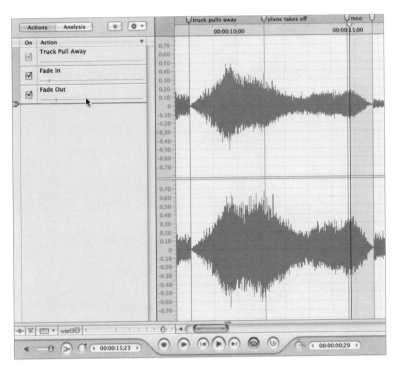

The waveform tapers down as it fades out at the gray marker. There is also a Fade Out action in the Action list.

6   Press Cmd-S to save your changes to the audio file project.

Extending a Selection

The Shift key allows you to extend a selection in several ways. You can Shift-drag to extend the selection or double-click the next selection to include it. Since there are two scoring markers between the current selection and the truck pulls away marker, let's use the latter method for more precision.

1   Shift–double-click the display area between the moo and plane takes off markers.

The selection extends to include that area.

2   Shift–double-click the display area between the plane takes off and truck pulls away markers to include that area as well.

3   Press the spacebar to play the selection and hear the sound fade in and fade out, noticing how well it works with the video clip.

4   Pause playback when you've seen and heard enough.

Well, what did you think? The sound fades in and out all right. There's just one big problem. The truck sound effect is way too long, and it doesn't work at all with the shots of the cows or the camel. The truck sound needs to end by the time the shot of the truck fades out. Looks like you'll need to modify the Fade Out and cut some of the excess audio.

Deleting Actions

Actions applied in the Waveform Editor are not only powerful but also an extremely flexible way to edit audio. You can add or delete actions, re-order them, and change them at will. For this exercise, you'll delete the Fade Out action, select the audio that you don't want to include in the Timeline and delete it, then add a new Fade Out in the appropriate place in the video so that the audio fades out when the shot of the truck fades out.

1   Clear the current selection.

> **TIP** ▶ It's a good idea to clear selections whenever they aren't necessary. That way you won't apply actions or delete a selected action by mistake.

2   Select the Fade Out action in the Action list.

3   Press Delete.

The Fade Out action is deleted from the list, and the Fade Out no longer appears on the waveform at the gray marker.

4   Move the playhead to the plane takes off marker.

This is a frame where the truck shot is fully faded out visually, and the plane shot has not yet started to fade in visually.

5   Drag the playhead to the right to create a selection a little beyond the gray marker.

NOTE ▶ Technically, the clip in the Timeline ends at the gray marker. But selecting the waveform a little beyond that marker won't affect the clip in the Timeline. Rather, it will ensure that you select everything you need before deleting part of the waveform.

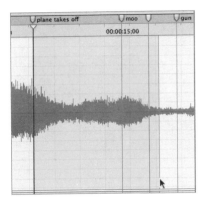

6   Press Delete.

Hmm. The selected waveform was deleted, but the remaining audio moved to the left and you still have the same issue—audio where you don't want it. Apparently, deleting was not the answer. That's because, just like in Final Cut Pro, the Waveform Editor's Delete key performs what is called a *ripple delete*, removing the selection and pulling the remaining audio to the left to fill the deleted space. But what you really wanted to do was silence that portion of the clip, which you'll do in the next exercise.

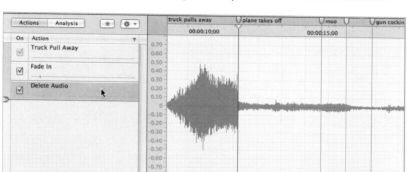

7   Select the Delete Audio action and press the Delete key.

Here you're essentially deleting a Delete Audio action. The playhead may have moved to the beginning of the file.

8   Drag the Visible Area rectangle in the Global view to the right until the Waveform display includes the truck pulls away and gray markers.

Moving Between Selections

We still need to ensure that there is no audio in between the plane takes off and gray markers, so in this exercise, you'll apply a Silence action using another very handy feature in the Waveform Editor. The Previous and Next selection buttons, located above the Global Waveform view, let you move back and forth between selections and navigate through your selection history.

1   Click the Previous selection button.

The selection should reappear between the plane takes off and gray markers.

> **NOTE ▶** If you made another selection since applying the Delete Audio
> action in the last exercise, click the Previous selection button again until
> the desired selection appears in the display area.

2   Choose Process > Silence or press Cmd-Delete to silence the selection.

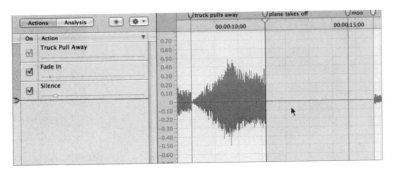

Mission accomplished. A Silence action is added to the Action list and
a flat line appears in the waveform, indicating no wave activity or dead
silence—like a flat line on a heart monitor.

Project Practice

It's time to put your new waveform selection skills to the test. First create a
selection that lasts one second (29 frames) and ends at the plane takes off
marker. Then apply a Fade Out action. Finally, create a selection between the
truck pulls away and plane takes off markers. Play the selection to see how it
works with the video. Once you've previewed the selection, don't forget to
save your changes to the audio file project. Have fun!

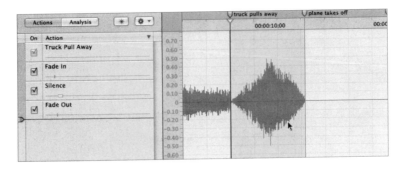

Playing an Audio File Project in the Timeline

Now that you've edited the audio file project, you should listen to the changes in the Timeline. In fact, it's already there waiting for you to hear it. Whenever you open a file from the Timeline and save it as an audio file project, the project replaces the original clip in the Timeline. Take a look and you'll see that the **5-1 TD Start** project is still open. All open projects (multitrack, or audio file) are accessible with tabs at the top-left corner of the Project window, just below the toolbar.

1   Locate the two project tabs.

The .stap file extension on the Truck Pull Away tab stands for Soundtrack Pro audio file project. Multitrack projects have an .stmp file extension for Soundtrack Pro multitrack project.

NOTE ▶ The .stmp file extension is not showing on the **5-1 TD Start** project because it was saved with the file extension hidden.

2   Click the **5-1 TD Start** tab to move that project to the front of the Project window.

3   Select the Truck Pull Away TD clip, if it's not already selected, and press Option-Z to fit the clip to the window.

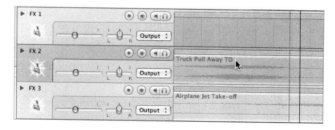

The name of the clip is **Truck Pull Away TD,** the same name as the audio file project.

4 Create a playback region from the truck pulls away marker to the moo
marker.

5 Press the spacebar to listen to the playback region, and then pause playback.

Nice work with the truck sound. Time to move on to the airplane clip, but
first, you should always close an audio file when you're finished with it.

6 Click the Truck Pull Away TD tab to make it active.

7 Choose File > Close Tab or press the shortcut Cmd-W to close that tab.

> **NOTE** ▶ If you missed any of the previous steps, feel free to open the
> project **5-2 TD Add Stretch** to catch up.

Creating Another Audio File Project

Your next editing goal will be to create an audio file project from the **Airplane
Jet Take-Off** clip and modify it in the Waveform Editor so that it works better
with the video. Instead of double-clicking this clip to open it as a project, let's
use the shortcut menu.

1 Ctrl-click the **Airplane Jet Take-Off** clip and choose Open as Project from
the shortcut menu.

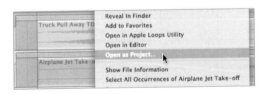

The Create Audio Project window opens.

2   Type *TD* at the end of the name in the Save As field and save the project in the My Soundtrack Pro projects folder.

The new audio file project opens in the Waveform Editor.

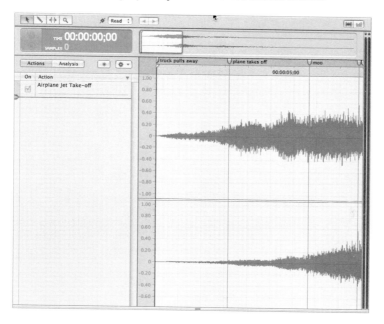

Graphically Editing Audio Files

Before you actually change the waveform, this is a good time to get acquainted with the Waveform Editor's four graphical editing tools: Selection, Sample Edit, Audio Stretching, and Zoom.

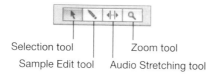

Selection tool   Zoom tool
      Sample Edit tool   Audio Stretching tool

Viewing the Waveform at the Sample Level

You're already familiar with the Selection tool, which you used to edit the previous audio file project. The Sample Edit tool allows you to edit a waveform with precision at the sample level. If you zoom all the way into a waveform, you'll see the actual digital samples used to create the file. Samples are the building blocks of digital audio. It's like viewing objects at the subatomic level.

1   Press the up arrow key repeatedly to zoom in to the waveform as far as possible.

The dots that you see are the digital samples.

2   Press Cmd-I or click the Details tab, and then click the File button on the Details tab to see the bit depth and sample rate for this file.

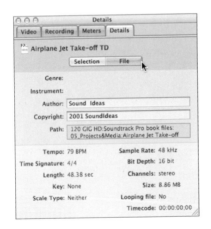

This project uses the same bit depth and sample rate—16 bit and 48 kHz—as Final Cut Pro.

NOTE ▶ Soundtrack Pro supports sample rates between 8 kHz and 192 kHz and bit depths of 8-bit integer, 16-bit integer, 24-bit integer, 32-bit integer, and 32-bit floating point. You can learn more about sample rates and bit depths in the Soundtrack Pro User Manual available through the Help menu.

3 Press Cmd-1 to return to the Video tab on the Utility window.

4 Click the Sample Edit tool, which is the second tool from the left and looks like a pencil.

5 Move the Sample Edit tool over the samples in the Waveform display area.

6 Click the Sample Edit tool near any of the samples, and drag the tool to draw a new waveform.

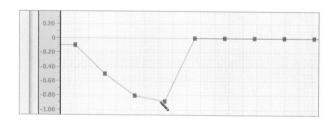

7 Press Cmd-Z to undo any changes you made to the waveform at the sample level.

8 Click the Selection tool, and then click anywhere in the display area to clear any selections your experimentation may have created.

9 Press Shift-Z to fit the waveform to the window.

Silencing the Beginning

The biggest problem with the jet plane sound effect is that the sound of the plane taking off is too long. Fortunately, the Audio Stretching tool can adjust the length of the audio waveform. Since it only resizes from the right edge of a selection (the end of the waveform), it's a good idea to first decide where the waveform should begin. In this exercise, you'll use some of your new skills to silence the beginning of the waveform and add a Fade In at the plane takes off marker. Once the beginning of the waveform is completed, you'll be ready to use the Audio Stretching tool in the next exercise.

1   Press the up arrow key once to zoom in one level horizontally.

2   Double-click the display area between the first two markers to select that section of the waveform.

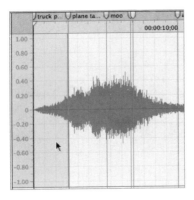

3   Choose Process > Silence or press Cmd-Delete to silence the selection.

4   Move the playhead to the plane takes off marker.

5   Type *29* in the Selection Length value slider, and press Return to select 29 frames starting at the marker.

6   Click the Fade In button.

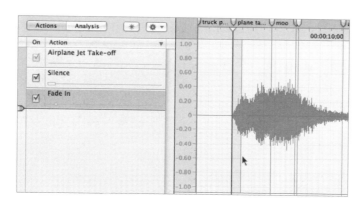

7   Save your progress.

Now the waveform is ready to use the Audio Stretching tool.

Working with the Audio Stretching Tool

Using the Audio Stretching tool, you can shorten the length of the waveform so that you'll get the full "take-off" part of the waveform in a much shorter amount of time. This will also make it sound like the plane is moving really fast, which works fine with this X-treme film trailer. First you'll use the Selection tool to select the portion of the waveform that you'd like to stretch—about 10 seconds of the file from the plane takes off marker through the fattest part of the waveform. Then you'll use the Audio Stretching tool to stretch the wave-form within a selection to make it shorter without changing the pitch.

1   Move the playhead to the plane takes off marker, if it's not already there.

2   Type *10.00* (10 period 00) in the Selection Length value slider and press Return.

The first 10 seconds of the file have been selected. The Selection Length value slider changes to 9;29, which is equivalent to 10 seconds in NTSC drop-frame timecode.

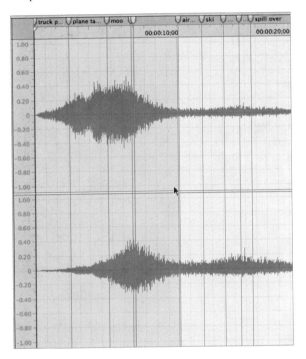

3   Play the selection once to see and hear how it works with the video.

Clearly the plane taking off sound is too long for the video.

4   Click the Audio Stretching tool, which is the third tool from the left.

Remember that the Audio Stretching tool only works from the end of the waveform, not the beginning.

5 Move the Audio Stretching tool over the right edge of the selection and click-hold the edge of the selection.

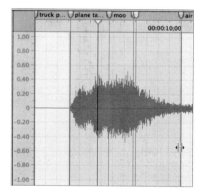

6 Drag the right edge of the selection to the moo marker.

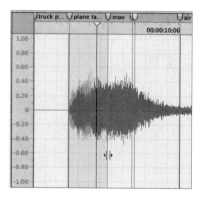

NOTE ▶ Be sure to drag from the middle of the display so that you stretch both the left and right channels of the stereo file. Although the figure above only shows the left channel, both are affected when you use the Audio Stretching tool.

The waveform within the selection compresses so that it ends at the moo marker.

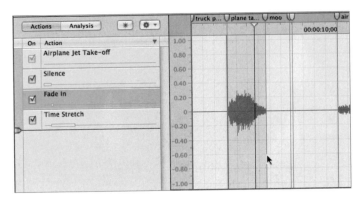

7   Play the newly stretched selection.

It ends sooner and is faster, but it's still too long. Sounds like another stretch job to me. Let's stretch it to about half the current size.

8   With the Audio Stretching tool, click the right edge of the current selection and drag to the left about halfway between the plane takes off and moo markers.

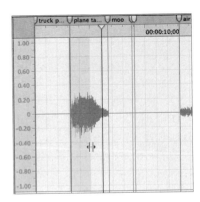

The waveform stretches again to fit the current selection.

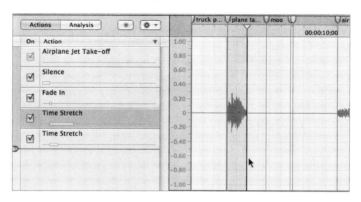

9 Play the selection to hear the result.

Perfect. Notice that there are two separate Time Stretch actions in the Action list.

10 Save your audio file project.

11 Click the 5-1 TD Start tab or the 5-2 TD Add Stretch tab, depending on which version of the multitrack project you are working on.

The multitrack project appears in the Project window.

12 Play the project playback region to hear the truck and plane effects.

The timing is good and the effects work, but the volume is too low on the plane effect, so let's fix that next.

Adjusting Amplitude in the Waveform Editor

You can always go back and change an audio file project. In this exercise, you'll go back to the **Airplane Jet Take-off TD** audio file project and adjust the amplitude of the waveform. The depth or intensity of a sound is called its amplitude, and is expressed in decibels (dB). Human ears can hear amplitude as the volume or loudness of a sound. The range of audible loudness is roughly 0 to 130 dB. The higher decibel levels are actually painful to human ears.

In Soundtrack Pro, amplitude is displayed visually by the height of the wave-form: The higher the amplitude, the louder the audio waveform will be per-ceived. You can adjust amplitude with a simple action available in the process menu, or by using the keyboard shortcut Shift-Cmd-L.

1   Click the Airplane Jet Take-off TD tab or double-click that project in the Timeline to view the audio file project in the Waveform Editor.

2   Select all of the Airplane Jet Take off waveform, if it is not already selected.

    You can also click the Previous Selection button.

3   Choose Process > Adjust Amplitude or press Shift-Cmd-L.

The Adjust Amplitude control opens. The control shows the default level of 0 dB, which indicates there has been no change to the default levels. The 0 dB in the Amplitude Level field does not show the actual value of the waveform's amplitude, only the amount that it is adjusted.

4   Type *10* in the Amplitude Level field and click OK to raise the amplitude of the waveform by 10.000 dB.

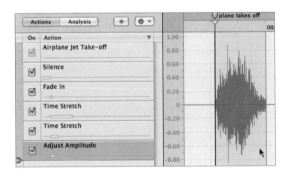

The amplitude of the waveform increases by 10 dB.

5   Save the change to the audio file project.

6   Play the selection to hear how it sounds with the adjusted amplitude.

7   Click the tab for the multitrack project, and play the playback region to hear the effect.

Sounds great. Good enough to flatten.

TIP ▸ If a Disk Limit dialog appears while you are playing the multi-track project, it indicates that your hard disk can't deliver all the audio in time. Mute the top 3 dialog tracks to save processing for the sound effects tracks. You can always unmute them later, or you can solo the FX 2 and FX 3 tracks to play only those tracks. Another way to optimize the processing is to flatten the actions of an audio file project in the Waveform Editor, which you're about to do in the next exercise..

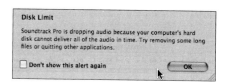

8   Click the audio file project's tab to return to the project in the Waveform Editor.

Flattening Actions

Actions are very flexible and powerful, but they can also take a lot of processing power to play. If you're satisfied with the changes that you've made to an audio file project and you'd like to free up the computer's processor, you can *flatten* the actions in your project to a single action. Flattening actions renders the actions into the file, reducing the file size and complexity so that your project takes up less room—just like when you flatten a beach ball so you can fit it in your beach bag. You can always blow up the beach ball again, but once you've flattened the actions there's no going back. All existing actions are removed from the Actions list and you can no longer reorder or edit their settings.

1   Click the Actions pop-up menu above the Action list.

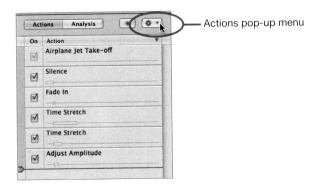

Actions pop-up menu

2   Choose Flatten all actions from the pop-up menu.

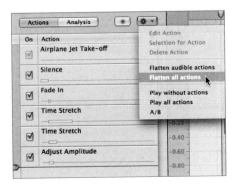

The actions flatten and become part of the file within the project. All that is left in the Action list is the name of the audio file.

3 Select the last 15 frames of the visible waveform and add a Fade Out to clean up any rough endings.

4 Choose Flatten all actions again to flatten the Fade Out.

> **TIP** ▶ If you're not sure you're happy with the overall sound, play the audio file project in the Multitrack project to hear the result before flattening in the Waveform Editor. Once you save a flattened audio file project, you won't be able to undo it.

5 Save your project and close the audio file project.

6 Play the current play range in the multitrack project to hear the changes.

7 Clear the playback region in the Time ruler.

8 Save the multitrack project.

> **NOTE** ▶ If you didn't complete all of the previous steps, feel free to open the project **5-3 TD Add Paste** to catch up.

Editing an Audio Waveform

The Waveform Editor also allows you to cut, copy, and paste portions of a waveform just as you would words in a word processor or clips in the Timeline. In fact, the shortcuts are the same as in virtually any of the Apple Pro applications.

In the next series of exercises, you'll cut and paste an audio waveform to fix the timing of footsteps with the video. Then you copy and paste audio from several different waveforms to create an entirely new sound.

Opening and Saving an Audio File Project

The first step in editing the waveform is to open the file and save it as an audio file project. You'll be working with the **Footsteps Snow Scuff** clip on the FX 1 track.

1 Move the playhead to the second green Time marker at 01:01:03:00 in the Timeline.

2   Press the up arrow key several times to zoom in to that area of the Timeline.

3   Double-click the **Footsteps Snow Scuff** clip.

4   Click OK in the Double-Click Preferences dialog to open it as an audio file project.

5   Type *TD* after the name of the clip in the Save As field, and click Save.

The new audio file project opens in the Waveform Editor.

6   Press Shift-Return to play the clip from the beginning and listen to it as you watch the accompanying video of two skiers walking in the snow.

As you can see and hear, the footsteps match okay at the beginning, but not for the full clip of the skiers walking. Foley effects often fit well, but in this case, you'll need to copy and paste a few footsteps to make it even better.

Setting a Marker in the Waveform Editor

It might be helpful to set a marker in the Time ruler where you'd like to hear a footstep sound. You can set markers in the Waveform Editor the same way you set them in the Timeline—the only difference is that you can only set the type of markers that match the time format for the audio file. Since this is a time-based (timecode) non-looping audio file, you can only set a time marker (M).

1   Press Shift-Return to play the beginning of the clip again, but this time, pause playback as soon as you see a skier step without hearing a sound to go with it.

It seems that the skier in the red jacket takes a silent step around 2;06.

2   Press Cmd–right arrow or Cmd–left arrow as needed to move the playhead one frame at a time around 2;06 to see the movement of the skier.

3   Move the playhead to 2;06 and press M to set a marker.

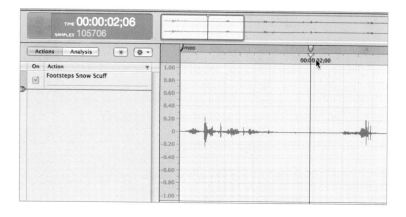

4   Press the down arrow key once to zoom out one level and locate the gray marker that indicates the end of the clip in the Timeline.

Next, you'll copy a footstep from the waveform on the right side of the gray marker.

Copying a Selection

In this exercise you'll select one of the two nearest footsteps at the right of the gray marker and copy it to the clipboard.

1   Move the playhead to the gray marker (3;27).

2   Press the spacebar and listen to the first two steps.

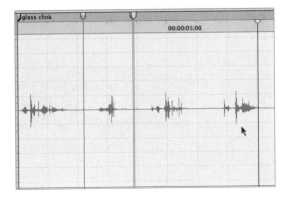

The first step is fine, but the second one sounds a little heavier, like some-one stepping down with the extra weight of a ski. You can choose either footstep for this exercise. I'll use the second step in the figures.

3   Drag the Selection tool over one of the footstep waveforms to select it.

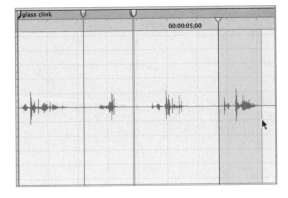

Be sure to include the entire waveform from before it starts to after it ends to make sure you select the entire thing.

4   Press Cmd-C or choose Edit > Copy, to copy the selection to the clipboard.

Pasting a Selection

Now that you've copied the selection to the clipboard, you can move the playhead to the position where you'd like to paste the clip. You don't actually want to paste on the marker because that would start the stepping sound *after* the skier starts to step. Instead, paste the middle of the waveform around the marker.

Your goal is to paste the copied waveform into the empty waveform space between the first two stepping sounds. To paste in a specific area without affecting the rest of the waveform, you'll need to make a selection where you'd like to paste. This is referred to as a *paste over* edit, similar to an overwrite edit in Final Cut Pro. If you paste in the waveform without making a selection, the pasted clip is inserted into the waveform and moves the rest of the waveform down to accommodate. Pasting without a selection is similar to an insert edit in Final Cut Pro.

1   Create a new selection in the empty waveform space around the green marker. Make the selection approximately the same length as the selection that you copied.

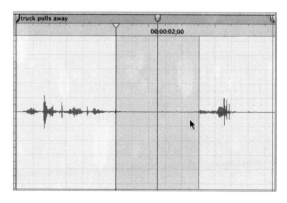

2   Press Cmd-V to paste the copied waveform into the selection.

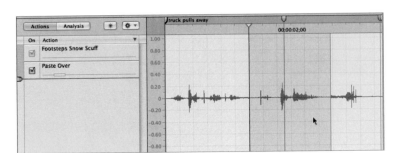

The pasted waveform appears in the selection area, and a Paste Over action appears in the Action list.

NOTE ▶ If the copied selection and pasted over selections are different lengths, the Paste Over action may slightly move the waveform to the right of the pasted section.

3   Click anywhere in the display to clear the selection.

4   Press Shift-Return to play the file from the beginning, watching the video as you play the newly modified footsteps.

It's good. The steps work well with the picture. However the audio level could use a little amplitude adjustment.

Project Practice

It's time to apply more of your new skills to select the waveform between the first two scoring markers and raise the amplitude by 10 dB. Once you've selected the waveform, choose Process > Adjust Amplitude, or press Shift-Cmd-L. Save the edited audio project, close the tab, and play that section of the multitrack project to see how it turned out. The footsteps are subtle, but they add to the overall soundtrack. Once you've played that section of the Timeline, save the multitrack project.

NOTE ▶ If you didn't complete all of the previous steps, feel free to open the project **5-4 TD Add Files** to catch up.

Combining Waveforms to Customize Effects

The grand finale of this waveform safari is to create a customized crash-scream-hit effect by copying parts of two different files into another. First, you'll create an audio file project, and then open two other files from the Media and Effects Manager.

1   Move the playhead to the crash combo marker (51;02) in the Timeline, and zoom in a level or two for a clear view of the marker.

2   Locate the **Auto Crash Metal 2** clip on the FX 1 track that starts at the marker.

This is the clip you'll be customizing as an audio file project.

3   Create a playback region a little before the crash combo marker to the end of the **Auto Crash Metal 2** clip.

4   Play it to see and hear the current effect.

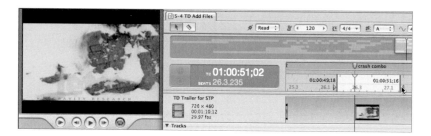

Ouch. The skier hitting the rock before falling over the ledge looks painful, and the current auto crash sound effect certainly echoes that feeling. Sure, it's not really an auto crash, but often in sports films, especially X-treme sports, sound editors take a few audio liberties with effects. This is one of those times.

5   Double-click the **Auto Crash Metal 2** clip and save it as **Auto Crash Metal 2 TD** in the My Soundtrack Pro projects folder.

Searching for Additional Effects

In this exercise, you'll locate and open a body hit and a scream file. Unlike the audio file projects, you won't save these files as audio file projects because you aren't changing them. All you're doing is opening them and copying some of the waveform.

1   Click the Search tab and select the Sound Effects category from the Keywords pop-up, if it is not already selected.

2   Type *Body Hit* into the Search text field.

There are 12 different Body Hit files to choose from.

3   Click the first file in the list, **Body Hit 01,** to hear the file. Press the down arrow key to move to the next file in the list until you have previewed all 12 files.

All of them are good, but I'm partial to the ones with an extra bone-crunching umph at the end. (Use your imagination when listening to sound effects—it comes with the job.) For now we'll go with **Body Hit 09,** and you can always rebuild the effect with any file you choose after the lesson.

4   Ctrl-click the **Body Hit 09** file on the Search tab and choose Open in Editor from the shortcut menu.

TIP ▶ Opening a file in the editor, without opening it as an audio file project, means you will be working with the actual file. Any changes you make to the file will permanently (destructively) change the audio file. So be careful. If you think you might accidentally mess up the original file, you can always open it as a project instead.

Body Hit 09.aiff opens in the editor.

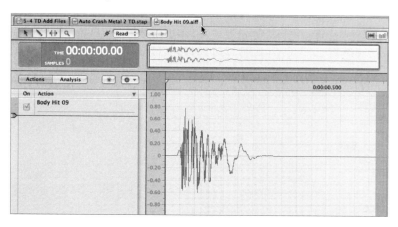

Notice that the tab shows an .aiff file extension, which means it is the actual file, not an audio file project. One file open, one to go.

5 Type *scream* in the Search Text field.

Soundtrack Pro comes with over 50 scream files. Curiously, they all seem to be named after a person, followed by the word *helm*. Curiously, many of the first names of the scream files in the list correspond with the brilliant Soundtrack Pro team at Apple. The helm is most likely an audio homage to the famous Wilhelm scream often used by Hollywood sound editors.

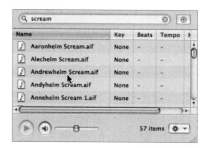

With so many screams to choose from, why not audition them all—or at least several of them—with the crash and the video clip?

6 Click the Auto Crash Metal 2 TD.stap tab to make the audio file project active.

NOTE ▶ Among sound editors and sound designers in Hollywood, one of the most famous and cliché sound effects is the Wilhelm scream. It was originally recorded by Warner Brothers for the film *Distant Drums* directed by Raoul Walsh in 1951. It appeared again in *The Charge at Feather River* (1953), where it was heard when a soldier named Private Wilhelm (played by Ralph Brooke) was shot in the leg with an arrow. The scream was so distinctive that it was recognized by sound editors and dubbed the "Wilhelm" scream after the character. Since then, the Wilhelm scream has appeared in many features including the *Star Wars* films, the *Raiders of the Lost Ark* series, and even animated films like *Aladdin*. You can find volumes about this on the Internet, including a QuickTime video with samples from different movies using the Wilhelm scream. Check it out at http://download. theforce.net/video/wilhelm_27mb.mov.

7   Press the spacebar to begin playback of the project.

While the project is playing, select the first scream in the list to audition it with the video and the crash sound. Press the down arrow key to audition as many screams as needed until you find one you like best. My choice is the **Tomhelm Scream** file because it sounds more like someone wiping out, rather than someone who sees something really scary.

8   Ctrl-click the scream of your choice and choose Open in Editor.

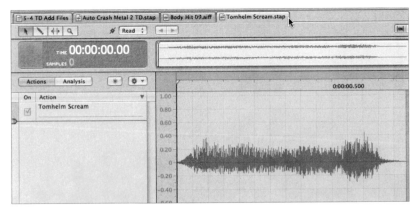

The file opens in the Waveform Editor.

Pasting a Mix

The last step in creating the crash-hit-scream effect is to select the audio files you'd like to combine and paste them one at a time as a mix into the Auto Crash Metal 2 TD audio file project. This is not an ordinary paste insert or paste over procedure. Pasting one waveform into another without overwriting the original waveform is a Paste Special feature. Let's start with the scream.

1   Double-click the scream file to select the entire waveform.

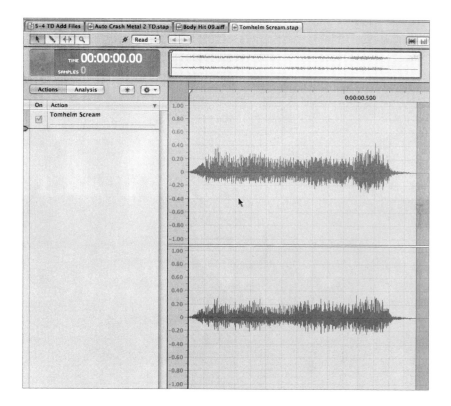

2   Press Cmd-C to copy the selected waveform.

3 Click the **Auto Crash Metal 2 TD** tab to make the audio file project active.

4 Double-click the display area of the auto file project to select the entire thing.

> **NOTE ▶** There are no gray markers in this audio file project because the entire audio file was used in the Timeline. Without markers in the Time ruler, you can select the entire file by double-clicking.

5 Choose Edit > Paste Special > Paste Mix, or press Shift-Cmd-V.

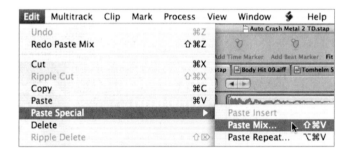

A Paste Mix control appears.

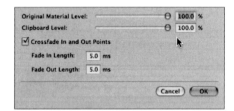

You can use the Paste Mix control to adjust the volume levels of the Original Material (Auto Crash Metal 2) and the Clipboard Level (scream file). The scream probably shouldn't overpower the crash, so how about leaving the Original Material Level at 100% and lowering the Clipboard Level to around 60%?

6   Drag the Clipboard Level slider to around 60% or type *60* in the
Clipboard Level field.

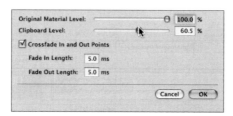

7   Click OK to paste the mix of the scream waveform with the crash waveform.

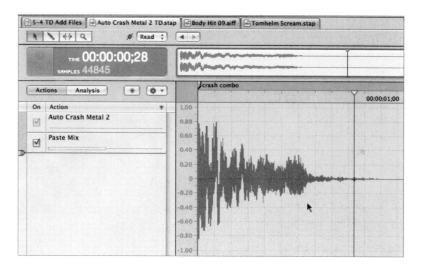

The waveforms combine to create something new.

8   Play the project to hear the mixed waveform.

Good stuff, and works well with the video.

> **TIP**   If you don't like the mix levels, you can double-click the Paste Mix
> action in the Action list and change the levels to modify it to your liking.

Project Practice

It's your turn to perform one more paste mix. Click the Body Hit 09 tab, select the whole waveform, and copy it. Then select the audio file project tab and paste mix the waveform to the current mix. Feel free to adjust the mix levels however you like by double-clicking the Paste Mix action and changing the settings. Save the Auto Crash Metal 2 TD audio file project once you're finished.

Closing and Saving

Now that you've completed creating your custom effect, you can save it with a different name to make part of your own collection in Lesson 10, "Exporting, Managing Media, and Preferences." Also, now is a good time to close the other open files in the Waveform Editor.

1   Click the tab for the scream file and close it.

2   Click the Body Hit 09 tab and close it.

There should only be two tabs remaining, the audio file project tab, and the multitrack project tab.

3   Click the Auto Crash Metal 2 TD tab if it is not already active.

4   Choose File > Save As to open the Save As window.

5   Change the name to Crash-Hit-Scream and save it in the My Soundtrack Pro projects folder.

6   Close the audio file project.

The renamed project is saved in your projects folder. The original audio file project is in the Timeline.

7   Press the spacebar and watch the playback region in the Timeline and enjoy your sound-designed custom effect.

8   Save the final changes to the project.

That concludes this lesson, but should spark your imagination on the many ways you can use the Waveform Editor to modify your audio clips. While the multitrack project is open, feel free to try out your new techniques with some of the other sound effects. Several have filters applied to them, which you'll learn how to do yourself in the next lesson.

> **MORE INFO** ▸ For more information about the film *Tangerine Dream*, or to see the actual trailer, go to: http://tetongravity.com.

Lesson Review

1. Which Apple Pro application creates scoring markers, and what makes them different than other Soundtrack Pro markers?

2. What is the difference between a multitrack project and an audio file project?

3. What are the four different Ruler units that you can set in the Sample ruler, and which is the default?

4. What are the two different ways that you can view an audio file in the Waveform Editor display area?

5. When processing an audio file, what determines where the action is applied?

6. What modifier key can be used to extend a selection in the display area?

7. Can you select just the left or right channels of an audio file?

8. Which graphical editing tool allows you to change the length of a waveform as you resize the selection?

9. What type of paste allows you to combine more than one waveform?

Answers

1. Scoring markers are created in Final Cut Pro and cannot be edited, moved, or deleted in Final Cut Pro. Another thing that makes them different is that you can see them in both the Timeline and the Waveform Editor.

2. A multitrack project is edited in the Timeline and contains up to 128 tracks. An audio file project contains only one file and is edited in the Waveform Editor.

3. The four different Sample ruler units in the Waveform are Sample Value, Percent, Decibels, and Normalized. The default setting is Normalized.

4. You can view audio files in the display area in waveform view or frequency spectrum view.

5. Actions are always applied to the selected portion of the waveform, or the entire waveform if no selection has been made.

6. The Shift key allows you to extend a selection in the display area by either dragging the edge of the selection, or double-clicking another area to include it.

7. You can select only the left channel by dragging the top of the display area, or only the right channel by dragging the bottom of the display area.

8. The Audio Stretching tool allows you to change the length of a waveform as you resize the selection.

9. The Paste Mix feature allows you to combine more than one waveform.

Keyboard Shortcuts

Waveform Editor

Shift-Cmd-V	paste mix
Shift-Cmd-L	adjust amplitude
Delete	ripple delete
Cmd-Delete	silence

Keyboard Shortcuts

Cmd-C	copy
Cmd-V	paste over selection, paste insert if nothing selected
Cmd-Z	undo previous step
Cmd-A	select all
Shift–right arrow	selects one gridline to the right
Shift–left arrow	selects one gridline to the left

Navigation

Cmd–right arrow	moves playhead one frame to the right
Cmd–left arrow	moves playhead one frame to the left
Shift-M	moves to the next marker
Option-M	moves to the previous marker

Zooming

Up arrow	zooms in horizontally in the display area
Down arrow	zooms out horizontally in the display area
Ctrl–up arrow	zooms vertically in to the waveform
Ctrl–down arrow	zooms vertically out of the waveform
Shift-Z	fits the waveform to the display area
Option-Z	fits the selection to the display area

6

Lesson Files   Soundtrack Pro book files > 06_Projects&Media > 6-1 ADA PSA Start, 6-5 ADA PSA Final

Time   This lesson takes approximately 1 hour and 35 minutes.

Goals   Normalize voiceover and production sound

Work with the Frequency Spectrum view

Select and set a noise print

Use the Reduce Noise feature

Analyze an audio file

Find and fix clicks and pops in the Analysis Pane

Use the Zoom tool

Adjust selections to zero crossing points

Set an ambient noise print

Add ambient noise to a selection

Lesson 6

Modifying and Repairing Dialog in the Waveform Editor

Whether you're working on a commercial, feature film, training video, or music video, dialog and vocals are usually the most important audio element of the project. Without spoken words, the characters have no voice, the narrator has no story, the vocalist has no song.

Audiences don't know your production budget or what equipment you used, only what they see and hear when they watch the final project. As the sound editor, it's your job to make everything sound as professional as possible by cleaning up the audible glitches, pops, clicks, distracting noises, erratic levels, overpowering ambience, or distorted dialog. Fortunately, the Waveform Editor comes equipped with all of the tools you'll need to fix these problems and repair your dialog tracks.

In Lesson 5, "Designing Sound in the Waveform Editor," you learned how to modify sound effects. In this lesson you'll work with the dialog tracks of a real-world Public Service Announcement (PSA) for the American Diabetes Association (ADA). You'll also learn some new shortcuts and tricks for enhancing dialog that you can apply to your own projects.

Preparing the Project

Begin by opening and playing the **6-1 ADA PSA Start** project located in the 06 Projects&Media folder. Once you've seen and heard the starting project, you will save it to the My Soundtrack Pro projects folder on your desktop.

1   Quit all open applications, except for Soundtrack Pro.

2   Close any open Soundtrack Pro projects.

3   Open the multitrack project **6-1 ADA PSA Start,** if it's not already open.

4   Save the project uncollected to the My Soundtrack Pro projects folder on your desktop.

5   Play the **6-1 ADA PSA Start** project once.

As the project plays, notice the different types of dialog that you hear, as well as any distracting sounds that may detract from the overall project.

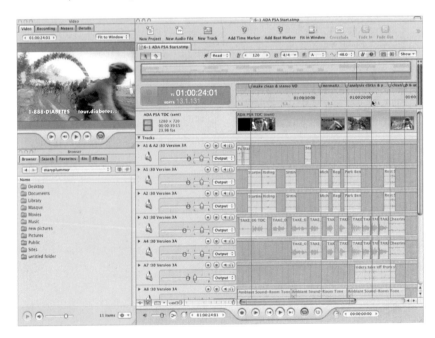

This project is an actual PSA for the ADA's Tour de Cure event. The project was taped using HDV format at 23.98 fps and edited in Final Cut Pro. The finished video edit was then sent to Soundtrack Pro for final sound editing and mixing. The music tracks were created in a separate Soundtrack Pro multi-track project, then mixed down and exported for this PSA. You can find the **diabetes mix** project in the 6 PSA_MUSIC folder located in the 06 Projects& Media folder.

> **NOTE** ▶ HDV requires a lot of processor speed to play. If you're working on a laptop or slower computer, you may see a slight stutter in the video as you watch it in Soundtrack Pro. The final video will play perfectly when exported from Soundtrack Pro through compressor, which you'll do in Lesson 10, "Exporting, Managing Media, and Preferences." Some of the sound issues that you'll be working on in this lesson were added to the project for the purposes of the exercises and were not actually part of the original recordings.

Working with Voiceover Recordings

Generally, the best quality recordings that you'll work with are those made in a controlled environment. Audio recorded in a sound booth isn't contaminated with external ambient noise or sounds such as car horns, cell phones, or dogs barking, so the biggest issue you'll face when editing professionally recorded voiceover is the audio levels. If you've never worked with professional voiceover recordings, here's your chance. The real-world voiceover recordings you'll work with in this lesson were professionally recorded with a voiceover artist.

Over the next series of exercises you'll open a voiceover clip as an audio file project. Then you'll silence the portions of the waveform that don't include dialog and normalize the dialog levels. Finally, you'll double the audio by converting it to stereo. To make the projects in this lesson easier to find, each has been marked with a green time marker. The audio file project you'll be starting with is called **TAKE_6 TDC** and is located on the fourth track from the top.

1 Press Return to move the playhead to the beginning of the project.

2 Press Shift-M to move to the make clean & stereo VO marker (2;12).

3 Double-click the **TAKE_6 TDC** clip at the playhead position on the fourth track to open the audio file project.

The audio file project opens in the Waveform Editor. The section of waveform between the gray markers is the portion showing in the Timeline clip.

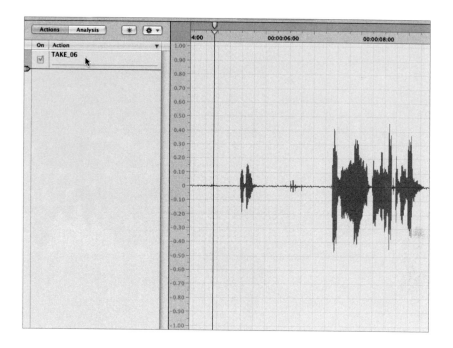

NOTE ▶ For this lesson, many of the audio file projects have already been created and saved so that all you'll need to do is open them and begin working.

Silencing Unwanted Sound

You could use the Razor tool to split the clip and delete the portion with the unwanted noise, or you could simply silence it in the Waveform Editor, which you'll try now. As you learned in the previous lesson, you can silence a selection by either choosing Process > Silence, or pressing the shortcut Cmd-Delete. Here's your chance to practice.

First, let's determine what needs to be silenced, then select it and apply the Silence process. You only need to modify the waveform between the gray markers, since that is the only portion that will be audible in the Timeline.

1   Double-click the display area between the gray markers to select the entire waveform in that section of the Timeline.

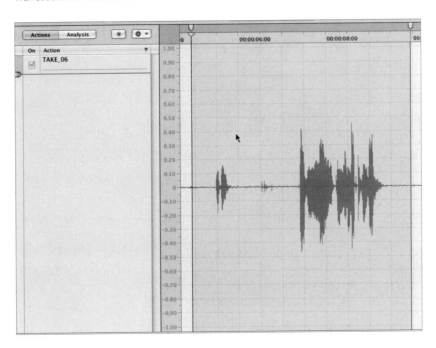

NOTE ▶ The amount of the waveform visible in the Waveform Editor may differ from what's shown in the figure above, depending upon your current level of zoom and screen resolution.

2   Press the spacebar to play the selection and listen to the voiceover segment.

It's nearly perfect, except for the talent clearing his throat before he speaks.

3   Move the playhead to the beginning of the first word of dialog in the waveform display area (07;09).

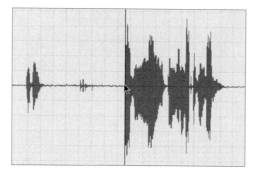

4   Press the up arrow key several times to zoom in for a closer look at the beginning of the dialog waveform at the playhead position.

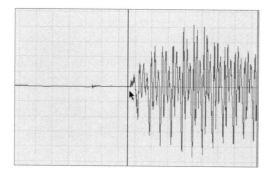

It's important that the playhead is positioned *before* the dialog begins. That way you won't have to worry about accidentally silencing part of the dialog by mistake. This playhead position is fine, and you can clearly see that it is before the dialog waveform starts.

5   Press the down arrow key to zoom out until you can see the gray marker at the left of the playhead.

6   Press Shift–left arrow several times to move left until the gray marker is
included in the selection.

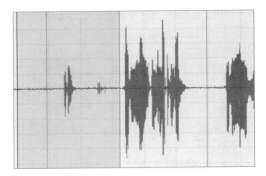

NOTE ▶ Don't worry if the selection extends beyond the gray marker.
This selection method selects by gridlines, not markers. Also, it doesn't
matter if you silence beyond the gray marker because that section won't
be audible in the Timeline anyway.

7   Choose Process > Silence or press Cmd-Delete to silence the selection.

The waveform with the selection becomes a flat line to indicate total
silence.

8   Press Cmd-S to save your progress.

Since you silenced the waveform in front of the voiceover, it's a good idea
to also silence the end of the waveform for consistency.

Project Practice

Now it's your turn to hone your selection and silencing skills. Move the playhead to the end of the dialog (09;09) and create a selection from the playhead
through the gray marker at the right of the waveform. Silence the selection and
save your progress.

Normalizing Voiceover Levels

A conversation that starts soft and quiet but ends up in a heated debate will have radically different volume levels. Maintaining that dynamic range is important for the reality of the scene. Voiceover dialog, on the other hand, is very consistent and needs to be the strongest and clearest audio in the project, making it ideal for the normalization process.

Normalization raises the maximum level of a digital signal to a certain amount—typically to its highest possible level without introducing distortion. How? Soundtrack Pro's Waveform Editor finds the point with the highest volume in audio and determines how far it is from the maximum possible level. The entire level of the selection is then raised by this amount so that the dynamic balance remains unaltered—it merely gets louder.

Although the levels in the current project are good, they have room for more amplitude without exceeding the maximum level of 0 dB. Let's try normalizing them.

1   Double-click between the two gray markers to select that section of the waveform.

2   Ctrl-click the Sample Value ruler at the left of the display area and choose Decibels from the shortcut menu as the display units.

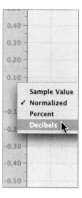

Notice where the highest and lowest peaks of the waveform are on the decibel scale.

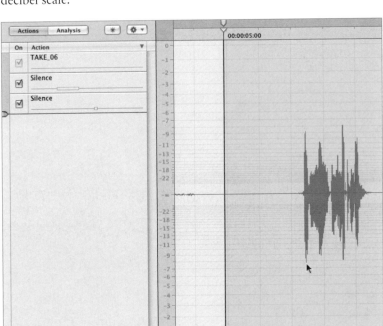

3   Choose Process > Normalize or press Cmd-L.

The Normalize dialog opens. For this exercise, you'll use the default level, 0.000 dB. In digital audio, 0 dB is the maximum level you can set without causing distortion (also known as *clipping*). When you normalize a waveform to 0 dB, you're increasing the amplitude of the entire waveform so that the highest and lowest peaks are just below 0 dB.

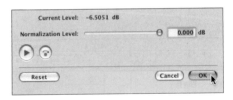

4   Click OK to normalize the waveform.

The amplitude (height) of the waveform increases until the highest or lowest peaks reach 0 dB.

5   Save your progress.

Doubling Dialog Tracks

Just as you doubled the music clips in Lesson 4, "Building Suspense with Editing Techniques," to fatten the track, the same process works to make the dialog sound stronger. Video editors often double the dialog while editing either by duplicating the clips in the Timeline or doubling mono dialog within a clip and converting it to stereo.

For this exercise, you'll convert the waveform from mono to stereo in order to double the audio within the clip. But first, let's take a look at the multitrack project to see what doubling techniques are already present in the Timeline.

1   Click the 6-1 ADA PSA Start tab to make the multitrack project active in the Project window.

Notice that the voiceover clips on the fifth track are duplicates of the clips on the fourth track. The clips on the second and third tracks were also doubled to increase the volume. These clips contain production sound dialog, which you'll be working with later in this lesson. For now, I just wanted you to see that there are different ways to double dialog tracks.

2   Find the first two voiceover clips on the fourth track from the top.

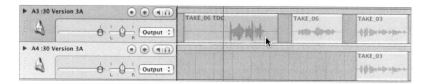

These two clips have not been doubled on a separate track. Instead, you'll double them by converting them from mono to stereo. You'll start with the first **TAKE_6 TDC** audio project, which is already open in the Waveform Editor.

3 Click the TAKE 6 TDC tab to make the audio file project active in the Project window.

Now you'll apply a Convert To Stereo process to the entire waveform. Up to this point, you've always selected part of the waveform before applying an action. If no selection is present, the process will be applied to the entire waveform.

4 Click anywhere on the waveform display area to clear any selections that may be present.

5 Choose Process > Convert To Stereo.

The Convert To Stereo dialog appears with a warning that your actions will be flattened, rendering everything into one audio file. This is a necessary part of the process of converting to stereo, and since the waveform has been expertly silenced and normalized, you don't have to worry about the fact that flattening is undoable once you've saved the project.

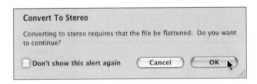

Convert To Stereo

Converting to stereo requires that the file be flattened. Do you want to continue?

☐ Don't show this alert again   (Cancel) (OK)

6 Click OK to flatten the actions and convert the waveform from mono to stereo.

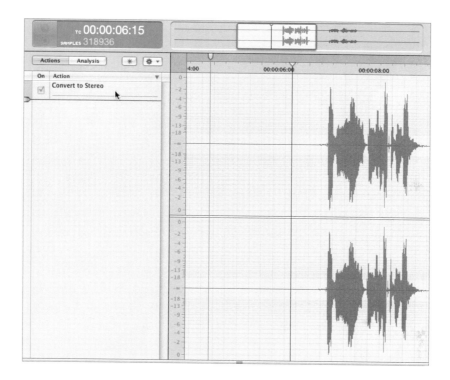

Violá! The waveform has been doubled, which boosts the overall level for a stronger, richer sound.

7 Save and press Cmd-W to close the audio file project.

8 Play the beginning of the project in the Timeline and listen to the first three pieces of voiceover (around 12 seconds).

As you listen to the voiceover with the other tracks, compare the perceived volume levels between the first, second, and third voiceover clips.

Both the first and third were doubled and seem to be the same level. The first was doubled as an audio file project normalized and converted to stereo in the Waveform Editor, while the third was duplicated to a different track in the Timeline. The second voiceover clip seems less powerful because it is still only a single mono audio track. What a difference a doubled track makes!

TIP ▶ Technically there's nothing wrong with doubling tracks over and over to boost their levels in the Timeline, but the more tracks and files you play simultaneously, the more processor intensive the project becomes. By modifying the waveform in an audio file project and then flattening it, you will reduce processor demands in the long run.

Project Practice

Now that you know how to normalize and convert a file to stereo in the Waveform Editor, try it on your own with the second voiceover clip. First double-click the clip and open it as an audio file project. Save the project as **Take_6 Stereo** to the My Soundtrack Pro projects folder. Then normalize the entire waveform and convert it to stereo. Finally, save the finished project, close the audio file project, and listen to the revised voiceover clip in the Timeline. Enjoy.

NOTE ▶ If you didn't complete all of the previous steps, feel free to open the **6-2 Remove Noise** project to catch up.

Working with Production Sound

Earlier in the lesson you worked with voiceover that was recorded in a controlled environment. A movie set is the next best thing to a sound booth, giving you a lot of control over things that could possibly contaminate sound recordings. But production sound recorded on location is at the mercy of everything from buzzing flies to airplanes passing overhead, car horns to people in the distance—even a good breeze can wreak audio havoc.

Nature happens on location, but luckily it's no match for the power of the Waveform Editor. Not only can you isolate and silence unwanted sounds, but you can also reduce the overall noise level. For the remainder of the lesson you'll work with production sound recorded on a set or on location. First you'll open an audio file project containing a production sound recording on location. You'll raise the overall level of the audio and use the Reduce Noise process to eliminate most of the background noise. Along the way you'll also use the frequency spectrum view for a better look at the noise.

1   Move the playhead to the normalize & remove noise marker (second marker from the left).

2   Double-click the Michael Berry – channel 1 clip below the marker on the second track to open it in the Waveform Editor.

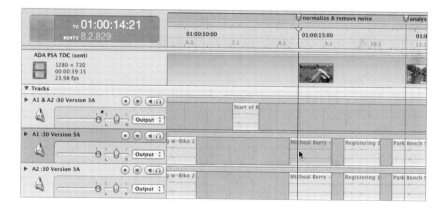

3   Play the project in the Waveform Editor to hear the current levels.

4   Ctrl-click the Sample Value ruler and change the sample units to Decibels in the shortcut menu.

Notice the current decibel level of the waveform peaks at around –20, which is fairly low.

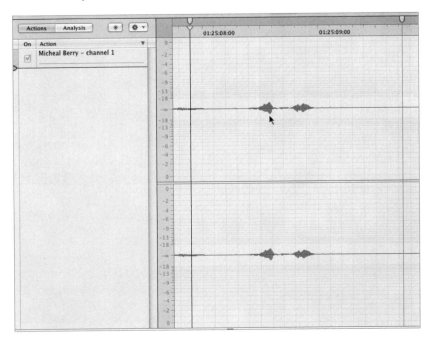

This signal may be doubled as a stereo track and is doubled again in the Timeline, but there is still no reason to leave the waveform low when it is so easy to modify it.

Normalizing Location Recordings

When an audio waveform is low in decibels, such as the one you're working with now, it's hard to tell how much ambient noise is in the recording until you boost the levels and take a look. Let's normalize the waveform and see what's there.

1   Click once to clear any selections that you may have created.

2   Choose Process > Normalize or press Cmd-L to open the Normalize dialog.

3   Click OK to normalize the file to 0 dB.

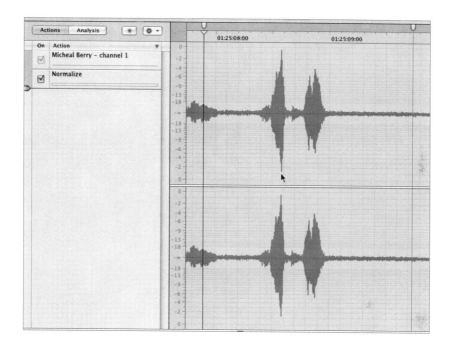

Yikes! The waveform is definitely amplified, and so is the ambient noise. Notice the thick band of noise between the lines of dialog. The rule in audio is that if you can see it, you can hear it, so the bigger the noise waveform, the more you'll hear it.

4   Play the normalized waveform.

The dialog is much stronger and so is the noise level. Perhaps 0 dB is too much for this waveform.

Modifying an Action

Since voiceover is the most important audio in the project, it makes sense that it's normalized to 0 dB. This dialog is also important, but should be less prominent in the overall project. Lowering the normalization level will also lower the level of the noise. You can modify most actions by simply double-clicking the action to reopen the dialog and changing the settings.

1   Double-click the Normalize action to reopen the dialog.

The current level displayed at the top of the dialog shows the peak levels of the original recording.

2   Type –6 in the Normalization Level field to normalize the highest and lowest peaks to –6 dB.

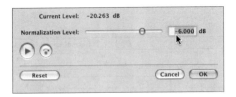

3   Click OK to apply the new normalization level.

4   Play the waveform to hear the dialog and noise normalized at –6 dB.

It's still a bit noisy, but much better than it was at 0 dB. Some noise is expected, since the scene takes place outside at an active location, so this is what sound editors call motivated noise.

Evaluating Noise in the Waveform

Unfortunately, sound that is recorded on location often contains a lot of background noise. As you just demonstrated, raising the level of the dialog also raises the level of the noise. If there's too much noise, the dialog drowns in the roar of the background. Not enough and the dialog feels fake, like it was recorded in a sound booth instead of on location. Clearly this cyclist isn't riding in a sound booth or deep space, so some ambient sound is expected. In fact, if it's too quiet, you'll likely need to add ambient sound to make it feel more realistic. Much of a sound engineer's time is spent removing noise, only to add more later as ambience, making the scene sound real without compromising the integrity of the dialog.

It's all part of the delicate audio balancing act. If hearing the dialog clearly means amplifying the embedded noise, you'll likely need to use the Remove Noise process to clean up the noise a bit. First, however, let's silence part of the waveform and take a look at the noise in the frequency spectrum view.

1 Move the playhead to the beginning of the dialog waveform (25:08:09).

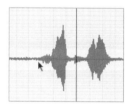

It's difficult to see where the noise stops and the waveform begins. That's partially because the noise never actually stops; it carries right on through the dialog and continues throughout the waveform.

2 Click the Frequency Spectrum view button to change the display area to the spectrum view.

In frequency spectrum view, you can clearly see the noise that looks like snow flurries near the bottom of the waveform. Remember, the lower the frequency, the lower it appears on the frequency spectrum. The dialog is displayed as bars representing the vocal sounds of each word, and looks more like a vocal skyline.

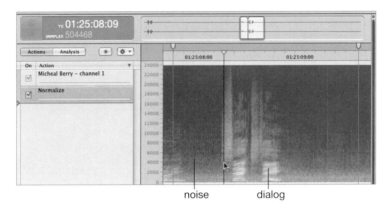

noise   dialog

Looking at the frequency spectrum, you can clearly see that the playhead is actually over part of the dialog and should be moved before silencing any of the waveform.

3   Press Cmd–left arrow twice to move the playhead two frames earlier (25:08:07).

Now that your playhead is definitely before the dialog, you can select and silence the noise at the beginning of the clip.

4   Press Shift–left arrow until the selection includes the first gray marker.

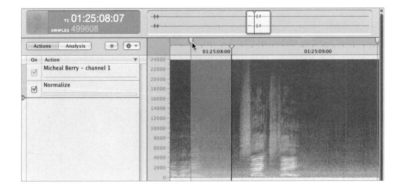

5   Press Cmd-Delete to silence the selection.

6   Click anywhere in the display area to clear the selection, then look at the silence in the spectrum view.

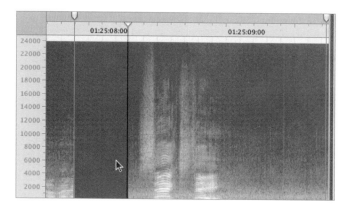

Sometimes you don't appreciate how noisy an audio file is until you see it!

Setting a Noise Print

While you're still in spectrum view, let's take this opportunity to select some of the noise and create a noise print. The noise print provides a signature of the frequencies to reduce or remove from the file using the Reduce Noise command.

1   Zoom out one level until you can see the second gray marker on the right side of the display area.

The secret of getting a good noise print is to select a section of noise that is representative of the noise throughout the waveform. In this case, the noise is fairly consistent and there is plenty of noise without dialog around the gray marker that will work well for the noise print.

2 Create a selection around the gray marker.

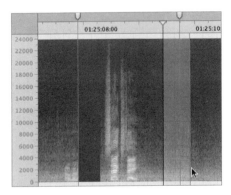

The length of the selection won't matter as long as the sound is representative of the noise throughout. Around 15 frames to 1 second will be fine.

3 Press the spacebar to play the selection and make sure it only includes noise.

If there is any dialog in the selection or sounds that aren't part of the overall noise, click outside the selection and try again.

4 Choose Process > Set Noise Print.

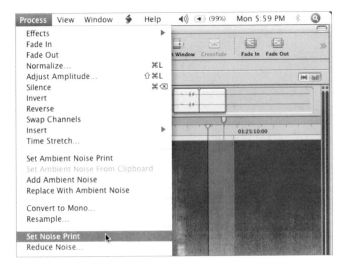

The selected noise is saved in memory and will be used to reduce the noise in the next exercise.

NOTE ▶ You can remove noise from an audio file in the Soundtrack Pro Waveform Editor the same way as you remove color when keying a video image. If this was an image and you were trying to remove the blue screen, you would first select the blue color, and then remove it. The noise print is the same as the selected blue color.

Reducing Noise in a Waveform

Now you can use the Reduce Noise command to preview (listen to) the waveform as you adjust the noise. You can also hear only what is being removed, similar to looking at the matte of a color key. Let's apply the Reduce Noise command and then make adjustments as needed to clean up the noise. First, you'll need to select the portion of the waveform where you'd like to reduce the noise, or else you'll only be reducing noise from the current selection.

1   Double-click between the gray markers to select that portion of the waveform.

2   Choose Process > Reduce Noise to open the Reduce Noise dialog.

The Reduce Noise dialog appears, giving you a chance to preview the noise selection.

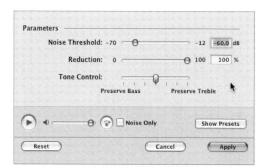

3   Click the Preview Play/Pause button to listen to the waveform with the noise print applied.

4   Drag the Noise Threshold slider to the left to lower the threshold (amount of noise frequencies removed).

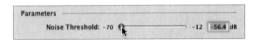

The noise threshold determines the level below which audio in the noise print is considered to be noise. Lowering the threshold results in only very low signals being reduced, while raising it results in more high signals being reduced. When you reduce noise, some of the frequencies are also present in the dialog. Raising the threshold too high will remove the frequencies shared by the dialog and the noise.

5   Drag the Noise Threshold slider all the way to the right to hear the highest threshold level.

As expected, the noise frequencies are greatly reduced, but the dialog sounds awful because it was altered in the process. Any frequencies the dialog shared with the noise have been stripped away, making it sound like you were better off with the noise. If solving one audio problem only creates another, try adjusting your threshold levels.

Previewing Noise Only

Another option is to preview only the noise as you adjust the threshold. That way you can hear exactly what is being reduced, and you'll know if the vocals are included in the frequency threshold.

1   Select the Noise Only checkbox.

2   Click the Preview button to continue previewing, if it's not still playing.

Now, all that you hear are the parts of the waveform that will be removed, so you can clearly hear the cyclist's voice along with the noise.

3   Drag the Threshold slider to the left until you can barely hear any of his voice amid the noise (38.2 dB).

4   Click Apply to apply the action.

5   Clear the current selection to see the area between the gray markers with the reduced noise.

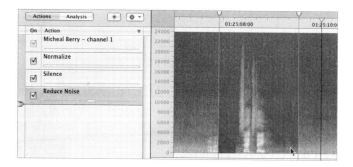

You can see a big difference in the spectrum view where the noise has been removed. Let's take a look at the difference in waveform view.

6 Click the Waveform View button and play the revised waveform.

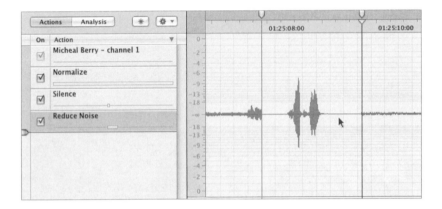

The noise is much less evident and the dialog is louder and clearer. What a difference! Wouldn't it be nice if you could easily hear the waveform before and after the actions so that you could evaluate the improvement?

Working with the Actions Insert Bar

Now that you've normalized, silenced, and reduced the noise on this audio file project, you can compare and evaluate the file before and after the actions. Actions are extremely flexible and allow you to turn them on and off, reorder, and even preview their results one at a time by moving the Action insert bar. In the next series of steps you'll experiment with these features.

1 Double-click the display area between the gray markers to select that section of the waveform.

2 Press the spacebar to begin playback of the selection.

3 Click the Actions menu in the top-right corner of the Action list and choose Play without actions.

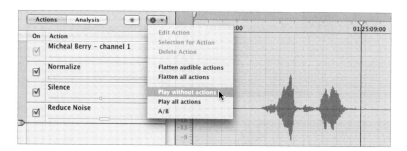

The actions all become disabled, and the waveform sounds the way it did when you first started.

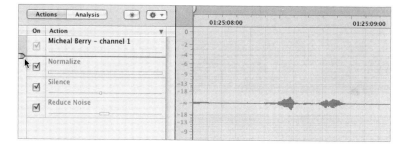

The actions weren't deleted or even turned off, so how were they disabled? The answer is the in the horizontal purple Action Insert Bar.

4 Locate the horizontal purple marker just below the Michael Berry – channel 1 file in the Action list.

The Action Insert Bar can be moved up and down the Action list between the different actions. Any actions below the bar are disabled; actions above the bar are enabled.

5   Drag the Action Insert Bar down below the Normalize action.

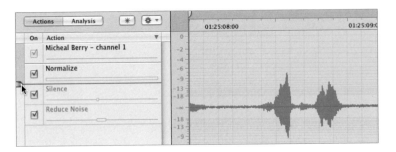

The waveform transforms instantly from before to after the Normalize action.

6   Pause playback, and then drag the Action Insert Bar to the bottom of the Action list below the Reduce Noise action.

All of the actions are now enabled. Each action also includes a checkbox so that you can selectively turn actions on or off.

7   Deselect the Normalize checkbox to turn off that action in the list.

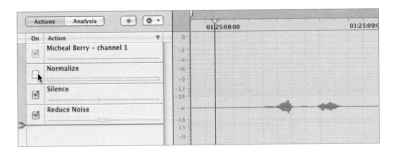

The other actions are still applied to the waveform, but it is no longer normalized.

8   Play the selection without the Normalize action.

9   Select the Normalize checkbox again to turn it back on.

10 Save and close the audio file project.

11 Play the modified file in the Timeline.

Not only did you improve the file, but it also sounds better than some of the other production sound clips that were simply doubled on two different tracks.

NOTE ▶ If you didn't complete all of the previous steps, feel free to open the **6-3 Fix Click** project to catch up.

Analyzing Files in the Waveform Editor

The techniques that you've learned so far will help you modify and repair sound levels. The Waveform editor can also analyze files for a range of common audio problems, including clicks and pops, hum, and phase issues. Better yet, it can automatically fix them.

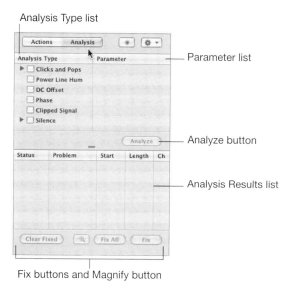

The Waveform Editor can perform six types of audio analysis:

Clicks and pops are sudden, short peaks in the audio file that can result from variety of causes, including Timeline editing in a video application or mechanical defects in analog recordings. You can set the threshold above the level at which Soundtrack Pro considers peaks to be clicks or pops.

Power Line Hum includes power lines and other electrical equipment that can produce a steady hum, often at 50 or 60 Hz.

DC Offset is a shift in the audio that causes the positive (upper) and negative (lower) parts of the signal to average above or below zero. DC offset can limit the dynamic range of an audio file.

Phase Issues can result from a distorted or inaccurate stereo image caused by poor microphone placement and other issues. When converting a stereo file to mono, the presence of phase issues can cause the left and right channels to partially or completely cancel each other out.

Clipped Signal or overloaded signal above the digital volume limits can result from several causes, including poor gain staging in a preamp during recording, bad electrical cables, or surface damage to an analog recording.

Silence detects parts of the audio file where the audio signal falls to zero (0). You can set the threshold below the level at which Soundtrack Pro considers the signal to be silence.

Eliminating Clicks and Pops

In this exercise, you'll open a clip at the analysis clicks & pops marker, which contains a nasty click. Next you'll run a Clicks and Pops analysis on the waveform to find the click and fix it—all in a matter of seconds. This may sound too good to be true, but it's not. Really.

1 Move the playhead to the analysis clicks & pops marker in the Timeline (19;14).

2 Double-click the upper Park Bench Stretching clip on the second track below the marker to open the audio file project in the Waveform Editor.

3 Play the waveform between the gray markers and listen to the click at the beginning of the dialog.

There are actually two sounds right before the cyclist says "Fifty." The first is a pedaling sound from a cyclist riding through the background of the shot, which is part of the production sound that goes with the scene. The second sound is the nasty click that you're hoping to eliminate. The analysis tool is sensitive enough that it can detect the difference based on the severity of the change in sound. The pedal sound is quick, but not loud, and doesn't spike in the waveform the way the click does.

4   Move the playhead close to the click that looks like a vertical spike in the waveform.

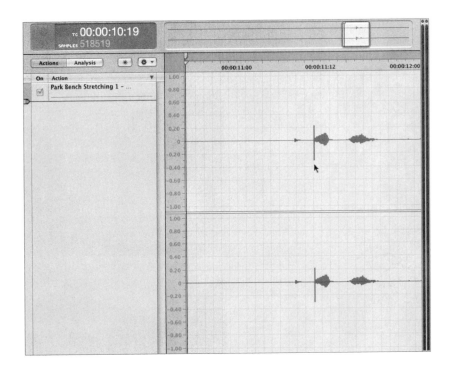

5   Press the up arrow key several times to zoom in for a closer look.

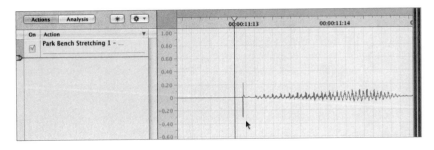

The click is right on the edge of the first word and might be difficult to remove manually without inadvertently trimming the dialog too. This is definitely a job for analysis.

6 Click the Analysis button to access the Analysis pane.

The Analysis Type list, Parameter list, and Analysis Results list replace the Action list in the window.

7 Drag the handle that looks like an equal sign at the bottom of the Analysis Type list to view all six tools in the Analysis Type list.

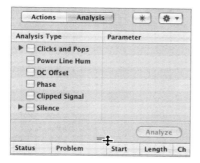

8 Press the down arrow key several times to zoom back out of the waveform until you can see both gray markers in the display area.

9 Select the Clicks and Pops checkbox in the Analysis Type list.

10 Click the Analyze button to begin the Clicks and Pops analysis.

NOTE ▶ The analysis tools will analyze a selection or the entire file. The time it takes depends upon the length of the file. Since you're working on a short clip, the analysis will be over in seconds.

Soundtrack Pro finds the click and marks the problem area in red in the Waveform display area.

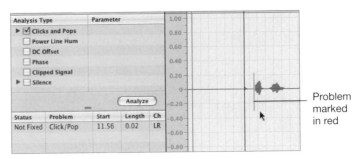

Problem marked in red

Reading and Fixing the Problem

Two things happened when you performed the analysis. A problem was detected and added to the Results list, and the problem was marked in red in the waveform. If the analysis had detected multiple problems, the problem areas would all be red in the waveform and would all appear in the results list in the order in which they were detected.

The Results list includes five columns of information:

Status	Problem	Start	Length	Ch
Not Fixed	Click/Pop	11.56	0.02	LR

▶ Status shows whether the problem is fixed or not.

▶ Problem shows to which type of analysis the problem belongs. This is especially useful if you were performing multiple types of analyses at the same time.

▶   Start shows where the problem begins.

▶   Length shows the duration of the problem.

▶   Channel shows whether the problem occurs in the left channel (L), right channel (R), or left and right (LR).

Only one problem was detected when you performed the analysis. If you select the item in the Results list, the part of the audio file around the problem becomes selected. Then you can zoom in to inspect the problem closer.

1   Click the problem in the Results list to select that area in the waveform.

2   Click and hold the Zoom button at the bottom of the Analysis pane to zoom in to the selected problem.

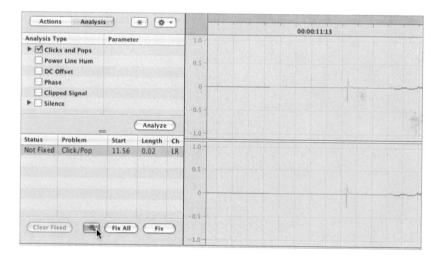

The Zoom button gives you a focused view on the exact problem.

3   Release the Zoom button to return the waveform to the previous zoom level.

4   Click the Fix button to fix the selected problem.

A fixing status window appears to show that the problem is in the process of being fixed.

Once the problem is fixed, it is marked as fixed in the results list, and the red part of the waveform disappears, along with the audible click. Amazing! Especially if you consider the effort it would take to try to eradicate that click manually.

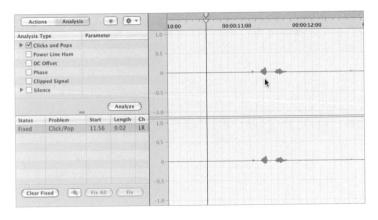

5   Save the fixed audio file project and close the tab for the audio file project.

6   Play the fixed audio file project in the Timeline to hear it with the other tracks.

> **NOTE ▶** If you didn't complete all of the previous steps, feel free to open the **6-4 Add Ambience** project to catch up.

Working with Ambience

The final series of exercises in this lesson are devoted to working with ambience in the Waveform Editor. In Lessons 3 and 4 you learned about adding ambient sound effects to a project to enhance the realism of the space, such as crickets or traffic. Now you'll focus on ambience recorded in production sound. Voiceover is supposed to be clean dialog and generally doesn't include any ambience. Production sound, especially when it's recorded outdoors, will almost always contain some form of background ambience.

Motivated ambience is okay as long as it is expected in that location or there is a reference to what is making the noise. For example, watching an interview with a surfer next to the beach, you expect to hear the waves in the background. That's fine, as long as the waves don't overpower the spoken dialog.

It's always better to have some sort of ambience running throughout a scene. Without consistent ambience, you'll hear every cut from shot to shot because each has a slightly different ambient background. A general rule for recording production sound is to record thirty seconds or so of ambient sound or "room tone" that can be added to the mix in a separate track to mask any gaps in ambience from shot to shot. Music can be used to do the same thing. Let's look at the ambience clips that were added to the multitrack project, then work with ambience within a clip in an audio file project.

1   Click the Solo button on the third track from the bottom of the Timeline to isolate the **Ambient Sound – Room Tone** clips in the track.

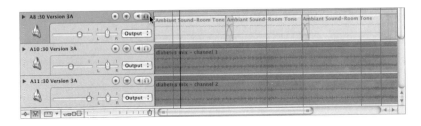

2   Play the project and listen to it with only the ambient sound audible.

The ambient sound is the same clip repeated three times with crossfades in between to smooth the overlap. The room tone ambient sound doesn't need to be anything dramatic, just a constant overall presence that will be consistent for the entire scene. If the scene changed to cyclists at the ocean, the room tone would also change to include ambience that would be more representative of that location.

3   Unsolo the track and click the Mute button so that the ambient clips will not be audible.

4   Play the project and listen to it without the added **Ambient Sound – Room Tone** clips.

5   Now mute the two music tracks and play the project again without music or ambience.

Ack! Why does it sound so bad? Well, the quality of the recordings didn't change. Nor did the levels of each clip. Instead, you're hearing, painfully clearly, every time the ambience changes between the different location shots. Not to mention the obvious gaps in ambient sound whenever there isn't ambient noise present. This was virtually unperceivable before because the ambience clips were filling the void and giving the audible illusion of consistency between shots. Music helps to mask the change in ambience, but can't mask everything.

6   Unmute the tracks and play the project again once with the **Ambient Sound – Room Tone** clips in the mix.

You can still hear slight changes in ambience from shot to shot, but they are much less apparent. Now that you've focused your attention on ambient sound, you'll be more sensitive to hearing it in this and future projects.

TIP ▶ To ease in the ambience sound within a clip, you can add a Fade In and Fade Out to the beginning and end of the clip, or try the Reduce Noise process to reduce the level of the ambient sound.

Setting an Ambient Noise Print

Earlier you set a noise print to hold the noise frequencies in memory so that they could be reduced from the waveform. You can also set an ambient noise print, which saves a copy of the ambient noise that can then be added when needed to an audio file project. This method is very useful for adding ambience to silenced portions of a waveform.

In this exercise you'll open an audio file project at the clean up & add ambience marker, then select a portion of the file to set as an ambient noise print.

1   Move the playhead to the clean up & add ambience marker and double-click the **Rest Stop Break 1** clip on the second track from the top below the marker.

The audio file project opens in the Waveform Editor.

2 Press the down arrow key to zoom out until you can see both gray markers.

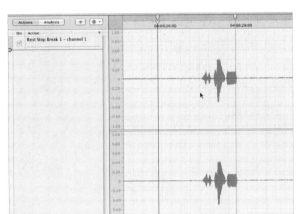

3 Select the waveform between the two gray markers and play the selection.

What do you think? Pretty good. The ambient sound is consistent throughout the file, without being distracting. However, the motorcycle horn honking at the end *is* a distraction, and needs to be silenced. Also, the word *twenty* is much lower in amplitude (volume) than the word *five*. Since you know that you'll be silencing the honking sound, let's set an ambient noise print that can be used to fill the silence later.

4 Move the playhead to the first gray marker and drag it toward the right to create a selection about one second long.

The Selection Length value slider in the bottom-right corner of the Project window will display the length of your selection.

5   Choose Process > Set Ambient Noise Print.

That's it. The ambient noise print has been created so that you can use it later. First, let's take a few minutes to put your new skills to work and adjust the problems you've already identified.

Working with the Zoom Tool

The next series of exercises will allow you to utilize many of your new skills as you modify the project to fix the problems. Along the way you'll also learn how to use the Zoom tool and adjust your selections to the zero point cross-ings for more precision and cleaner editing.

Let's start by using the Zoom tool to select the horn honking sound at the end of the dialog in the waveform. Previously, you've always created selections by dragging the Selection tool, then used the up or down arrows keys to zoom in and out. The Zoom tool allows you to create a selection and instantly zooms that selection to fit the display area.

1   Click the Zoom tool, which looks like a magnifying glass, to select the tool.

2   Click-drag the Zoom tool over the horn honk portion of the waveform to create a selection.

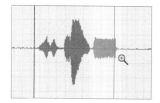

The Zoom tool creates a light shaded area to show what is being selected for zoom, rather than a dark blue selection such as the one created by the Selection tool.

3 Release the mouse button, and the zoom selection will instantly fit the display area.

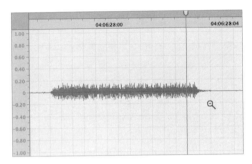

There you have it, instant zoom.

4 Press A to return to the Selection (arrow) tool.

Now that you have a clear view of the horn sound, you can select it.

5 Click-drag the Selection tool from the beginning to the end of the horn waveform to select it.

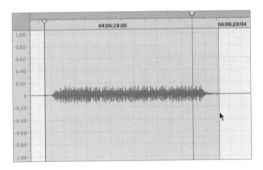

It's almost ready to silence. First, let's check to see if the selection starts and ends at the zero crossing point.

Selecting at the Zero Crossing Point

A sound wave begins at zero (dead center) and then begins a wave pattern with equal parts above and below the zero point. Selecting the waveform where it crosses the zero point will allow the cleanest edit. Creating random selections or slicing up audio files with the Blade tool doesn't always cut the waveform at the zero point, so you might hear audio remnants, or pop at the edit point. To see how the waveform crosses the zero point, let's zoom in further to the beginning of your selection.

1   Press Shift-Cmd-+ several times to zoom in to the waveform vertically.

2   Press the up arrow key several times to zoom in to the waveform horizontally.

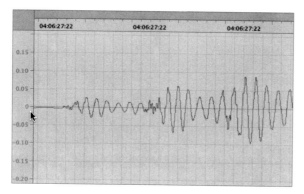

NOTE ▶ You may need to use the zoom scroll bar at the bottom of the window to keep the waveform in view as you zoom horizontally. The amount of adjusting you'll need to make depends on your screen size, resolution, and zoom level.

As you zoom in, notice that the sound waves become more defined. The horizontal line passing through the center of the sound waves is the zero point. The height of the sound wave is the amplitude, and the length of the wave from zero point to zero point is the frequency. Now that you know what the zero point is, let's see if your selection In point is at a zero crossing point. You can see this by looking at the waveform at the sample level.

3   Press Home to move the playhead to the In point of your selection, if it is not already in that position.

NOTE ▶ If the playhead moves to the beginning of the project, press End to move to the end of the selection, then Home to move to the beginning of the selection. Home and End only move to the beginning and end of the selection if the playhead is already within the selection.

4   Press Z to zoom all the way in to In point of the selection at the sample level.

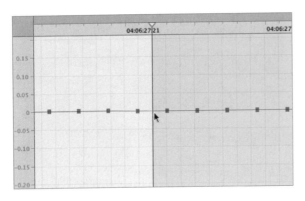

My selection looks like it is at the zero crossing point. Is yours? Don't worry if it is not, because Soundtrack Pro includes a handy set of shortcuts and menu items to help.

5   Choose Edit > Adjust Selection to Zero Crossing > Outward.

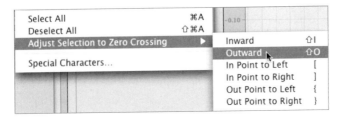

The selection extends outward so that the In point and Out point are both at a zero crossing point.

6   Press End to move the playhead to the selection Out point.

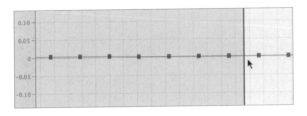

The selection should end exactly at a point where the waveform crosses the zero position. There you have it. Your selection is now precisely within zero crossing points.

NOTE ▶ The shortcuts for adjusting selections to the zero crossing points are: Shift-I to trim the In and Out points inward, Shift-O to trim both In and Out points outward, [(left bracket) to trim the In point to the left,] (right bracket) to trim the In point to the right, Shift-[(left bracket) to trim the Out point to the Left, and Shift-] (right bracket) to trim the Out point to the right.

7 Click anywhere on the display area to clear the selection, then press the down arrow key to zoom out until you can see the full horn honk part of the waveform again.

Wait—you just cleared the selection! All that zero crossing work… gone! Or is it? Remember Soundtrack Pro's Waveform Editor has a long selection history, so you can simply click the previous selection button to get your precise selection back again. Whew! (I just threw that in for review because you haven't used it in a while.)

8 Click the Previous Selection button to reactivate the previous selection.

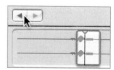

9 Press Cmd-Delete to silence the selection.

10 Click the previous selection button again until the entire waveform between the gray markers is selected.

11 Play the selection and listen to it without the horn honk.

It sounds much better without the horn. Of course, now you've created a silent gap in the ambience. No problem.

Pasting Ambience to Replace Silence

Remember the ambient noise print that you created a few minutes ago? Well it's time to put it to work. Sure, you could have waited until now to set the ambient noise print. It doesn't matter when you set it; as long as you don't quit Soundtrack Pro or set a different ambient noise print, it will be retained in memory.

1   Click the forward selection button to return to the selection that you used to create the silence.

2   Choose Process > Add Ambient Noise to add the ambient noise print to the selection.

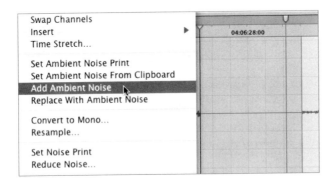

Ambient sound is added to the selection.

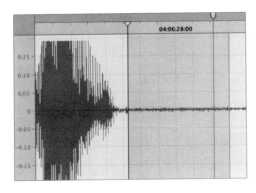

3   Save your progress, clear the selection, and play the edited project.

NOTE ▶ The Process menu offers several choices for pasting ambient sound. You can choose Add Ambient Noise to add ambience to the waveform in the selection without replacing it. You can also choose Replace With Ambient Noise to replace the waveform in a selection with the ambient noise print. You could have used the Replace With Ambient Noise process to replace the horn sound with ambience without ever needing to silence it first. In the previous exercise, you performed the extra step of silencing in order to learn how to use the Add Ambient Noise option and make zero crossing point selections.

Project Practice

Now it's your turn to select the waveform representing the word "twenty" and raise the amplitude until it matches the amplitude of "five." Press Shift-Cmd-- (minus) to zoom out vertically from the waveform. Feel free to use the Zoom tool to zoom horizontally for easy access to that part of the waveform, and don't forget to adjust the selection to the nearest zero crossing points. Once you've selected the word, press Shift-Cmd-L, or choose Process > Adjust Amplitude to raise the amplitude by around 7 dB. Save the audio file project, close the Waveform Editor, and watch the finished multitrack project.

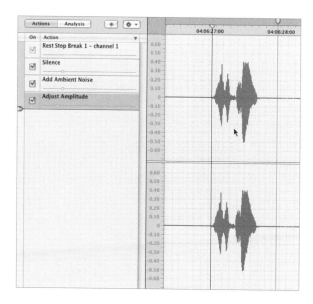

Congratulations! You now have a valuable set of dialog-fixing skills that you can apply to your own projects.

Lesson Review

1. What two methods can you use to silence a selection in the Waveform Editor?

2. If you do not select part of the waveform before applying an action, where will the actions be applied?

3. What two steps can you take to boost the overall volume level of a dialog clip and make the sound richer?

4. Can you modify actions once they are applied in the Waveform Editor?

5. How do you determine which actions are currently applied to the Waveform?

6. How do you determine which noise frequencies to reduce from the waveform? Can you set the noise that will be reduced?

7. What are the two ways that you can apply an ambient noise print to a selection?

Answers

1. You can silence a selection in the Waveform Editor by choosing Process > Silence or pressing Cmd-Delete.

2. Actions will be applied to the entire file if no selection has been made.

3. You can boost the volume level of the dialog and make it sound richer by normalizing or amplifying the level and doubling the waveform by converting it to stereo, or duplicating the clip in the Timeline.

4. To modify actions in the Waveform Editor, double-click the action in the Actions list and change the values in the shortcut menu.

5. The Actions Insert Bar determines which actions are applied to the waveform.

6. The Reduce Noise process uses the noise print to determine which fre-
    quencies to reduce from the waveform. You can set the noise that will be
    reduced by selecting a section of noise in the waveform and choosing Set
    Noise Print from the Process menu.

7. Ambient noise can be added to a selection or used to replace the selection.

Keyboard Shortcuts

Waveform Editor

Cmd-L	Normalize
Cmd-Delete	Silence
Z	zoom in to Sample Level, or back to previous zoom level

Adjust Selection to Zero Crossing Points

Shift-I	trim the In and Out points inward
Shift-O	trim the In and Out points outward
[	trim the In point to the left
]	trim the In point to the right
{ (Shift-[)	trim the Out point to the left
} (Shift-])	trim the In point to the right

Tools

A	Selection tool

7

Lesson Files

Time   This lesson takes approximately 45 minutes to complete.

Goals   Work with single take recording in the Timeline

Record a single take

Explore multitake recordings

Record a multiple take

Switch between takes in a multitake file

Edit both single take and multitake recordings

Recording Audio

You already know how to arrange and edit clips in the Timeline and modify audio file projects in the Waveform Editor. Now you'll learn to record, edit, and save your own recordings. In Soundtrack Pro, whether you're working with voiceover, sound effects, or music, you can record files directly into the Timeline, Mixer, or Waveform Editor. You'll learn the basics for setting up your equipment and editing techniques for single take and multitake recordings. Along the way you'll also pick up some new shortcuts and techniques that you can apply to your own projects.

Preparing the Project

You will begin this lesson by opening the 7-1 **Single Take** and 7-2 **Multitake** project files. Both files are located in the 07_Projects&Media folder.

1   Quit all open applications, except for Soundtrack Pro.

2   Open the projects 7-1 **Single Take** and 7-2 **Multitake**.

    Both project tabs should be showing in the Project window.

3   Click the 7-1 Single Take tab to make it the active project.

    Don't play the project yet. Just leave it open until we get to it in a few minutes.

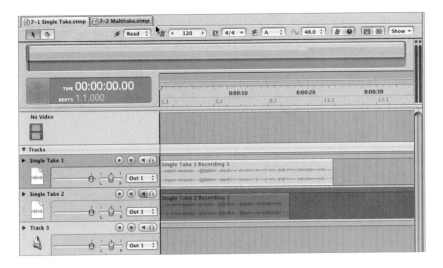

Planning Your Recording Session

Although you won't be prompted to record until later in the lesson, it's a good idea to get everything set up in advance so that when you're ready to record you can go for it. Before you begin a recording session, you've got to connect your equipment, check hard drive space, and set your recording preferences. Oh yeah, it's also a good idea to know what you are planning to record.

Connecting Your Audio Equipment

Soundtrack Pro supports a variety of audio equipment for both recording and playback. However, it does not support video input from devices such as camcorders or videocassette decks. If you own an iSight camera, you can also use it as a microphone. For information on connecting a specific piece of equipment to your computer, read the documentation that came with the equipment.

If you have equipment that cannot connect directly to the computer, you might be able to connect it to an audio interface and connect that to the computer. Audio interfaces can connect to both input and output devices such as microphones, musical instruments, speakers, amplifiers, or a mixer. When choosing an audio interface, check the manufacturer's specifications to make sure the interface is compatible with Mac OS X v10.3 or later. Some audio interfaces require driver software, while others are supported without the need for a driver. If the device requires a driver, make sure an up-to-date driver is included with the device or is available from the manufacturer.

> **NOTE** ▸ Soundtrack Pro supports input from digital audio interfaces up to a maximum sample rate of 96 kHz and a maximum bit depth of 24 bits. If your interface is outside that range, an alert message will tell you that it is not compatible with the application.

When using external audio devices, it's a good idea to connect them before opening Soundtrack Pro. Take a moment to plug in or set up your microphone or recording device now. If your computer has a built-in microphone, you can also use that for this exercise, but you can still follow along without one.

Checking for Hard Drive Space

What is your available hard drive space? Recording 44.1 kHz stereo audio files requires about 10 MB of disk space per minute. Stereo audio files that you would use for dialog recordings for video at 48 kHz are even larger. Fortunately, for this lesson the clips you record will be fairly short, and I don't imagine you will need too many takes. However, if you are a perfectionist and anticipate many takes, check your hard drive and plan accordingly.

Setting the Recording Preferences

You will also need to set the input device and output monitoring device for recording in either the Preferences Recording pane or the Recording tab. Let's open the Preferences Recording pane and modify the settings for your recording.

1   Choose Soundtrack Pro > Preferences or press Cmd-, (comma) to open the Preferences window.

2   Click the Recording tab at the top of the Preferences window to view the Preferences Recording pane.

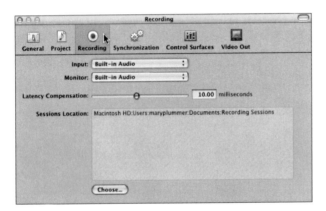

3   Click the Input pop-up menu and select the microphone you will be using.

If you are using the built-in computer microphone, select Built-in Audio.

> **NOTE ▶** If you have additional recording hardware installed, it should appear in the Input pop-up menu.

4   Click the Monitor pop-up menu and select what you will be using to listen to the recording.

If you are using the built-in computer speakers, select Built-in Audio.

Notice that the Sessions Location filed shows you that, by default, the files will go to a Recording Sessions folder in your Documents folder. If you need to move it, you can click Choose and change the location where the recordings will be saved. It's a good idea to leave them in the default location, though, so you don't need to move them right now.

5   Close the Preferences window.

Exploring Both Recording Methods

Soundtrack Pro offers two different recording methods: single take and multiple or multitake. Both of these methods create stereo or mono AIFF files that you can add directly to your project. You can also tag your recorded files in the Apple Loop utility so they will be recognized by the search database. You will work with the Apple Loop utility in Lesson 10, "Exporting, Managing Media, and Preferences." For now, let's focus on the recording process.

Recording a Single Take

Single take recording is a way to record audio into the Timeline based upon the current playhead position. Using the single take recording method, the recording begins at the playhead position once you click the record button, and ends when you press the Play/Pause button. By moving the playhead over a portion of audio that you wish to overwrite, you can click Record to *punch* in and out of record mode within the file while the playhead is moving. The recorded files are saved when you save the project. Let's take a look at two single take recordings in the **7-1 Single Take** project.

> **NOTE** ▶ For the record (pun intended), I recorded these in my hotel room using the little built-in microphone on my laptop. Also, I'm an editor and composer, and definitely not a voiceover artist. So don't expect much on the quality of the recorded content. This is only meant to be an example of a single take recording. You'll see an example of a professional recording later in the lesson.

1   Mute the Single Take 2 track, if it is not already muted.

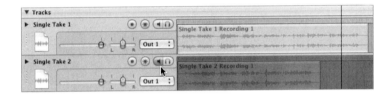

2   Play the project to hear the recording in the Single Take 1 track. This take is full of mistakes, which could be edited out, or you can record another take.

Notice that the name of the recording is nearly identical to the name of the track. The naming convention uses the track name, followed by the recording session. If this is the first recording session for a project, the name will be followed by Recording 1.

3   Mute the Single Take 1 track, and unmute the Single Take 2 track.

4   Play the second take.

It isn't great, but at least it is complete and has fewer mistakes.

5   Mute the Single Take 2 track so that both tracks have been muted.

You can only record one track at a time, and must click the Record Enable button on a track header to arm it for recording. Clicking the Record Enable button also automatically opens the Recording tab in the Utility window. Once a track has been record enabled you will be able to monitor (hear) the microphone input.

6 Click the Record Enable button on Track 3 to arm the track for recording.

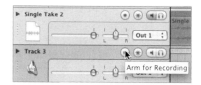

The armed track is highlighted in red and the Record tab becomes active in the Utility window.

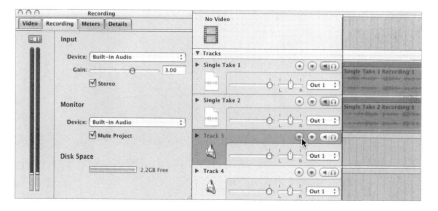

The Recording tab includes meters to view the input level of the recording, a Gain slider for adjusting the input level, pop-up menus for Input and Monitor Device, a Stereo checkbox that allows you to record stereo or mono files, a Mute Project checkbox that mutes the audio from the project as you record, and finally, a handy Disk Space meter to indicate how much free space you have on your hard drive. It's a good idea to leave at least 10% of your hard disk free for optimal performance. So the bigger the hard drive, the more space you need to keep open.

TIP ► If you hear feedback, the input or output levels may be too high on your computer. Turn off the Record enable button, and lower the monitor volume. You can also change the input or output levels in the audio pane of System Preferences. Once you've removed the feedback, re-enable the track. You may need to turn down the monitor volume considerably to avoid feedback if the speakers are close to the microphone.

7   Speak into your microphone, or play the instrument you wish to record and listen for a delay when you hear it through the output monitor.

NOTE ► All digital audio interfaces can be susceptible to latency, a noticeable delay between the time the audio signal is produced and the time you hear it. Connecting the interface through a hub or daisy-chaining it through another device can cause an unacceptable amount of latency, particularly with slower protocols such as USB. Instead, connect directly to the computer.

If you hear a delay, you can adjust it using the Latency Compensation slider in the Recording Preferences pane. If you don't hear a delay, skip down to step 10.

8   Press Cmd-, (comma) to open the Preferences window.

9   Drag the Latency Compensation left or right until you no longer hear the delay and then close the Preferences window.

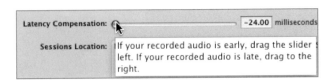

10   Press Return to move the playhead to the beginning of the Timeline.

Single take recording always begins at the playhead position on the enabled track. Technically, your project is ready to record.

11 Read through the voiceover text below before proceeding to the next step and recording a take. If you don't wish to record this voiceover, move on to the next section, "Working with Multiple Takes."

VO:

THIS IS A SINGLE TAKE RECORDING, WHICH MEANS I RECORD ONLY ONE TAKE.

IF I DON'T RECORD IT PERFECTLY I'LL NEED TO TRY AGAIN. I CAN ALWAYS EDIT AND SAVE THESE TAKES AS NEEDED.

EACH TIME I RECORD USING THIS METHOD, IT IS SAVED AS A SEPARATE AUDIO FILE IN THE RECORDING SESSIONS FOLDER.

NOTE ▶ Voice Over scripts are traditionally typed in all caps, where spoken dialog for actors is typed in upper and lower case letters.

12 Click the Record button in the Transport Controls and read the voiceover text above out loud.

13 Press the spacebar to stop recording when you are finished.

If you're not happy with your recording, mute Track 3, enable Track 4, and try again.

14 Choose File > Save As and save the project to the My Soundtrack Pro projects folder on your computer.

Working with Multiple Takes

The multitake recording method lets you record more than one take within the same file. Once you complete a multitake recording, you can view all of the different takes, or edit between takes in the Timeline or the Waveform Editor. To record using the multitake method, you must first create a playback region in the Timeline where you wish to record. You also need to make sure the

Looping button is on. If looping is off, you will only be able to make single take recordings.

Let's take a look at the multitake recording in the **7-2 Multitake** project.

1   Click the 7-2 Multitake tab at the top of the Project Window to view that project in the Timeline.

The multitake recording in the Timeline includes four different takes within the same recorded file. Notice that the recorded file is the same length as the playback region. The text in the bottom-right corner of the file indicates which take is currently showing in the Timeline.

2   Play the project to hear the current take.

Believe it or not, that's the best take (feel free to chuckle). Next, look at the other takes that can be accessed by either dragging the edge of the file, or using a shortcut menu.

3   Ctrl-click the file and choose Take > 3 from the shortcut menu.

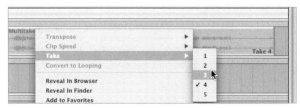

The file changes to show Take 3 in the Timeline. Did you happen to notice that the menu showed 5 takes? Just a moment ago I said there were only 4.

4   Ctrl-click the file again and choose Take > 5.

As you can see, Take 5 doesn't show much potential as a viable take. In fact, it doesn't include a waveform because I didn't speak. This take is human error. Basically, I didn't stop recording fast enough after the end of Take 4, so it started a fifth take. No problem, as long as you don't use Take 5 in the final project.

5   Ctrl-click and change the file to Take > 1.

To view all of the takes at once, simply extend the edges of the clip to reveal the other recordings.

6   Press the down arrow key to zoom out of the Timeline until the file is about one fourth of the length of the Timeline.

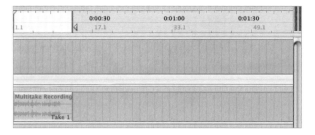

7   Drag the right edge of the file to the right to extend it and reveal the other takes.

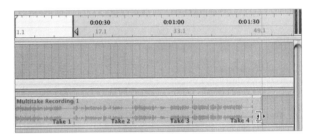

Each take is separated by a dotted line and take number.

8   Press Cmd-Z to undo the resizing of the file and return it to its original size.

9   Double-click the recording to open it in the Waveform Editor.

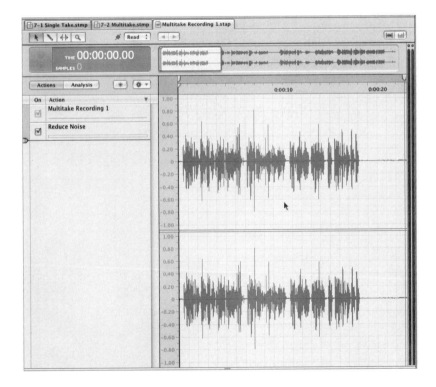

As you can see, I've already saved this as an audio file project and applied the Reduce Noise process. When you open a multitake recording in the Waveform Editor, the zoom level is set to fit the current take in the display area.

10   Drag the Visible Area Rectangle in the Global view to the right to see the other takes one at a time.

11   Press Shift-Z to fit all of the takes in the Waveform display area at once.

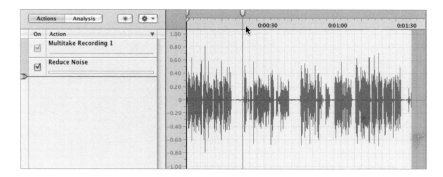

Just like other audio file projects, the gray markers show which portion of the file is currently showing in the Timeline.

12   Close the audio file project.

Recording Multiple Takes

The Record tab functions the same for both single take and multitake recordings. You also need to enable the track to which you'd like to record. To try a multitake recording of the voiceover script, continue with the following steps.

If you'd like to skip the recording, move on to the next section, "Tips for Recording Audio."

1   Mute the Multitake track in the Timeline.

2   Click the Record Enable button on Track 2.

3   Read through the Multitake VO script once for practice.

MULTITAKE VO:

THIS IS A MULTITAKE RECORDING WHICH USES A PLAYBACK REGION AS A BOUNDARY TO MARK THE BEGINNING AND END OF EACH TAKE. ONCE THE PLAYHEAD REACHES THE END OF THE PLAYRANGE, IT RETURNS TO THE BEGINNING AND STARTS A NEW TAKE.

MULTITAKE RECORDINGS ARE ALSO STORED IN THE RECORDING SESSIONS FOLDER. HOWEVER, ALL OF THE TAKES ARE PART OF THE SAME AUDIO FILE.

4   Click the Record button on the Transport controls when you're ready to begin.

Record at least two full takes of the voiceover.

5   Press the spacebar to stop recording.

6   Press Shift-Cmd-S to save the file uncollected to the My Soundtrack Pro projects folder.

The project will reference the recording that is saved in the Recording Sessions folder. Unless you plan to move it to a different computer that doesn't have the folder with the original recordings, there is no need to save the file as collected (with audio files).

7   Listen to your different takes in the Timeline.

TIP You should always save the projects with finished recordings as soon as you finish recording a new file. Remember, the files aren't saved in the Recording Sessions folder until the project is saved. That way, in the event of a sudden power outage, rolling blackout, or other phenomenon that may shut down your computer unexpectedly, your recorded files will be saved.

Tips for Recording Audio

▶ If you are using an external microphone, move it away from the computer for your recordings. Computer towers emit a low sound that may end up on your recording. Obviously you can't turn the computer off—but moving or shielding the microphone will help.

▶ When recording sound effects that may be useful for future projects, vary the takes. Try different intensities, durations, and distances from the microphone to give you more choices later.

▶ Start your own effects and loops libraries. Create master folders to store and organize your recordings. You never know when you may need them again.

▶ When you are recording a specific music loop or sound effect for a project, if you plan to fade the sound in or out, make sure you record enough sound at the beginning of your loop or single take to make room to fade in or fade out. If you are not sure whether you will fade in or fade out, record it both ways. It's much better to plan ahead and record too many takes, than not enough.

▶ When you are recording an instrument part to go with the music already in the Timeline, set the recording loop at least a measure or two earlier than you need, to give yourself plenty of time to get into the groove. If your loop is too tight, you won't have time to reset mentally or physically between takes.

▶ Practice playing your instrumental part along with the music in the Timeline several times to see how long it takes you to get up to speed and in time with the song. Then set your recording loop accordingly. Plus, it never hurts to practice.

▶ More is better when you record multiple takes. It's easier to throw things out later than to set up and record again because you didn't get what you needed the first time.

▶ When you are recording a music loop, make sure it doesn't start and stop abruptly. The idea of a loop is seamless, repeatable music. Music loops should also be recorded in musical time, and start and end on a beat.

Preparing the Project

Now that you understand the difference between single take and multitake recordings, let's take a look at a real-world example that was professionally recorded.

You'll be working with an unmixed version of the song *Something About You* by the band Turn to Stone, produced by Adam Green. This is an early version of the song that has not been through a final mix, and there have been no effects applied—yet.

The original song contains over thirty separate audio tracks. For this exercise, many of the tracks were exported as groups and imported as single tracks to simplify the project. You'll learn more about that process in Lesson 10, "Exporting, Managing Media, and Preferences." Also, you'll work with many of the separated music tracks in the mixing lessons coming up in Lessons 8 and 9.

1   Close all open Soundtrack Pro projects.

2   Choose File > Open.

3   Select **7-3 Something Start** from the 07_Projects&Media folder.

4   Save the file uncollected to the My Soundtrack Pro projects folder on your computer.

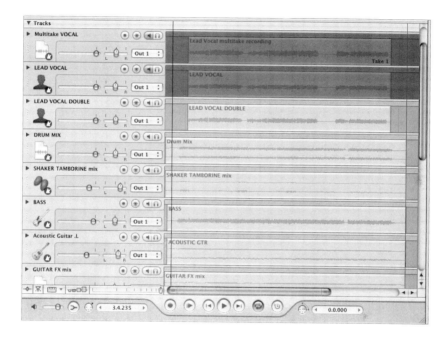

Editing Recorded Files in the Timeline

There is no real mystery to editing single take recorded files in the Timeline. In fact, all the files that you have edited thus far in the book were all recorded at one time or another. You can cut them with the Razor tool or the split feature and arrange the clips on different tracks. Editing multitake recordings is a flexible way to cut the clip then switch between takes as needed. Over the next series of steps you'll preview the different vocal takes and try editing both the single take and multitake recordings in the Timeline.

Previewing the Different Takes

Before you start cutting up the lead vocals for this song, you should know what you're working with. In this case, all of the takes are good, so it's just a matter of gauging the different performances at different points in the song.

The Solo and Mute buttons come in quite handy when previewing takes because you can click different takes on and off while the playhead is moving. You already know how to use the Mute and Solo buttons and switch between takes in a multitake recording. Now you can use those skills to preview the different takes in the song. For the purposes of this exercise, the top three tracks will be referred to as Track 1, Track 2, and Track 3 from top to bottom, regardless of the actual track name.

1   Mute Track 1 and Track 2 if they are not already muted.

2   Begin playback of the song and listen to the **LEAD VOCAL DOUBLE** file in Track 3.

3   Unmute Track 2 and mute Track 3 to hear the song with the **LEAD VOCAL** file from Track 2.

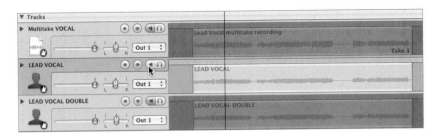

4   Unmute Track 3 again to hear both vocal tracks at the same time.

Interesting. There's a bit of echo between them because they aren't in exactly the same time, but it might be a cool effect during the chorus or to accentuate specific vocal phrases. Now on to the multitake recording on Track 1.

5   Continue playback and unmute Track 1, and then mute both Tracks 2 and 3.

    You're currently listening to Take 1 of two different takes.

6   Deselect the multitake clip if it is selected on Track 1, and continue playback.

7   Ctrl-click the multitake clip, and choose Take > 2 from the shortcut menu.

    NOTE ▶ If the file was selected before you Ctrl-clicked it, there's a good
    chance that you'll get a disk warning dialog. You'll also notice a moment of
    vocal silence as the file switches from Take 1 to Take 2 during playback.

8   Pause playback.

    So what did you learn from this vocal preview experience? How about the
    fact that you *can* preview both single take or multitake recordings while
    the playhead is moving. Using Mute or Solo buttons and clicking between
    two separate recordings on different tracks is more seamless than trying to
    switch between multiple takes during playback.

Using the Razor Tool to Edit Recordings

Your goal in this exercise is to use the Razor tool to cut the files so the song
begins with Take 2, then changes to Take 1, then finishes with Take 2. You'll
start with the multitake file, then perform the equivalent on the single take
recordings. To keep the editing simple, you'll cut the recording at the pauses
between the lead vocal parts.

1   Mute Track 1 and Track 2, if they are not already muted.

2   Move the playhead to 33.1.000 in the Timeline.

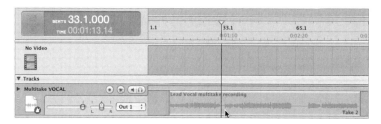

3   Press B for the Razor (blade) tool and click the Razor tool on the
Lead Vocal multitake recording clip at the playhead position.

4   Move the Razor tool to the second gap in the **Lead Vocal multitake recording**
waveform (approximately 65.1.000) and click again to split the clip.

5   Press A for the Selection (arrow) tool.

6   Crtl-click the middle **Lead Vocal multitake recording** clip, and choose
Take > 1 from the shortcut menu.

The middle section of the **Lead Vocal multitake recording** changes to
Take 1 and is labeled as such in the lower right corner of the clip.

7   Play the portions of the song around the edits in the vocals.

That was easy. Now how can you re-create the same thing from the two
separate single take recordings? Better yet, how do you use both takes at
the beginning of the third segment?

NOTE ▶ This is a pretty big file so it might push the limits of your
processor if your computer is slower. If you see a disk warning dialog,
select the checkbox in the dialog that says Do Not Show This Warning
Again. You won't be bothered by the warning again.

Project Practice

If you thought that was easy, this will be a slightly bigger challenge. Use the Razor tool or select and split the clips in the same location leaving a slight overlap in the last segment of the Lead Vocal clip. Rather than step you through it, I'll provide a picture of the finished edit. Have fun. When you finish, play the edits. The overlapped section works really well. If you like the slight echo sound during the overlapped section, you can increase it by nudging the upper clip slightly to the left or right. Save and close the project.

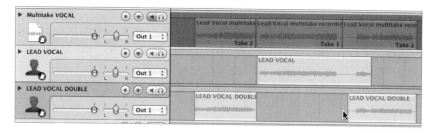

Nice editing! As you can see there are advantages to both recording methods.

> **TIP** ▶ If you like the ease of switching a multitake recording but also the flexibility of separate files, you can always extend a multitake recording, split it into separate pieces with the Razor tool, and place the parts you wish to overlap on separate tracks.

Once recorded, you can open the new files in the Apple Loops Utility and add metadata tags, such as key, tempo, or general to the file so it can be indexed and searched in your Soundtrack Pro database. In Lesson 10, you'll learn how to export your recordings as files or loops and tag them in the Apple Loops utility so they can be indexed in the Search tab.

Lesson Review

1. What steps are necessary to record a single take recording in the Timeline?

2. What step is necessary for a multitake take recording, that differentiates it from a single take recording in the Timeline?

3. Where is the default location for recordings to be saved on the computer?

4. What are three ways that you can view different takes of a multitake take recording?

5. If a multitake take recording includes six takes, how many files will be stored on the computer for that recording?

6. Can recordings be edited and modified in the Waveform Editor once they have been saved?

Answers

1. Before you record a single take recording in the Timeline, you must first turn on the Record Enable button for the track where you'd like to record, and move the playhead to the position in the Timeline where you'd like the recording to start. Finally, you need to click the Record button in the transport controls to begin recording.

2. It is necessary to first create a playback region in the Timeline in order to create a multitake take recording. Multitake recordings use the boundaries of the playback region, rather than the playhead position, to record to the armed (record enabled) track.

3. Soundtrack Pro recordings are stored in the Recording Sessions folder located in the Documents folder. You can change the default location of recordings in the Recording Preferences.

4. You can view the different takes of a multitake take recording by Ctrl-clicking the recording in the Timeline and choosing a different take in the shortcut menu. You can drag the right or left edges of a multitake take recording to reveal the other takes. Also, you can open the recording in the Waveform Editor and view all of the different takes within the recorded file.

5. A multitake take recording is saved as one file in the Recording Sessions folder, regardless of the number of takes within the recording. For example, a multitake recording with six takes would be saved as one file.

6. Recordings can be edited and modified in the Waveform Editor as audio files, or audio file projects, the same as any other audio files.

Keyboard Shortcuts

Editing

B	Razor tool
A	Selection tool

Preferences

Cmd-, (comma)	opens Preferences window

8

Lesson Files   Soundtrack Pro book files > 08-09_Projects&Media > 8-1 Basic Mix Start

Time   This lesson takes approximately 90 minutes to complete.

Goals   Evaluate a song

Understand basic mixing

Balance volume and panning levels for each track

Automate volume and panning levels over time

Adjust track levels in the Mixer

Record automation in the Timeline and Mixer

Lesson **8**

Mixing Audio

Mixing is one of the most important steps in finishing a project in Soundtrack Pro. Balancing the volume levels within the song and making it sonically interesting are essential to the overall sound regardless of the type of project. An unmixed soundtrack is like an audio sketch that is lacking color and dimension. The mixing process blends the audio from the different tracks together artfully to create a full overall acoustic image.

Over the next hour and a half you will learn to balance the relative volume levels of the tracks, pan tracks to create perspective in the stereo field, and use automation to create changes over time. Fortunately, Soundtrack Pro's user-friendly interface puts the tricks of the trade at your fingertips with the track controls in the Timeline and the channel strips in the Mixer.

Preparing the Project

You will begin this lesson by opening the **8-1 Basic Mix Start** project file located in the 08-09_Projects&Media folder. For the music mixing section of this lesson, you'll work with a part of the song "Something About You" by a band called Turn to Stone.

The project only contains a third of the song to save processor and hard drive demands. The skills you learn mixing the beginning of the song can be applied to any song that you work on in the future.

1   Quit all open applications, except for Soundtrack Pro.

2   Open the project **8-1 Basic Mix Start**.

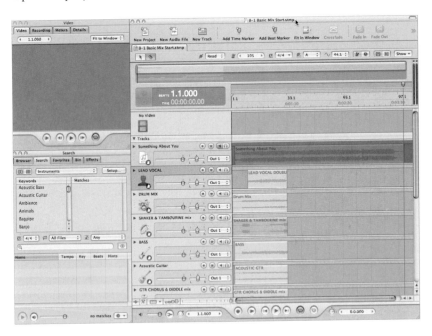

The project opens with 12 tracks in the Timeline, including a mixed MP3 version of the song on the muted top track that you can use as a reference.

The original song included over 50 different tracks. To simplify the project for these exercises, many of the tracks were combined (mixed down) to demand less from the computer and hard drive.

Since this is a music project, and does not include a video clip, let's take a moment to hide the Video track, and change the Utility window to the Meters tab. Otherwise, you'll be wasting space at the top of the Timeline with an empty video track, as well as an empty Video tab in the Utility window.

You can use the Show drop-down menu located in the upper-right corner of the Project window to show or hide different elements within the Timeline.

3   Choose Video Track from the Show drop-down menu to hide the video track.

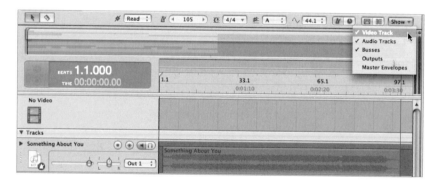

The Video Track is no longer visible at the top of the Timeline.

4   Click the Meters tab on the Utility window.

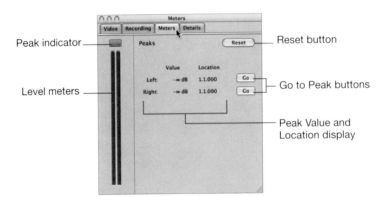

The Meters tab displays stereo level meters that can be used to observe the overall output volume for a multitrack project or the output for an audio file project.

▶ *Peak Indicator:* Shows the highest level reached as the project plays. The peak indicator becomes red to indicate if the level rises above 0dB, to indicate clipping.

▶ *Level meters:* Show the output volume of the overall project as it plays.

▶ *Peak Value and Location display:* For each channel (left and right), displays the highest value played, and its location.

▶ *Go to Peak buttons:* Moves the playhead to the channel's peak.

▶ *Reset button:* Resets the Peak Value and Location display and the peak indicator to their default values.

5   Press Shift-Cmd-S and save the project uncollected to the My Soundtrack Pro projects folder on your desktop.

The changes that you made to the Timeline and Utility window will be saved with the project so that the next time you open the project, it will open with the Meters tab active and the Video track hidden from the Timeline.

Evaluating a Song

Once all of the tracks have been recorded, and the files arranged, you are ready to begin mixing tracks. At this moment, there are many instruments all playing at about the same volume and panned to the same location in the stereo field. You will make adjustments to the levels in a few minutes. First, you should look at the different elements of the song. Almost every piece of music comprises different fundamental parts. These parts include melody, rhythm, background, lead, and supporting tracks. In the next series of exercises, you will actively listen and evaluate tracks to help you gain hands-on, ears-focused knowledge of the building blocks for this song.

Isolating Tracks with Mute and Solo

As you learned earlier in the book, there are two ways to isolate tracks in Soundtrack Pro. The first is the Mute function, which makes a track silent. The second is Solo, which makes all the tracks silent except for the solo track (or tracks).

You can toggle these buttons on and off anytime, even when the project is playing.

Keep in mind that solo always overrides mute. So if you solo a track, you can't click the Mute button on a different track to unmute it; you need to use the Solo button.

> **TIP** ▶ Think of what you are trying to do before you start to solo and mute tracks. If you want to isolate one or two tracks, use solo. If you want to leave everything on except for a couple of tracks, mute the tracks you don't need.

Feeling the Rhythm Tracks

Let's start with the rhythm tracks. The rhythm is the heartbeat, or pulse, of the song. When you tap your foot to a song, you are tapping to the beat of the rhythm. When the rhythm slows, the entire song feels slower. When the rhythm beats fast, the entire song feels more alive and quicker. A song without rhythm would be a song with no pulse and would sound pretty dead.

1   Click the Solo button on the DRUM MIX and SHAKER & TAMBOURINE mix tracks in the Timeline.

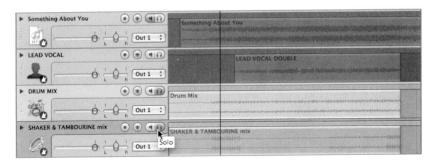

The Solo button darkens to indicate that it is on, and all of the other tracks darken to show that they have been muted.

2   Listen to the rhythm tracks. You don't have to play the entire track, just enough to get a feel for the rhythm.

By themselves they do not make up much of a song.

Let's reverse the process and mute them instead. This way you will hear how empty the song is without the rhythm tracks.

3   Click the Solo buttons for both rhythm tracks to unsolo them.

The buttons lighten to show they are no longer on.

NOTE ▸ If you see an Alert that your hard drive is not able to play all of the tracks, try pausing playback and saving the project uncollected. Then try muting some of the extra tracks such as: Guitar FX, Distorted Guitar, GTR CHORUS & DIDDLE mix, and SHAKER & TAMBOURINE mix. If you still have trouble playing back the remaining tracks, pause playback when you make changes to the volume and panning levels.

4   Click the Mute buttons for both rhythm tracks.

5   Play the ten seconds or so of the song without the rhythm. Listen to see if another instrument carries the rhythm in place of the drums.

The song still works without the rhythm tracks; it's just different. Did you notice that the bass and acoustic guitar parts have taken over the role of the rhythm tracks?

NOTE ▶ Rhythm can be created by many different instruments, not just drums. The bass track often works as support for the rhythm tracks. A guitar part used to support the song's rhythm is referred to as a rhythm guitar part. A song can have only one instrument, such as a piano or a guitar. In that case the piano or guitar would play the melody and rhythm.

6   Solo the BASS and Acoustic Guitar tracks to hear them maintain the rhythm of the song. Continue listening to the song.

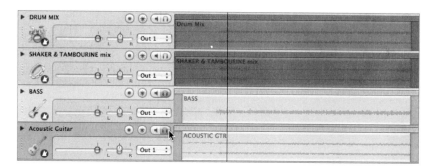

TIP ▶ Soloing and muting tracks while the song is playing provides a more direct comparison of the song with and without certain tracks. If you prefer, you can pause playback before soloing or muting a track. Use either technique during these exercises.

7   Unmute, then Solo both the DRUM mix, and SHAKER & TAMBOURINE mix tracks to hear them with the other rhythm tracks.

8   Unsolo all four tracks and listen for the rhythm in the song.

9   Pause playback.

Listening to the Melody and Supporting Tracks

The melody is the main theme or memorable part of the song and can be played by any instrument, including vocals. If you find yourself humming a song, or whistling the theme music to your favorite music, chances are it's the melody. Supporting tracks can be any instrument such as a guitar or piano that mirrors the melody either loosely or exactly. A very basic musical arrangement may only include the melody and supporting tracks, such as a singer playing only the guitar or piano.

1   Move the playhead to the beginning of the 10th measure in the Timeline (Bar 10) and solo the LEAD VOCAL track.

2   Begin playback and listen to the melody of the vocals. Continue to the next step.

3   Solo the Acoustic Guitar and STRAT mix tracks to hear them supporting the melody.

4   Unsolo the LEAD VOCAL track, and listen only to the supporting
Acoustic Guitar, and STRAT mix tracks.

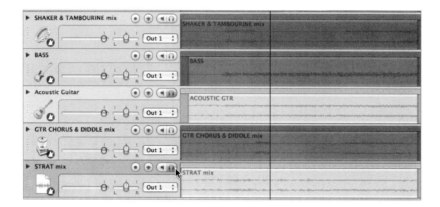

Can you still hum, or anticipate the vocal melody even without hearing
the vocal tracks? If so, that's because you remember the melody, and the
supporting tracks are acting as a reminder of the vocals.

5   Pause playback and unsolo all tracks.

Recognizing Lead, Solo, and Harmony Tracks

Lead and solo parts are exactly what they sound like. The *lead* instrument is
like the leader and stands out above all of the other tracks. In a traditional pop
song there is often a lead guitar or keyboard. If there are multiple vocalists, the
lead vocalist is the one that stands out from the other tracks.

Solo parts involve the other instruments taking a break, or dropping down in
the mix to let another part take the center of attention. If you've ever seen a
live band, you've seen the different musicians getting their moment in the
spotlight.

Harmony tracks can be either background vocals, or instruments that perform
different notes of a chord in the same key as the lead vocal or lead instrument
to create a richer sound. This is similar to the result you created in Lesson 4,
"Building Suspense with Editing Techniques," when you doubled the piano

part and transposed it to another key. The same musical progression is played, but as a harmony to the original part.

This song has several lead and solo parts, including a lead guitar solo in the second half of the song that you listened to in Lesson 7, "Recording Audio." The background vocals were recorded as harmony tracks for the lead vocals. The combination of all the tracks gives you the overall sound of the song.

> **NOTE ▶** If you missed any of the previous steps, feel free to open the **8-2 Balance Volume** project to catch up.

Understanding Basic Mixing

The art of mixing typically includes five steps: balancing relative volume levels; panning tracks to create left-to-right perspective; adding EQ, compression and other effects; using automation to create changes over time; and setting the overall project volume. These steps do not necessarily need to be performed in this order, and you'll often move back and forth between steps throughout the mixing process. For this lesson you'll focus on balancing volume and panning tracks, and then use automation to create changes over time. You'll learn to apply effects and set the overall project volume in Lesson 9, "Working With Audio Effects and Finishing the Mix." You'll start with balancing the levels.

Volume is the perceived loudness of a track. Pan is the perceived location of the track between the left and right speakers.

Each track is currently set to the default volume and panning levels. When all of the levels are the same, it's harder to distinguish the different instrumental parts.

Each track has individual volume and panning controls located in the track header. You can use these controls to adjust the levels for an entire track. The goal in the next series of exercises is to combine the different track levels to create a balanced mix of all the tracks.

Project Practice

Before you start, take one more opportunity to compare the mixed MP3 version of the song to the unmixed tracks. Keep in mind that the mixed version also has effects applied to the tracks, so the instruments and vocals will sound slightly different.

Unmute the MP3 version of the mixed song on the top track, and click the solo button to hear only the top track. Begin playback and listen to the balance between the vocals and the other instrumentation. While the song is playing, mute, then unsolo the top track to hear the unmixed song. Do you notice the difference? The volume levels in the unmixed version are more chaotic, some instruments are louder than the vocals, and all of the tracks are competing for attention, rather than working together.

Now that you've found your mixing motivation, pause playback, and make sure that the top track is muted and that no other tracks are soloed or muted.

Balancing Volume Levels

In Lesson 4 you learned that the volume control is the long, horizontal bar at the bottom center of each track. The Volume slider is the round control button.

By default all of the tracks are created with a relative volume level of 0.00 dB. This does not mean that the tracks are all actually playing at zero decibels. A value of 0.00 dB on the slider means that the volume of the track has been altered by 0.00 dB since the track was originally recorded or imported to the Timeline. In other words, it hasn't been altered at all. Raising or lowering the Volume slider will alter the volume level relative to the original recording level.

Each track starts at 0.00 and you have the ability to raise and lower the volume. A volume value of 0.00 is relatively high considering that +6 is highest you can raise the value, yet you can lower it as much as –96 (silence). The volume range of +6 to –96 is an audio industry standard.

> **TIP** ▶ To reset a track's volume level to the default setting, you can double-click the Volume slider, or Ctrl-click the slider and choose Set to 0 dB from the shortcut menu.

The default level of 0.00 is a good starting point for tracks when you are arranging the song. Once you're finished with the arrangement, it's time to begin modifying the levels.

This project has 13 different tracks. How do you know where to start?

When it comes to balancing volume levels (music or soundtracks) you need to prioritize the tracks. Generally the most important tracks are the main voice (dialog) or vocal tracks. You can solo those tracks and set their volume levels. A good starting level is around –6dB: that gives you room to raise the levels later if needed.

Next, you'll add the other voice and middle ground tracks such as dialog, voiceover tracks, or background vocals one at a time until their levels sound good with the main vocal tracks.

Once the vocals and middle ground tracks are balanced, you can add background tracks, and finally adjust the overall volume.

Recap of volume-balancing priorities:

- ▶ Start with the lead vocals, or voice (dialog) tracks
- ▶ Mix in additional middle ground tracks, instruments, and voice tracks
- ▶ Add the remaining background tracks
- ▶ Adjust the overall level as needed, which you will do in Lesson 9.

Now that you have a strategy, let's try it.

1 Create a playback region from the first beat of the 10th measure (bar 10) to the end of the clips in the instrument tracks.

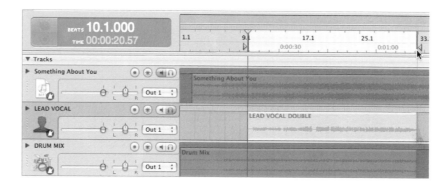

The playback region ensures that the playhead will cycle from the beginning of the first Lead Vocal clip to the end of the instrument clips while you balance the volume.

2 Solo the LEAD VOCAL track. Begin playback and listen to the isolated vocal track.

The track's volume level is the default 0.00 dB. Next, you'll lower the level to –6 by dragging the Volume slider.

3 On the LEAD VOCAL track, drag the Volume slider to the left until the gray indicator shows a level of –6.

The LEAD VOCAL track is set. Now is a good time to set the output level on your computer to a comfortable level before adding any more tracks to the mix. Continue playback.

4   Adjust the computer output volume using either the volume keys at the top of the computer keyboard, or the Output volume slider at the upper-right corner of the screen. Make sure the level is comfortable for listening to the vocals of this song, or the dialog of a scene. If you plan to mix with headphones, make sure you are listening through the headphones as you adjust the output level.

There's one very important thing to remember. Once you've adjusted the output levels on the computer, don't touch them again until you've balanced the volume levels of all the tracks. Really. Don't touch! If you constantly adjust the output level on the computer you'll never be able to gauge how loud the tracks are because they are constantly changing. Make sure you adjust the output to your own personal liking.

NOTE ▶ If you listen to your mix with headphones, you will hear the prominent placement of the instruments and volume levels. However, headphones concentrate the sound too much for mixing and don't let you really feel the true interaction of the different track levels. It's not a good idea to mix your tracks using headphones, because you want to hear the sound the way others will when the project is finished. Most people will probably listen to your projects through speakers (television, computer, or stereo system). Professional music producers always mix and master projects using speakers (monitors) to hear the full quality and value of the mix.

5   Continue playback and notice the output levels displayed on the
Meters tab.

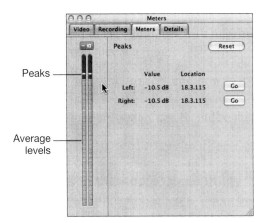

These are considered *"sticky"* meters because the white bars stick to the
highest peaks in volume level, while the solid meters show the average level
as it changes during playback. Green levels are low to medium, yellow
levels are above medium and recommended for a solid level, and red is bad.
If the meters reach red they are overdriven, or clipping and the signal will
be distorted. The levels of the Lead Vocals look great. They're solid yellow
and loud enough to be heard clearly, with a little room left at the top to
make them louder if needed.

Now that you've seen the Vocal levels on the Meters tab, let's add some
more tracks to the mix.

6   Continue playback and solo the HARMONY Mix 1 and HARMONY Mix 2
tracks at the bottom of the Timeline.

At the current level, the Harmony vocals sound a little like a barber shop
quartet, which isn't the sound we're going for in this pop song. You could

turn up the lead vocals to try to match them, or lower their volume levels to fit better in the mix.

7 Pause playback and lower HARMONY Mix 1 to –11.25 and HARMONY Mix 2 to –13.50.

8 Move the playhead to the beginning of the 24th measure and begin playback.

The harmony vocals are at a much better level with the lead vocals and are no longer competing for attention, or drowning out the lead vocal.

NOTE ▶ Adjusting track volume is like adjusting water temperature in a shower with separate cold and hot controls. If you are running both hot and cold water, and you want to make the overall temperature hotter, you can just turn down the cold instead of turning up the hot. The same goes for volume—instead of making a track louder to hear it better, you might need to turn the other tracks down a bit instead.

Modifying Volume Levels in the Mixer

You can also adjust volume and panning levels for each track in the Mixer window. Since you haven't seen the mixer since Lesson 1, "Working with the Interface," let's adjust the remaining volume levels using the Mixer.

1 Press Cmd-2 to open the Mixer.

The Mixer appears in front of the Project window. There is a channel strip for each track in the Timeline, plus one channel strip for the project's overall output.

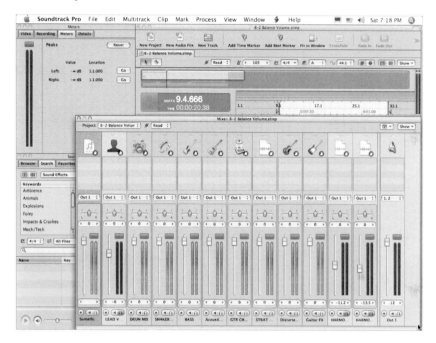

NOTE ▶ If you can't see the channel strips for all of the tracks, move the Mixer to the left and drag the resize handle in the lower-right corner to extend the window. Make sure that you place the Mixer low enough that you can still see the time display in the Project window. Otherwise, you can show a time display or Transport controls in the Mixer by selecting them in the Show dropdown menu at the upper-right corner of the Mixer.

2   Notice the Solo and Mute buttons at the bottom of each channel strip. The same three tracks are soloed in the Mixer that were soloed in the Timeline.

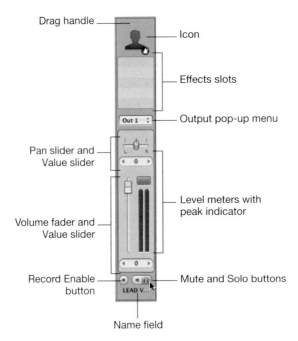

The same navigation shortcuts work in the Mixer that you use in the Timeline.

3   Press the spacebar to begin playback.

NOTE ▶ The spacebar will not work to start playback if you have selected any of the pan or volume Value sliders to enter values on the Mixer.

4   Solo the Acoustic Guitar track to add it to the mix.

5   Drag the Volume fader on the Acoustic Guitar track down until the Value slider shows about −7.03.

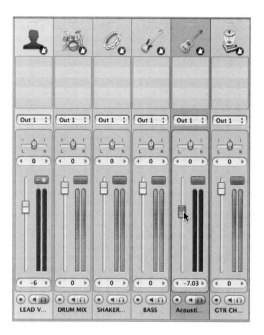

You can set an exact volume by typing it into the Value slider.

6   Click the Value slider and type *−7.13*, then press Return.

As you can see, the Mixer is an easy and flexible way to adjust volume levels to balance the tracks.

7   Press Cmd-S to save your progress.

Project Practice

Now that you understand the concept of slowly adding more tracks to the mix and balancing the levels, it's your turn to finish adjusting the tracks. You can adjust levels using the Mixer or the Track headers in the Timeline. The bullet points below will indicate the order that you'll add tracks to the mix, and the volume level that you'll need to set. If you can't set the same exact level, you should be able to set something close to the suggested level. Keep in mind that some of the tracks (such as GTR CHORUS & DIDDLE and Guitar FX) don't include musical parts for the entire duration of the project. Be sure to look at the waveform in the track and play a section that includes audio so that you can balance the track's volume.

▶   STRAT mix track, −8.25

▶   DRUM MIX track, −6.00

▶   BASS, −6.75

Those were the middle ground tracks that make up the basic tracks. The remaining tracks are more background tracks to enhance the song with interesting musical nuances.

▶   SHAKER & TAMBOURINE mix, −18.00

▶   GTR CHORUS & DIDDLE mix, −13.50

▶   Distorted Guitar, −12.00

▶   Guitar FX, −8.25

There you have it. You finished balancing the volume levels for the tracks. Now you can clear the playback region. Be sure to save your progress and close the Mixer.

> **TIP** ▶ When you are mixing volume levels, think about the type of instrument you are working with and how prominently you want to hear it. Keep in mind that some instruments—like horns—have a sharper sound and can be easily heard even when they are lower in volume than the other tracks.

NOTE ▸ If you didn't complete all of the previous steps, feel free to open the **8-3 Balance Panning** project to catch up.

Using the Exclusive Solo Feature

You've probably noticed that at this point every track in the Timeline is soloed except the top track, which has been muted. No problem until you want to unsolo all of the tracks. You could do it the hard way and click the solo button on each track until they are all unsoloed, or you could use the Exclusive Solo feature. Exclusive Solo overrides (turns off) all of the other solo buttons, except the selected track.

The first track that you'll be working with in the panning exercise is the Acoustic Guitar track, so let's try the Exclusive Solo feature on that track.

1   Ctrl-click the Acoustic Guitar track header and choose Exclusive Solo from the shortcut menu, or Option-click the Solo button.

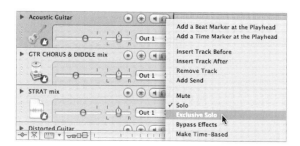

The Acoustic Guitar is now exclusively soloed, and all the other solo buttons have been turned off.

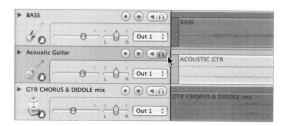

Balancing Panning Levels

Pan stands for "panoramic." A panoramic photograph is an image that includes your full visual spectrum from the far left to the far right. In other words, it's everything you can see without turning your head. A stereo field is everything you can hear from the far left to the far right, without turning your head.

Soundtrack Pro has a panning range from −100 to +100. These numbers represent the stereo field from the extreme left (−100) to the extreme right (+100). Zero (0) is the center of the stereo field.

By default, all tracks are panned to zero or center, which means you will hear them equally out of both the left and right speakers, and they will sound as though they are in the center of the room.

Your goal when you are mixing tracks for music, film, or video is to give the different elements a realistic feel and location in the mix. For example, if an F-14 does a flyby traveling left to right, the audio should also sound as though it is traveling from the left to the right speaker. Similarly, at a live music performance, whether rock band or orchestra, you *see* the actual location of the different instruments, as well as *hear* their sound coming from a specific location in the performance area.

It's time to imagine the song "Something About You" as if the band Turn to Stone was performing onstage. Where are the different musicians located?

NOTE ▶ Turn to Stone is, left to right, Hector Rios (Lead Guitar), Thor Jeppesen (Bass), Steve Purtic (Drums), Jose Ortiz (Lead Vocal), and Gus Rios (Rythum Guitar).

The drummer is almost always in the center of the stage toward the back, and the lead vocalist is center stage near the front. The bassist is also near the center of the stage. The two guitarists are on the left and right sides of the stage. Even if you didn't have a visual reference, instrument panning follows the same general principles.

Although rules are always meant to be broken, the image below represents the typical placement for instruments in a stereo mix.

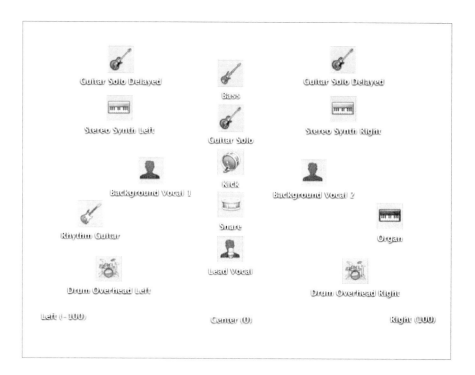

Now that you understand the basics of panning, let's start with the Acoustic Guitar track, which also represents the rhythm guitar.

> **NOTE ▶** If you are working with headphones, take a moment to make sure that you're wearing them with the left (L) side on the left ear and the right (R) side on the right ear. Otherwise, your panning results will be the opposite of what you may expect.

1   Create a playback region from the beginning of the Timeline to the end of the instrument clips and begin playback.

2   On the Acoustic Guitar track, drag the Pan Slider all the way to the right (+100).

In the stereo field +100 is the farthest right that you can place a sound. If you were looking at a stage, an instrument panned +100 would be just offstage to the right. If you were panning a sound effect to +100 it would seem that the sound is coming from something offscreen to the right.

3   Drag the Pan Slider all the way to the left (–100).

Now the guitar is panned all the way to the left speaker.

4   Pan the Acoustic Guitar track to around –63.

The rhythm guitar sound now feels like it is coming from the left side of the stage, without being completely offstage to the left.

5   Turn off the Solo button on the Acoustic Guitar track.

Next you'll open the Mixer and pan the STRAT mix track to the right about the same amount.

6   Press Cmd-2 to open the Mixer.

7   Solo the STRAT mix track and drag the Pan slider right to 62.

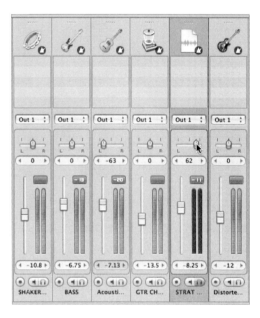

8   Solo the Acoustic Guitar track in the Mixer and listen to both guitar tracks.

The sound of each guitar is more pronounced now that they are coming from different positions in the stereo field.

NOTE ▶ Panning tracks toward the left or right may make them sound louder because the sound stands out more in the mix. If needed, you can tweak the volume levels after panning the tracks.

9   Unsolo both tracks and listen to the more distinctive guitar parts in the mix, then pause playback.

Project Practice

Take a moment to pan the remaining tracks that need adjustment. Remember, you don't have to pan all of the tracks. It's just important to spread the sound of some of the tracks to make the overall sound more interesting. You can pan the tracks using the Mixer or the Track headers in the Timeline. Also, the numbers are approximate so feel free to adjust them to your liking.

▶   GTR CHORUS & DIDDLE mix track, −40

▶   Distorted Guitar track, +40

▶   HARMONY Mix 1, −23

▶   HARMONY Mix 2, +23

Nice work. Can you hear the difference now that you've panned the tracks? The more attuned you are to things like volume levels and panning, the more trained your ear will be for mixing projects in the future. When you finish, save the project uncollected and close the Mixer.

> **NOTE** ▶ If you didn't complete all of the previous tasks, feel free to open the **8-4 Add Volume Points** project to catch up.

Automating Volume Level and Pan Envelopes

In the everyday world, envelopes are rectangular containers made out of paper that hold documents, letters, bills, and so on. If you are an audio engineer, an envelope is the volume curve of a sound that can be represented on a graph or meter. Envelopes have yet another meaning if you are editing or mixing audio.

Envelopes in Soundtrack Pro are elements of the interface that you can use to dynamically adjust and automate volume, panning, tempo, and effects parameters.

Earlier you learned how to use the volume and panning controls to mix the overall levels of the individual tracks. Our goal in this exercise is to learn how to use envelopes to adjust the volume levels at certain points *within* a track.

Track envelopes are hidden from view to maximize your workspace. To reveal the track envelopes, click the automation disclosure triangle in the upper-left corner of each track header.

You'll start by automating the volume levels on the GTR CHORUS & DIDDLE mix track to raise the level of the guitar chorus, yet leave the guitar diddle part at the current volume level.

1   Click the automation disclosure triangle at the upper-left corner of the GTR CHORUS & DIDDLE mix track header to reveal the Volume and Pan envelopes for that track.

The purple volume and pan envelopes appear below the GTR CHORUS & DIDDLE mix track.

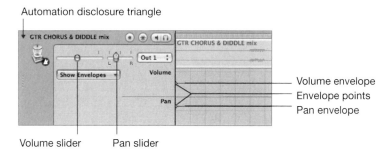

Each envelope includes an envelope point with the starting value of that envelope.

2 Click the envelope point at the beginning of the Volume envelope to select the point and see its value (−13.50 dB).

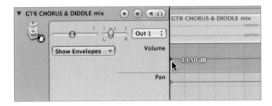

3 Click the Pan envelope point to select the point and see its value (40% L, or −40).

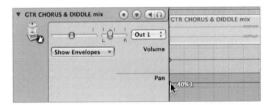

The Show Envelopes drop-down menu in the track header allows you to show all envelopes, or choose which envelopes will remain showing in the Timeline. Since your goal is to change the Volume envelope, let's go ahead and hide the Pan envelope on the GTR CHORUS & DIDDLE mix track.

4 Click the Show Envelopes drop-down menu and choose Pan to uncheck the Pan envelope.

The Pan envelope is no longer showing in the track.

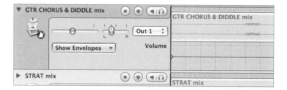

You can adjust the entire envelope value of a track by dragging the Volume slider left and right, or the envelope point up and down.

5　Drag the track's Volume slider all the way to the left (–96 dB). As you drag the slider, the envelope point moves accordingly.

6　Drag the envelope point upward to around –13.33 dB. You may not be able to drag it to exactly its original value.

7　Ctrl-click the Volume envelope point and choose Set Value… from the shortcut menu.

A dialog opens that allows you to enter a specific value for the envelope point.

8 Change the value in the field to −13.50 then click OK.

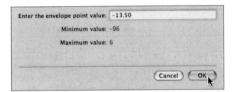

The envelope point value changes to exactly −13.50.

Adding Envelope Points

In the previous exercise, you adjusted the entire track envelope by dragging the slider in the track controls. You can also bend the envelope to change the value over time by adding envelope points. To add an envelope point, double-click the envelope line at the desired location.

The process of changing envelope values over time is called *automation*. First, it's a good idea to turn off the snap feature so that you can create envelope points anywhere you wish. Otherwise with snap on, you can only create envelope points on the nearest gridline.

1 Press N, or click the Snap button at the bottom of the Timeline to turn off snapping, if it's not already turned off.

2 Solo the GTR CHORUS & DIDDLE mix track.

3 Move the playhead to 22.2.000 in the Timeline.

The playhead should be just before the guitar chorus part starts. If you look carefully at the waveform in the clip, you'll see the beginning of the chorus.

4   Press Ctrl–up arrow once to view the tracks one size larger.

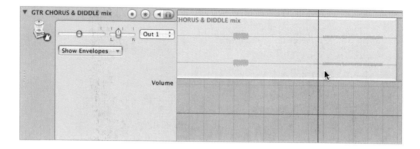

Now you should clearly be able to see where the guitar chorus begins.

5   Double-click the Volume envelope at the playhead position to add an envelope point at that position.

6   Add another envelope point about one gridline to the left of the first point that you added.

Now that you've added two envelope points, you can modify one of them to raise the level for the guitar chorus.

7   Drag the envelope point closest to the guitar chorus upward to a value of –9.10.

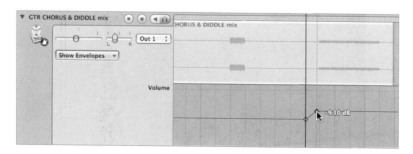

The envelope point on the left maintains the original volume level value, and the envelope point on the right has the new value. The envelope bends in a diagonal line between the envelope points to show the change in volume over time.

8   Unsolo the track and listen to the louder guitar chorus section with the rest of the tracks in the mix.

9   Click the automation disclosure triangle on the GTR CHORUS & DIDDLE mix track to hide the Volume envelope.

10 Save your progress.

> **NOTE** ▶ If you didn't complete the previous steps, feel free to open the **8-5 Add Pan Points** project to catch up.

Automating a Panning Effect

You already know how to add and adjust envelope points to the Volume envelope. In this exercise you'll create a panning effect by changing the panning of a track quickly from left to right. This is a fairly common effect used by audio engineers, and as you'll see in a minute, it's quite easy to create in Soundtrack Pro.

1   Solo the Guitar FX track, which contains three duplicates of the same guitar clip.

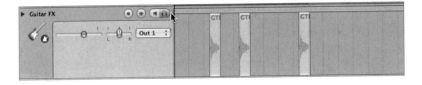

2   Select the first clip in the track and press the up arrow key several times to zoom in to the clip.

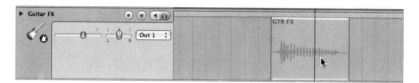

3   Click the automation disclosure triangle on the track to view the envelopes.

4   Click the Show Envelopes drop-down menu and uncheck Volume to hide the Volume envelope.

The Pan envelope is currently set to the center position (0). Your goal is to set three envelope points at the beginning, middle, and end of the wave-form, then change the values so the sound pans from the left, to the right, and back.

5   Double-click the Pan envelope at the beginning of the waveform in the GTR FX clip to add an envelope point.

6   Drag the envelope point up to a value of 80% L (80% to the left, or –80).

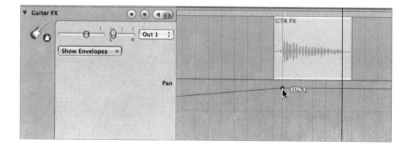

7   Add another envelope point around the center of the waveform and drag it down to 80% R (80% to the right, or +80).

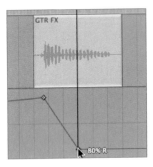

8   Add one more envelope point at the end of the waveform and set it to 60% L.

9   Play the clip with the automated panning to hear how it sounds.

The audio travels from the left speaker to the right and back. Pretty cool effect.

10   Save your progress uncollected.

Project Practice

It's your turn to recreate the panning effect on the second GTR FX clip on the track. This time you'll vary it a bit by panning from 80% R (right) to 80% L (left) then back to about 60% R. To really appreciate the effect, unsolo the track and listen to the panned GTR FX clip with the rest of the song.

Have fun. Be sure to save once you finish.

Editing Envelope Points

Once you've created envelope points, you can edit them just as you would clips. You can cut, copy, paste, move, or nudge them with the same commands that you use in timeline editing and arranging. To demonstrate, in this exercise you'll copy the Pan envelope points you placed under the first GTR FX clip, and paste them under the third GTR FX clip.

1   Press the down arrow key several times to zoom out of the Timeline until you can see all three of the GTR FX clips in the track.

2   Move the mouse pointer in the Pan envelope to the left of the first set of envelope points.

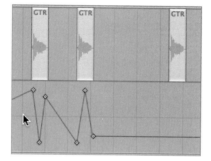

3   Click and drag the pointer to the right until you select all three envelope points under the first GTR FX clip.

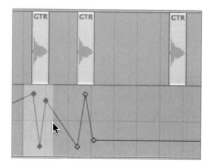

The envelope points turn darker purple when they are selected.

4 Press Cmd-C, or choose Edit > Copy, to copy the selected points.

5 Move the playhead to the beginning of the third GTR FX clip (17.4.000).

6 Press Cmd-V, or choose Edit > Paste, to paste the copied envelope points at the playhead position.

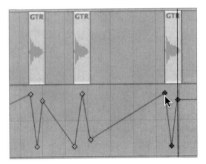

TIP ▶ If you aren't satisfied with the position that you pasted the envelope points, you can hold the Option key and use the left and right arrow keys to nudge the selected points into position.

7 Unsolo the track, reduce the track height, hide the Pan envelope, and play the project one last time to hear all of the changes.

8 Press Cmd-S to save the project.

What a difference a little mixing can make in the professional sound and feel of a project.

NOTE ▶ If you didn't complete all of the previous steps, feel free to open the **8-6 Record Automation** project to catch up.

Tips for Working with Envelope Points

Selecting and deselecting envelope points follow the same selection procedures as selecting and deselecting audio clips in the Soundtrack Pro Timeline.

▶ To delete an envelope point, click the point to select it, and then press the Delete key.

▶ To select multiple envelope points, hold the Cmd key and click the additional points you wish to select.

▶ To select a contiguous group of points, click the envelope area near a point and drag across all the points to select them, or click the first point, then Shift-click the last point you wish to include.

▶ Cmd-click a selected point to deselect it without deselecting the other points in a group.

▶ You can raise or lower the value of selected points by holding the Option key and pressing the up or down arrow keys. The up arrow key raises the value, while the down arrow key lowers the value.

Recording Envelope Points in the Timeline and Mixer

In the previous exercise you added envelope points manually by double-clicking the envelope in the Timeline. Soundtrack Pro can also record your actions so that envelope points are added automatically when you adjust the volume and panning controls during playback.

Your goal in this exercise is to dynamically adjust the volume level of the Distorted Guitar track so that the level changes with the song.

Modifying the Window Layout for Recording Automation

First, let's change the window layout to include both the Mixer and the Timeline.

1   Press F2, or choose Window > Layouts > Mixer.

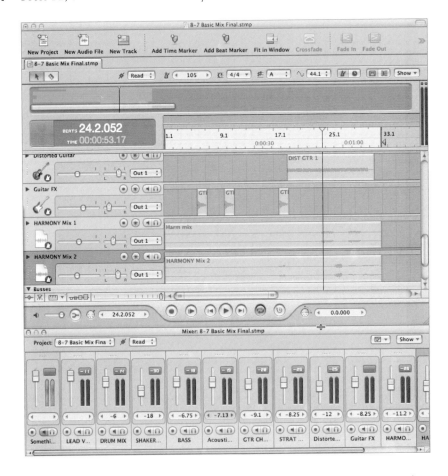

A very short Mixer appears below a reduced Project window. Fortunately you can resize the Mixer and Project windows dynamically.

2   Move the pointer between the two windows until it changes from an arrow (selection tool) to a resize tool.

3   Drag the resize tool upward until the top of the Mixer is in about the middle of the display and the Project window is in the upper half of the screen.

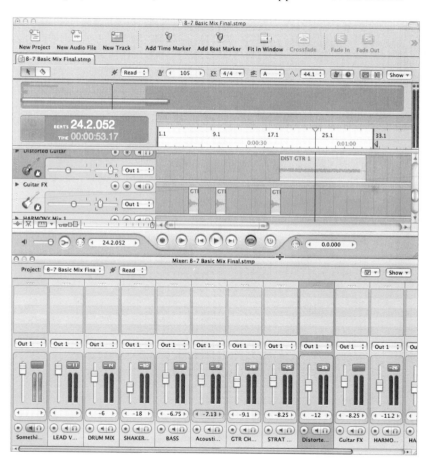

You can choose or hide different elements within the Channel strips from the Channel Strip menu.

4   Click the Channel Strip menu in the upper-right corner of the Mixer and uncheck Effects.

5   Click the Channel Strip menu again and uncheck Output.

As you can see, the Mixer and channel strips are customizable. You'll work with the Effects and Output in Lesson 9.

Since you will be working with the Distorted Guitar track, this is a good time to make sure that you can see it in the Timeline portion of the screen.

6   Drag the vertical scroll bar until the Distorted Guitar track is at the top of the Timeline in the Project window.

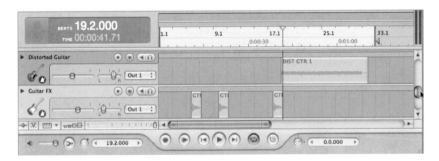

7   Drag the playback region In point toward the right until the playback
region is the length of the DIST GTR 1 clip in the Distorted Guitar track.

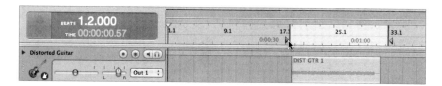

8   Click the automation disclosure triangle on the Distorted Guitar track to
reveal the envelopes.

9   Hide the Pan envelope on the track, so that only the Volume envelope is
showing.

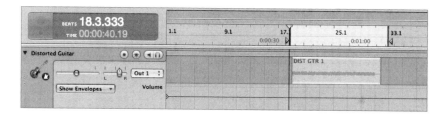

Working with Read, Touch, and Latch Automation

Soundtrack Pro includes three modes for recording automation: Read, Touch,
and Latch. Read is the default automation mode for normal playback, and it
only reads the automation data and does not record new data while you play
the project. Touch and Latch both record new data when you change the controls while playing the project. Both overwrite any current data with changes
to the controls while the project is played. The difference between Touch and
Latch occurs when you release the controls. Releasing the controls in Touch
mode returns them to the value they previously had at the point of release.

Latch, on the other hand, maintains the adjusted value at the time you released the controls. An easy way to remember the different modes is that Read only reads the automation, Latch latches on to your movements and records everything, and Touch is used for touch-ups because when you release the mouse it returns to its previous value.

For this exercise you'll use the Touch automation mode to record Volume envelope automation on the Distorted Guitar track.

1   Choose Touch from the automation mode pop-up menu.

2   Solo the Distorted Guitar track and begin playback so that you can hear what the distorted guitar sounds like before you start automating the levels.

3   Continue playback and unsolo the track.

4   When the playhead reaches the beginning of the play range, click and hold the Volume fader.

5   Drag the fader up slightly then back down during playback. At the end of the playback region, release the mouse.

Envelope points are recorded according to the movement of the fader.

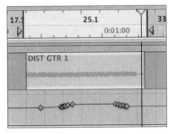

NOTE ▶ If you're not satisfied with the changes to the volume levels, you can press Cmd-Z to undo the recording and try again, or select the envelope points, delete them, and try again.

6 Press F1 to return to the standard window layout.

7 Clear the playback region, and hide the track envelopes in the Distorted Guitar track.

8 Press Cmd-S to save the project.

And that is envelope points made easy by recording them from the Mixer. You can also record envelope points by dragging the volume or panning controls in the Timeline. In Lesson 9 you'll learn to add effects to the tracks, and modify levels for the overall project.

NOTE ▶ Soundtrack Pro also supports Control Surfaces, which allow you to use approved mixing hardware for mixing and recording automation. You can learn more about working with Control Surfaces in Lesson 11, "Advanced Mixing, Editing, and Sound Design Techniques."

Lesson Review

1. What are the default volume and panning levels in the Timeline?
2. What panning values represent full left and full right?
3. On which track(s) should you balance the volume first in a multitrack project?
4. Where can you precisely change the volume and panning values?
5. Where are track envelopes, and how do you show/hide them?
6. What are two ways that you can add envelope points?
7. What are the three different automation modes?
8. What feature allows you to solo only one track, regardless of how many tracks are currently soloed?

Answers

1. The default volume level is 0.00 dB (no changes) to the file's volume level. The default panning level is 0 or center position in the stereo field.

2. −100 is the full left panning value, and +100 is the full right panning value.

3. When balancing volume levels in a multitrack project, you should start with the lead vocals for a song, or primary dialog tracks in a video or film project.

4. You can precisely change the volume and panning values in the Channel Strip Value sliders in the Mixer.

5. Track envelopes can be displayed by clicking the automation disclosure triangle. You can then choose which envelopes to show or hide using the Show Envelopes drop-down menu.

6. You can add envelope points by double-clicking the envelope line to manually add a point, or change the automation mode to record envelope points by changing the value while the playhead is moving.

7. The three different automation modes are read, latch, and touch.

8. The Exclusive Solo feature allows you to solo just one track, thus turning off the Solo button on all other tracks simultaneously.

Keyboard Shortcuts

Mixer

Cmd-2	opens Mixer window
F2	changes interface to Mixer layout

Track Headers

Double-click Volume control	resets the value to default (0.00)
Double-click Pan control	resets the value to center (0)
Option-click Solo button	exclusive solo of that track

Keyboard Shortcuts

Envelope Points

Cmd-C	copies selected envelope points
Cmd-V	pastes envelope points
Option–up arrow	moves selected envelope points up
Option–down arrow	moves selected envelope points down
Option–right arrow	moves selected envelope points right
Option–left arrow	moves selected envelope points left

9

Lesson Files	Soundtrack Pro book files > 08-09_Projects&Media > 9-1 Effects Start, 9-5 Final FX
Time	This lesson takes approximately 60 minutes to complete.
Goals	Add effects to a track
	Adjust effect parameters
	Turn off and bypass effects
	Automate effect parameters in the Timeline
	Work with effects in the Mixer
	Create a bus and send
	Set the overall Project volume level
	Listen to a temporary mono mix

Lesson **9**

Working with Audio Effects and Finishing the Mix

Sound designers and engineers use effects as tools to enhance, modify, and perfect a project's overall sound. Effects are the icing on the acoustic cake that adds flavor, color, and style to complete the sound mix. As with effects, too much icing can distract from, or even ruin the cake. Mastering audio effects and how they manipulate sound is enough for an entire book in itself. *The Soundtrack Pro User Manual* (accessible through the Help menu) includes a nice overview of effects and what they do.

In this lesson, you'll focus on the big picture: finishing the sound mix and adding effects to enhance the overall sound. First you'll learn to apply effects to a track. Then you'll modify the effect's parameters, automate parameters in the Timeline, add effects in the Mixer, and create busses and sends to apply effects to groups of tracks. Finally, you'll apply a nice EQ effect to the entire song and set the overall project volume to eliminate clipping. Let's get started.

Preparing the Project

You will begin this lesson by opening the **9-1 Effects Start** project file located in the 08-09_Projects&Media folder. You'll work with the same project that you mixed in the previous lesson, only this time you'll focus on applying and modifying effects.

1   Quit all open applications except for Soundtrack Pro.

2   Open the project **9-1 Effects Start.**

3   Save the project uncollected to the My Soundtrack Pro projects folder.

Some of the tracks have already had effects applied to them.

Working with Realtime Effects

Soundtrack Pro includes a complete set of professional-quality audio effects you can use in your projects. These audio effects can be used to add both dramatic and subtle changes to audio file projects or clips in a multitrack project. You can also apply effects to outputs, such as equalization, to enhance the entire project. In addition to the effects that come with Soundtrack Pro, you can also use third-party Audio Units effects plug-ins in both multitrack and audio file projects.

Processing effects are added as actions from the Process menu in the Waveform Editor and can modified in the Action list. Realtime effects can be added to tracks, busses, or outputs in a multitrack project, or to an audio file project. Realtime effects modify the audio as it passes through the effect, so you can hear any changes you make to the effect as the changes occur (in real time). All realtime effects include parameters that can be adjusted to control how the effect modifies the audio. You can also view and automate effect parameter envelopes in the Timeline to create changes to the effect over time.

In the next series of exercises, you'll explore and modify a realtime effect that has already been added to the DRUM MIX track, then you'll apply a series of realtime effects to the LEAD VOCAL track.

First, let's start with a close examination of the DRUM MIX track header.

1   Solo the DRUM MIX track.

Notice that the Effects button (*), which looks like an asterisk, is purple. When the Effects button is purple, it means that effects have been applied to the track. You can see which effects have been applied to the track on the Effects tab in the Media and Effects manager.

2   Click the Effects button (*) on the DRUM MIX track header.

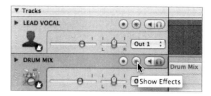

The Effects tab becomes active in the Media and Effects manager.

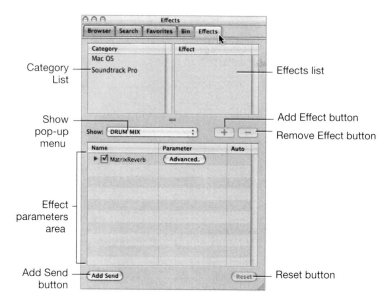

The Show pop-up menu shows which track, bus, or output the effect or effects have been applied to. In this case, the DRUM MIX track has been selected, and has the MatrixReverb effect applied to it.

3   Press the spacebar to begin playback of the DRUM MIX track and listen to the sound of the track with the MatrixReverb effect applied.

4   Deselect the MatrixReverb checkbox to turn off the effect and listen to the difference in the sound of the drums.

The effect no longer modifies the sound of the drums. Notice that the Effects button on the track header is still purple. That is because it still considers the track to have an effect applied to it, even if the effect is turned off.

5   Select the checkbox again to turn on the effect.

Viewing Effect Parameters and Presets

The disclosure triangle at the left of the effect allows you to view the parameters for that effect. Many effects also include an Advanced graphical interface.

1 Click the disclosure triangle next to the MatrixReverb effect to view the different parameters.

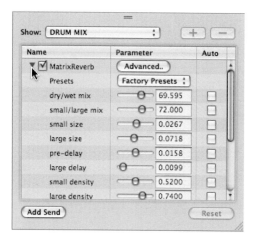

Each parameter can be modified individually. The Auto checkboxes in the right column allow you to select parameters to be displayed as envelopes in the Timeline. You'll work with that feature later in the lesson.

For now, let's look at the Factory Presets. The presets are handy settings that eliminate much of the guesswork in selecting the effect parameter settings. Not all effects include factory presets.

2 Begin playback, if it's not already playing, and click the Factory Presets pop-up menu to see the different MatrixReverb presets that come with the effect.

3   Choose one of the factory presets such as Large Room 2 and listen to how the effect changes the sound of the drums.

Notice that the parameter values change to accommodate the preset settings.

4   Choose another factory preset from the Presets pop-up menu.

5   Pause playback, and then click the disclosure triangle again to hide the MatrixReverb parameters.

Some effects, like the MatrixReverb, include an Advanced Settings button that shows the parameters in a floating Advanced Settings window.

6   Click the Advanced button located on the right of the MatrixReverb effect.

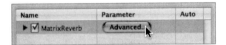

The AUMatrixReverb Advanced Settings window opens. You'll use this window to make the final parameter adjustments for this effect. The song's producer, Adam Green, used a Plate reverb on the drums during his professional mix. The MatrixReverb effect also includes a Plate preset, which changes the sound of the drums and makes them feel more distant rather than too dominant in the mix.

7 In the Advanced Settings window, choose Plate from the Factory Preset pop-up menu. Then press the spacebar to begin playback and listen to the effect on the drums.

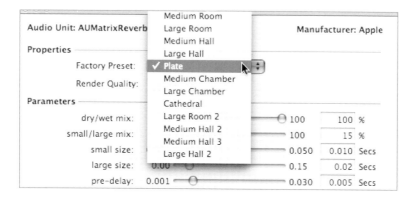

You can easily bypass an effect to hear the track without it by toggling on the Effect Bypass button in the lower-left corner of the Advanced Settings window.

8 Click the Effect Bypass button, which looks like a curved arrow jumping over a circle.

The Effect Bypass button darkens when it is on and the effect has been bypassed.

NOTE ▶ In the previous exercise, you learned that you can use the MatrixReverb checkbox to turn an effect on or off at any time. If you uncheck an effect, you can leave the effect applied to the track without turning it on. The Effect Bypass button, which is only available in the Advanced Settings window, controls the same checkbox in the Effects list. You can toggle it on and off to hear the track with or without the effect.

9   Click the Effect Bypass button again to turn it off and hear the full effect.

It's good, but a little extreme. Let's lower the amount of the dry/wet mix slider from 100% to 70%.

10   Drag the dry/wet mix slider to the left until the value is 70%.

Sounds pretty cool. Definitely a more stylized drum sound. Of course you only know how the drum sounds by itself. The real test is to hear it with the other tracks.

11   Click the Close button (x) in the upper-left corner of the Advanced Settings window to close it.

12   Unsolo the DRUM MIX track and play some of it with the other tracks to hear the effect.

The volume is a little low. Applying effects can change the perceived volume of a track in the mix. However, before you change the drum volume levels, let's first add effects to the lead vocals, since they are the backbone of the entire piece. Then you can adjust the drums accordingly.

Adding Realtime Effects to a Track

Now that you've seen what an effect looks like, and know how to bypass the effect and turn it on and off, it's time to add some realtime effects to a track. Lead vocals typically use three effects: compression to bring out the sound of the vocal frequencies, reverb, and a touch of delay. Of course, there is no limit to the number of effects that you can apply to a vocal track. The professional effects that come with Soundtrack Pro are powerful enough to completely change a voice. For example, you can change the pitch to make it lower, higher, or sound like an animated mouse or robot if that's what you're going for. Fortunately, the lead singer for Turn to Stone has a great voice, so you won't need to perform any dramatic effects to disguise (save) the vocals. Instead, you'll just enhance them a bit to make them stand out more in the song.

1   Solo the LEAD VOCAL track, and create a playback region over the entire LEAD VOCAL DOUBLE clip within the track.

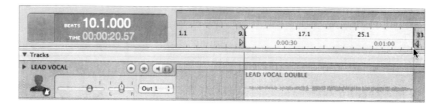

2   Click the gray Effects button on the LEAD VOCAL track to show that track in the Effects tab.

3   On the Effects tab, choose the Soundtrack Pro category, and then scroll down through the Effects list and click Compressor to select that effect.

4   Click the Add Effect button (+) to add the selected Compressor effect to the track.

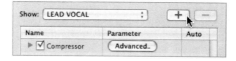

The Compressor effect appears in the Parameter list. The Advanced Settings window for some effects includes a Graphical Effects interface available through the Advanced button. These interfaces are designed to look and respond like comparable effects hardware used in professional recording studios.

TIP You can also double-click an effect to add it to the track.

5   Click the Advanced button to open the Advanced Settings window.

The Graphical Effects interface of the Advanced Settings window includes a variety of knobs, radio buttons, and sliders to modify the parameters. If you're not familiar with external compression hardware, you're in luck because this effect comes with a nice assortment of presets.

6   Click the Show Presets button in the lower-right corner of the Advanced Settings window to show the Presets drawer.

7   Click the disclosure triangle for the User Presets on the Presets drawer.

The User Presets are organized by four categories, including Vocal Compressors. Since you're working with a lead vocals track, the Vocal Compressors seem like a good place to find the perfect preset.

NOTE ▶ To expand the Presets drawer, you can drag the resize handle (three vertical dots) on the right edge of the drawer.

8   Click the disclosure triangle for the Vocal Compressors and drag the scrollbar at the right of the presets list down to view all of the different vocal presets.

9   Start playback, select the first preset, Rap Vocal Compressor, and then click the Apply Preset button to hear how it sounds with the lead vocals.

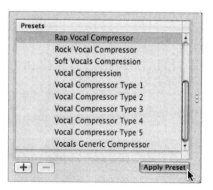

10   Continue playback and listen to all of the different Vocal Compressor presets.

Let's go with the Vocals Generic Compressor for this exercise. If you'd like to use a different one, feel free to change the compressor preset after the lesson.

11   Apply the Vocals Generic Compressor preset, and then unsolo the Lead Vocal track to hear how it sounds with the other tracks.

Sounds great! Compressors are designed to focus certain frequencies to make them stand out more in the mix, especially vocals. In this case, the lead vocals are really emphasized nicely.

> **TIP** ▶ Compressors can be extremely useful in bringing out a vocal track by raising the vocal frequencies, while limiting the peaks of other frequencies. Vocal compressors also work well to enhance poorly recorded voice over tracks, or dialog that may have been recorded too low. You can read more about compressors and other dynamic effects in the *Soundtrack Pro User Manual* accessible through the Help menu.

12   Toggle on and off the Effect Bypass button in the lower-left corner of the Advanced Settings window to hear the vocals with and without the effect.

13   Close the Advanced Settings window.

The compressor really focuses the vocals without distorting them. Of course, now the lead vocals sound a little loud in the overall mix. Before you change the volume level of the track, let's finish adding the other two effects to the track.

> **TIP** ▶ You can reset a selected effect back to the factory settings anytime by selecting the effect in the effect parameter area and clicking the Reset button on the Effects tab or Advanced Settings window.

Project Practice

Now it's your turn to add another effect to the LEAD VOCAL track. First, you'll need to solo the LEAD VOCAL track. Both of the effects that you'll add are located in the Soundtrack Pro category on the Effects tab.

Add the Stereo Delay effect. Open the Advanced Settings window. Lower the Left and Right Mixers each to 5%.

When you're finished adding the effect, be sure to save your progress.

> **NOTE** ▶ If you missed any of the previous steps, feel free to open the **9-2 Save Preset** project to catch up.

Working with Effects in the Mixer

You can also add effects to a track, bus, or output in the Mixer. First you'll open the Mixer and select the LEAD VOCAL track. Then you'll add the PlatinumVerb effect to the track in the Mixer. Once the effect has been applied, you'll modify the settings.

1   Press Cmd-2 to open the Mixer.

The LEAD VOCAL track shows both of the applied effects in the Effects list.

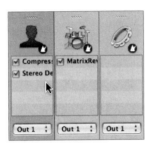

NOTE ▸ If you do not see the Effects list in the channel strips, you'll need to choose Effects from the channel strip menu in the upper-right corner of the Mixer next to the Show pop-up menu. Remember, in Lesson 8, "Mixing Audio," you deselected Effects and Outputs from the same menu.

You could add another effect using the Effects tab, as you did previously, or you could use a shortcut menu. Since you've already mastered the Effects tab method, let's try using the shortcut menu for this effect.

2   Ctrl-click the Effects list on the LEAD VOCAL track in the Mixer and choose Add Effect > Reverb/Delay > PlatinumVerb.

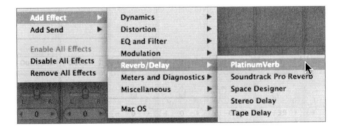

The PlatinumVerb effect appears on the LEAD VOCAL channel strip. Each effect in the Effects list also includes a checkbox to turn the effects on and off.

You can open the Advanced Settings window from the Effects tab, or double-click the effect in the Effects list in the Mixer window.

3 Double-click the PlatinumVerb effect to open the Advanced Settings window.

You'll only change two settings, both located on the upper half of the Graphical Effects interface.

4 Press the spacebar to begin playback.

5 Drag the Room Shape slider left to a value of 4.

The purple room shape changes to a room with four sides, similar to a recording studio.

6   Drag the Mix fader down to a value of 13%.

The Mix fader determines how much of the effect you are mixing into the original sound of the file. A mix of 0% would be no effect, while a mix of 100% would be 100% effected with none of the original file's sound mixed in.

7   Unsolo the LEAD VOCAL track and listen to the vocals with the full mix.

8   Pause playback and close the Mixer.

Nice effects! I bet the PlatinumVerb effect would sound great on the background vocal tracks.

NOTE ▶ Effects are listed in the order in which they are added, and their effects are cumulative. You can reorder the effects on the Effects tab, or in the Channel strip by dragging them up or down to a different position. Reordering effects is similar to reordering actions in the Action list.

Saving an Effect Preset

You've already seen how useful the presets can be for some of the effects settings. You can also save your own customized presets that can be applied to other tracks or projects. In this exercise you'll save the new PlatinumVerb settings as a preset, and then apply the preset to both of the HARMONY tracks. You can save presets in the parameters list on the Effects tab.

1   Close the Advanced Settings window and the Mixer if they are still open.

2   On the Effects tab, click the PlatinumVerb effect's disclosure triangle to view the various parameters.

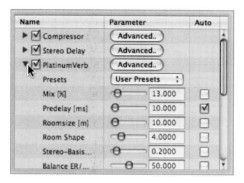

3   Choose Save Preset from the User Presets pop-up menu.

A Save Preset dialog opens.

4   Type *4x Room Mix 13% Vocals* in the Preset Name field.

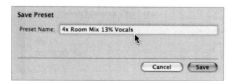

5 Click the Save button to save the preset.

> **TIP ▶** Try to name the saved presets with something that you will remember, such as an indication of the settings as you did above, or even name it after the song. The important thing is to be able to recognize the preset later if you'd like to use it again.

6 Click the disclosure triangle again to hide the parameters.

7 Press Cmd-S to save your progress.

Applying User Presets to Effects

Now that you've saved the effect preset, you can apply it the same way you would any other preset. First you apply the effect, and then choose the preset. Let's try it.

1 Click the Effects button on the HARMONY Mix 1 track.

The Show pop-up menu in the Effects tab changes to the selected track.

This time, instead of clicking the Add button (+) you'll double-click the desired effect to automatically add it to the track.

2 On the Effects tab, double-click the PlatinumVerb effect from the Soundtrack Pro category.

The PlatinumVerb effect appears in the Parameter list.

3   Click the disclosure triangle for the effect in the Parameter list.

4   From the Preset pop-up menu, choose 4x Room Mix 13% Vocals.

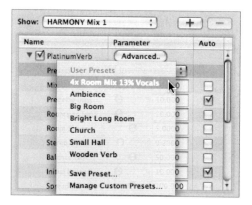

That was easy. Now let's add the preset to the other HARMONY Mix track, this time using the Mixer and the Advanced Settings window.

5   Press Cmd-2 to open the Mixer.

6   Ctrl-click the Effects list on the HARMONY Mix 2 track's channel strip and choose Add Effect > Reverb/Delay > PlatinumVerb.

The PlatinumVerb effect appears in the channel strip's Effects list.

7   Double-click the PlatinumVerb effect on the HARMONY Mix 2 channel strip to open the Advanced Settings window.

8   Click the Show Presets button in the lower-right corner of the Advanced Settings window.

9   Click the User Presets disclosure triangle and choose the 4x Room Mix
    13% Vocals preset. Then click the Apply Preset button.

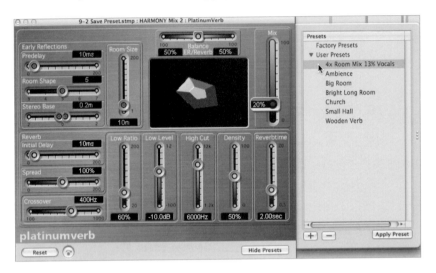

The effect updates with the preset settings.

10 Close the Advanced Settings window and the Mixer, and then listen to the
    last part of the song with the HARMONY tracks.

11 Press Cmd-S to save your progress.

> **NOTE** ▶ If you didn't complete all of the previous steps, feel free to open
> the **9-3 Automate Effect** project to catch up.

Automating Effect Parameters

In the previous lesson you learned how to automate volume and pan envelopes
over time using envelope points. Most effects parameters can also be automated as envelopes in the same way. Your goal in the next series of exercises is
to modify the PlatinumVerb mix parameter so that it gradually gets stronger at
the end of the LEAD VOCAL track. In other words, it's automation time! Not
only will you automate the envelope points on the Mix parameter, but you'll

also record them as you move the mix fader in the Advanced Settings window. Sound complicated? It isn't.

1   Solo the LEAD VOCAL track.

2   On the Effects tab, select LEAD VOCAL from the Show pop-up menu.

3   Click the PlatinumVerb disclosure triangle to show the parameters in the Parameter list.

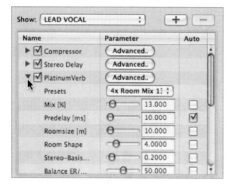

4   Deselect any checkboxes in the Auto column that are already selected.

Selected checkboxes in the Auto column appear as envelopes in the Timeline. If you're not careful, you could have a lot of envelopes to deal with.

5   Select the Mix checkbox in the Auto column.

6   On the Timeline, click the automation disclosure triangle on the LEAD VOCAL track to view the envelopes for that track.

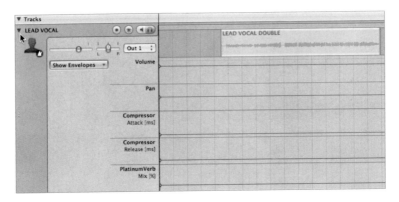

The LEAD VOCAL track includes five envelopes: Volume, Pan, Compressor/Attack, Compressor/Release, and PlatinumVerb/Mix.

As you can see, five envelopes can take up a lot of the Project window.

7   Deselect all of the envelopes under the Show Envelopes pop-up menu except for the PlatinumVerb/Mix. You'll need to deselect them one at a time.

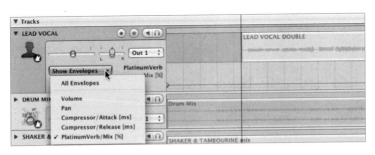

Press Cmd-S to save your progress.

Recording Effect Automation

Previously you recorded envelope points using the Touch automation mode. This time you'll use the Latch automation mode to record the changes that you make to the PlatinumVerb/Mix envelope in the Timeline.

Your goal is to raise the Mix level from 13% to 25% on the last vocal phrase "Feeling it oh so strong." If all goes well, the last word "strong" will be at the full 25% mix level.

You could change the level from the Effect Parameter list or the Advanced Settings window. The Advanced Settings window has a nice easy-to-use fader, which might lend itself to a smoother recording experience.

1   Click the Advanced button for the PlatinumVerb effect to open the Advanced Settings window.

   NOTE ▸ Before you start recording, this is a good time to make sure that you're working with the LEAD VOCAL track and not one of the HARMONY Mix tracks. Double check the Show pop-up menu to make sure you're working with the right track before you continue.

2   Move the Advanced Settings window to the left of the playback region and LEAD VOCAL DOUBLE clip in the Timeline so the Mix fader is close to the envelope you'll be automating.

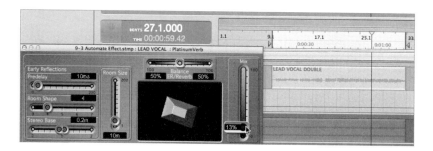

3   Set the Automation pop-up menu to Latch mode.

4   Use the right or left arrow keys to move the playhead to the beginning of the 27th measure.

5 Begin playback and listen to the vocals. When you hear the last phrase start (around 30.1.000), drag the fader up to 25%.

> **TIP** ▶ The slower you drag the fader, the more gradually the envelope points will be recorded. The faster you drag the fader, the more abrupt the change in envelope points will be. You can adjust the automation recording sensitivity (number of points recorded) in the General Preferences window.

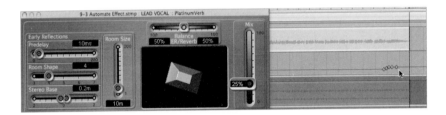

6 If you'd like to try again, press Cmd-Z to undo the automation, then move the playhead back to the beginning of the 30th measure and try again.

7 Once you have successfully recorded automation to the Mix envelope, close the Advanced Settings window. Hide the envelopes on the LEAD VOCAL track and change the automation mode back to Read.

> **TIP** ▶ It's a good idea to always return the project to the Read automation mode when you aren't planning to record automation. That way if you decide to tweak a few levels you won't accidentally record the changes as automation.

The LEAD VOCAL track sounds great with the new effects, but it's now a little loud in the mix.

8 Lower the LEAD VOCAL track's Volume slider to −10.50.

The LEAD VOCAL track still stands out acoustically, but is not as over-powering in the mix.

9   Press Cmd-S to save your progress.

NOTE ▶ If you didn't complete all of the previous steps, feel free to open the **9-4 Add Bus** project to catch up.

Working with Busses and Sends

You already know that you can apply effects to a track. You can also create busses to add effects to groups of tracks. For example, what if you wanted to add a compressor to all of the percussion and drum tracks? You could add the effect to the individual tracks, but then you could only adjust it at the track level one track at a time. Creating a bus allows you to modify the levels of that group of tracks using one fader.

This project includes a DRUM MIX track and a SHAKER & TAMBOURINE mix track. The volume and pan levels have already been adjusted on those tracks. Also, the drum track already includes a MatrixReverb effect. Your goal in this exercise is to create a bus that will then be applied to both tracks. Once you've created a bus, you can create a send, which determines the tracks the bus will affect. Any effects applied to the bus will automatically be applied to any tracks that are sent to that bus.

First, let's scroll down to the bottom of the Timeline to see where the busses and outputs are located.

1   Scroll down to the bottom of the Timeline.

Here you'll find Busses, Outputs, and Master Envelopes.

2   Click the disclosure triangles for Busses, Outputs, and Master Envelopes. You'll need to click them one at a time.

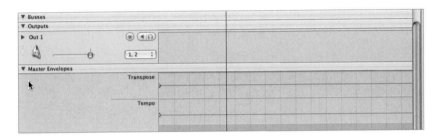

There are currently no busses in the project, and only one output called Out 1. The Master Envelopes allow you to automate the project's key (transpose) and tempo over time. You'll work with the Master Envelopes in Lesson 11, "Advanced Mixing, Editing, and Sound Design Techniques." For now, you'll focus on the busses.

3   Click the Master Envelopes disclosure triangle again to hide the Master Envelopes.

4   Click the Outputs disclosure triangle to hide the output.

That leaves the busses. You can leave it open for now because you're about to add a new bus.

5   Choose Multitrack > Add Bus, or press Ctrl-Cmd-T to add a new bus.

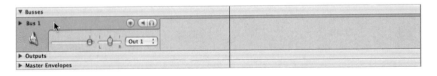

A bus called Bus 1 appears in the Timeline under the Busses Timeline divider.

You can change the name of busses and outputs, just as you change the names of tracks.

6   Click the name field (Bus 1) on the Bus, and type *Drum Compressor.*

Great. You've created the bus; now all you need to do is send the tracks to the bus.

Sending Tracks to a Bus

You can add a send to a track from either the track itself or the Effects tab. In this exercise you'll use both methods as you add sends to both the DRUM MIX and SHAKER & TAMBOURINE mix tracks. Let's start with the DRUM MIX track.

1   Click the Effects button on the DRUM MIX track to show it in the Effects tab.

2   Click the Add Send button at the bottom-left corner of the Effects tab.

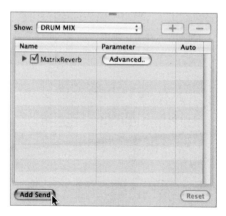

A send appears in the Parameter list, and it's automatically connected to the Drum Compression bus because that is the only bus. If you had multiple busses in the project, you could select a different bus from the pop-up menu.

3   Click the Send disclosure triangle to see the additional Send parameters.

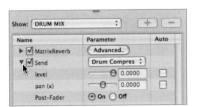

The level and pan sliders allow you to further adjust the DRUM MIX volume and pan settings on their way to the bus. These adjustments are independent of the volume and pan levels set on the DRUM MIX track header.

The Post-Fader on and off choices allow you to determine if the sound from the DRUM MIX track will be modified by the bus before or after it passes though the fader on the DRUM MIX track. For this exercise, you'll retain the default settings for the send parameters, including leaving the Post-Fader on. This means that the effect is applied after the sound has passed through the track's volume and pan levels.

Now let's send the SHAKER & TAMBOURINE mix track to the Drums & Percussion bus. This time you'll add a send from the track header.

4   Ctrl-click the SHAKER & TAMBOURINE mix track header and choose Add Send from the shortcut menu.

That's all there is to it. You've now sent both tracks to the bus. Now all you need to do is add the compressor effect to the bus.

Adding Effects to a Bus

You can add effects to a bus or output the same way that you add them to a track. In this exercise you'll add a Compressor effect to the bus, and then set it to one of the Drum Kit presets.

1   Click the Effects button on the Drum Compressor bus to show it in the Effects tab.

2   Choose the Compressor effect from the Soundtrack Pro category on the Effects tab, and add it to the bus.

3   Click the Advanced Settings button for the Compressor effect.

4   In the Advanced Settings window, click the Show Presets button.

5   Click the User Presets disclosure triangle, then click the Drum Compressors disclosure triangle.

6   Begin playback of all the tracks and try each of the different Drum Compressor presets. Feel free to click the Effect Bypass button in the Advanced Settings window to hear the song with and without the added compression on the bus.

7   Choose your favorite Drum Compressor for the bus. If you're not sure which one to pick, try the Percussion Compressor preset.

8   Close the Advanced Settings window and listen to the song.

How do the drums sound with the compressor? Mine sound great, but they're a little hot (too loud) in the mix. Instead of lowering the DRUM MIX track, you can simply lower the volume fader on the bus. Why adjust the bus instead of the DRUM MIX track's volume? Trace your steps. If the DRUM MIX track levels were okay before you added the bus, then the track level is fine. The drum compressor effect that you added to the bus is supposed to bring out the sound of the drums. You just need to adjust the level of the bus to make sure it doesn't add too much. You can also make adjustments to the levels in the Compressor that can affect volume levels.

9 Begin playback and lower the Drum Compressor bus as needed until the drums fit well in the mix.

NOTE ▶ Remember that music is very subjective and that everyone's taste will differ, so modify the levels to your own liking.

10 Clear the Playback region and save your progress.

Adding Effects to the Project

Once you've added effects to the individual tracks and busses, you can then add EQ or other effects to the output or outputs. In this song, there is only one output, which is common with music projects. For a video project, you may have multiple outputs to separate the dialog tracks from the Music and Effects. You'll work with multiple outputs in the next lesson. For now, you'll focus on working with the Equalizer effect (EQ) that has already been added to the song's output.

1 At the bottom of the Timeline, click the Outputs disclosure triangle to view the project's output.

2 Click the Effects button on the Out 1 output to show it in the Effects tab.

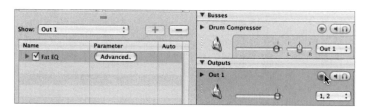

As you can see, a Fat EQ effect has already been applied to the output.

3   Click the Advanced Settings button on the Fat EQ effect.

The settings have already been modified slightly for this song, however you can easily reset them to factory standards by clicking the Reset button.

NOTE ▶ Fat EQ is a five-band equalizer and works like any equalizer you might have come across—like the EQ on your car or home stereo. The left sliders boost the bass end, and the right sliders boost the treble.

4   Press the Home key and spacebar to begin playback.

5   Adjust the different Fat EQ parameters as you play the project. See if you can come up with something better than the original. Do not adjust the master gain; it could make the overall volume too loud for the project.

6   When you're finished, close the Advanced Settings window.

TIP ▶ The best way to learn how the different effects work is to try them out. If you don't like an effect, you can always delete it or press Cmd-Z to undo it.

Project Practice

Before you do set the overall project volume level, make sure you're satisfied with the mix. Now is your chance to balance a particular track a little differently, make the harmony vocals a little louder, or raise the level of the acoustic guitar. And don't forget to adjust the drums. You can even try adding effects or modifying the existing effects. When you're happy with the mix, save the project uncollected and move on to the next exercise.

Setting the Overall Project Volume Level

Before setting the overall project volume, let's quickly recap what you've done so far to reach this point in the mix.

First you balanced the volume levels on each track, starting with the lead vocals. Then, you balanced the Panning for each track to spread the sound within the stereo field. Next, you added effects to some of the tracks to enhance their sound, and created a bus to group the two percussion tracks together and add compression to them at the same time. Finally, you adjusted the EQ of the entire song.

Nice work. The song has come a long way. You would follow the same process if you were mixing the sound for a dialog scene. The difference is that you'd be adding effects to the dialog, music, and sound effect tracks, rather than instrument tracks.

The final step to your mix is to check the overall project volume to make sure that it's loud enough, without clipping. Remember, clipping means that an audio signal is overmodulated and will cause distortion. Soundtrack Pro includes meters and Peak indicators in the Timeline, Meter's tab, and Mixer that you can use to gauge the overall project's volume. In the next series of exercises, you'll locate the different meters, and modify the output and Master Volume level.

1   Press Cmd-2 to open the Mixer.

2   Click the Meters tab, if they are not showing in the Utility window, then adjust the Mixer until you can see all of the tracks, plus the bus and output.

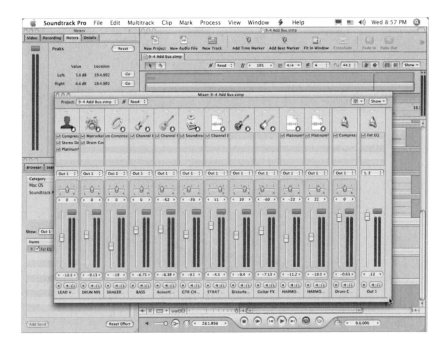

You can now see the Meters in the Meters tab, Mixer, and Timeline. The Timeline meters are the hardest to see because they are fairly small, and located on the far-right edge of the Time ruler.

If you think all of those meters seem uneventful now, wait until you start playback.

3   Press Shift-Return to begin playback from the start of the Timeline.

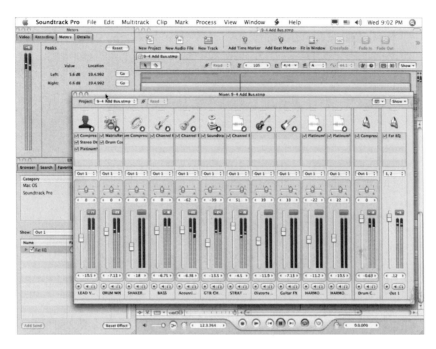

As the song plays, watch the meters in the Meters tab, Timeline, or the Output in the Mixer. These three show the same thing—the overall level of the song.

The lowest portion of the meter is green, which indicates the quietest levels. The highest part of the meter is red, indicating that the levels are dangerously high. The Timeline meters include clipping indicators that are the small circles above the meters. They light up anytime the levels are loud enough to distort.

All of the other meters include Peak indicators that look for the highest volume levels as you play your project. The highest levels are then recorded in the Meters pane and displayed in decibels for both the left and right channels. The precise location of the highest level is also recorded so you can find and fix the excessively loud clips.

There are also two convenient Go buttons on the Meters tab, which will instantly send the playhead to the loudest peak in the Timeline.

4   Notice the Peak indicators above the Out 1 volume fader in the Mixer, and the meters in the Meters tab.

The level within the Peak indicator is the highest peak that has been played since the meters were reset, using the Reset button on the Meters tab. If the amount in the Peak indicator is red, the level is dangerously high and clipping.

5   Continue playback until you finish playing the song, and look for any clipping (red) in the Peak indicators.

If you find any evidence of clipping, lower the Out 1 fader slightly, then click the Go buttons in the Meters tab to take the playhead to that position. If you'd rather work in the Timeline than the Mixer, you can also adjust the Out 1 fader in the Timeline. Click the Reset button on the Meters tab and play that section again to see if you eliminated the clipping. If not, lower the output level again and repeat the steps until there is no evidence of clipping in the song.

6   When the song levels are good, pause playback and save the song.

7   Close the Mixer.

An output is a flexible way to adjust a project's overall volume level when it is exported. It also includes a volume envelope so that you can automate the project's level over time. A project may have more than one output.

Listening to a Temporary Mono Mix

Now that you've finished the song, you might want to hear a temporary mono mix. With a temporary mono mix you won't hear any of the stereo nuances like the panning effect you created for the Guitar FX track. On the other hand, you will hear what the song might sound like over a single speaker, or non-stereo output. This is also useful to hear what the project will sound like if it's played on a television or computer with a mono speaker. It's always a good idea to hear a project in both stereo and mono, so you know the mix will hold up in either case.

To hear a temporary mono mix, click the Mono Mix button at the bottom left of the Project window at the right of the Master Volume slider.

> **NOTE ▸** The Master Volume *slider* adjusts the overall volume when you play the project. The volume level defaults to 0 dB when you create a project. Adjusting the master volume slider does not affect export volume, which is only affected by the project's output(s).

1 Begin playback of the song in the Timeline.

2 Click and hold the Mono Mix button during playback.

3 Release the Mono Mix button to hear the song in stereo.

4 Click and hold the button again to hear the Mono Mix.

   You don't have to play the entire project at this time to see if it works in mono and stereo. The point is that you now know the importance of checking a project in both stereo and mono in the future.

5 Pause playback and save the final project.

Nice mix! The mixing process may seem like a lot of work, but it's necessary to make your projects sound professional and be worthy of the work you put into creating them. In Lesson 10, "Exporting, Managing Media, and Preferences," you'll learn how to output the project so you can play it in iTunes.

Lesson Review

1. What are two methods for adding an effect to a track?
2. Where can you adjust effect parameters?
3. Once an effect has been applied to a track, what are two ways that you can listen to the track with and without the effect?
4. How do you determine which effect parameters can be automated?
5. What method can you use to group tracks together to share effects?
6. What are two methods can you use to add a send to a track?
7. Why would you want to listen to a temporary mono mix of the project?

Answers

1. You can add an effect to a track by clicking the Effects button on the track header. Or you can Ctrl-click the track header and choose Add Effect from the Shortcut menu, then select an effect in the Effects tab and click the Add button (+) or double-click the effect.
2. Effect parameters can be adjusted in the Parameter area of the Effects tab, or the Advanced Settings window when available.
3. Once an effect has been applied to a track, you can listen to the track with and without the effect by selecting the checkbox for the effect in the Parameter area, or selecting the Effect Bypass button in the Advanced Settings window for the effect.
4. You can determine which effect parameters can be automated by selecting the Auto checkbox for the corresponding parameter in the parameter area of the Effects tab.

5. You can create a bus to group tracks together so they can share effects.

6. You can add a send to a track by clicking the Add Send button in the Effects tab, or Ctrl-clicking the track header and choosing Add Send from the shortcut menu.

7. If your exported project may be played on a television, computer, or other device with a single mono speaker, it's a good idea to listen to a temporary mono mix to hear how it will sound.

Keyboard Shortcuts

Multitrack Project

Ctrl-Cmd-T   adds a new bus

10

Lesson Files   Soundtrack Pro book files > 01-02_Projects&Media > 1-2 Final,
2-2 Jazz Final files

06_Projects&Media > 6-5 ADA PSA Final

08-09_Projects&Media > 9-5 Final FX

10_Projects&Media > 10-1 Reconnect, 10-2 Files

Time   This lesson takes approximately 60 minutes to complete.

Goals   Export a song as a mixed audio file

Export selected tracks

Export a project with Compressor

Save a project and its media collected

Reconnect media to a project

Export tracks as looping and non-looping files

Tag files in the Apple Loops Utility

Index tagged files in the Search database

Distributing and Managing Soundtrack Pro Files

The fun is over. Now we get to the boring stuff—file management.

Actually, this chapter is necessary so that you can enjoy the fun stuff like sound design, scoring music, and mixing projects. In fact, there is a feeling of accomplishment when you've finished a project and are ready to prepare it for distribution. Think of file management as preventive maintenance or life insurance for your projects.

This lesson focuses on the different methods of exporting, saving, reconnecting, and managing files. You will also learn how to use the Apple Loops Utility to save and tag your own files and index them as part of your library. As you explore the different distribution options, you'll work with a variety of projects from the previous lessons to keep things interesting.

Come to think of it, exporting a finished project and seeing the result after all of your hard work is quite rewarding, and may be the most fun of all!

Preparing the Project

You'll begin this lesson by opening the finished project, **9-5 Final FX**, from Lesson 9, "Working with Audio Effects and Finishing the Mix."

1   Quit all open applications except Soundtrack Pro.

2   Close any open Soundtrack Pro projects, except the **9-5 Final FX** project.

3   From the 08-09_Projects&Media folder, open **9-5 Final FX**, if it's not already open.

Distributing Soundtrack Pro Projects

Distributing Soundtrack Pro projects isn't about starting your own record label and distribution company. Instead, it's about remembering the big picture of what the project is for and figuring out the best way to get it there.

Once you have finished your project and created a final mix, you have several choices for distributing the tracks: as a project or customized mix, as individual tracks, or with Compressor.

Let's try each of the three different ways to export a Soundtrack project, and also look at another option that lets you save your project and files together.

Exporting a Project Mix

Exporting a project mix is the most common way to export audio from a multitrack project. When you export a mix, all of the project's unmuted tracks are heard in the output file.

Soundtrack exports the mix as a stereo AIFF file, which can be imported into any of the Final Cut Studio applications. You can also convert it to an MP3 file to distribute over the Internet or play on an iPod.

The different Soundtrack Pro export options are located under the File menu. In this exercise you'll export the final mix of the beginning of the song "Something About You."

1   Make sure that none of the tracks in the project **9-5 Final FX** are soloed or muted.

2   Choose File > Export > Export Mix.

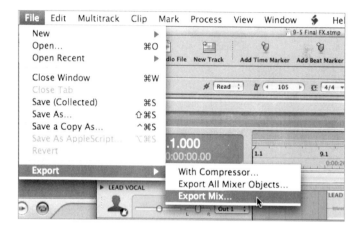

A Save As dialog opens to name the exported mix and determine where it will be saved. Before naming the file, let's first expand the Save As dialog, and create a new folder on the desktop for all of the files you'll export in this lesson.

3   Click the downward pointing triangle to expand the dialog window, if it is not already expanded.

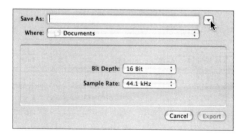

4   Click the Desktop icon on the Sidebar of the expanded Save As dialog.

You've now selected the Desktop as the location for the saved file.

5   Click the New Folder button in the bottom-left corner of the dialog to create a new folder on the desktop.

A New Folder window appears.

6   In the Name of new folder field of the New Folder window, type *Exported Files*. Then click the Create button to create that folder.

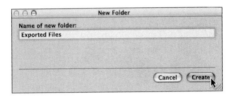

The new folder has now been created and selected on the Desktop. Now that you've created a folder to store your exported files, you'll need to name the file you're about to export.

7   In the Save As field at the top of the dialog, type *SomethingAboutYou-mix*.

> **TIP ▶** By creating file names without spaces, you can help keep down the number of characters and avoid excessively long file names.

Notice the Bit Depth and Sample Rate pop-up menus near the bottom of the dialog.

These allow you to export the mix at a Bit Depth of either 16 or 24 Bit, with a choice of Sample Rates: 32 kHz, 44.1 kHz, 48 kHz, or 96 kHz.

Since this multitrack project contains only music, and most professional music is burned to a CD, you'll use the standard CD sample rate of 44.1 kHz.

8 Change the project sample rate to 44.1 kHz if that is not the current setting.

9 Click the upward pointing triangle to compress the dialog window.

10 Click the Export button to export the project.

An Exporting Mix progress window appears to display the estimated time to export the file.

Voilà! You exported the project as a single mixed file.

Exporting a Customized Mix

Once you export the mixed version of the project, you may wish to export a few additional customized mixes. There are many different types of mixes. You may export a version that has heavier effects and EQ, and another with almost no effects at all. If you wish to exclude tracks from the mix, mute them before you export. For example, say you're mixing music for a band that also plays live. You can make customized versions of the project for each band member to use for practice. Perhaps the lead singer wants to practice singing his part against the full song. You can mute the LEAD VOCAL track before exporting the mix. That way, the vocalist will have a karaoke version for rehearsing. Let's try it.

1 Mute the LEAD VOCAL track.

2 Choose File > Export > Export Mix.

3 Name the file *SomethingAboutYou-vocals* in the Save As field.

In this file name, "-vocals" stands for minus the vocal tracks. If you prefer, you can call it "no vocals," as well.

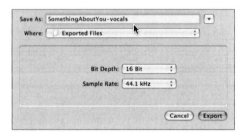

4 Click the Export button, or press Return to export the project.

When the project finishes exporting, you can take a look at both exported files.

5 Press Cmd-H to hide Soundtrack Pro.

Once you export a mix, you can determine in which application the file will open. If you want to hear the file, Ctrl-click the file and choose Open with QuickTime Player or Open with iTunes—or play it directly in the Preview column in the Finder column view. The last option is the easiest.

6 Double-click the Exported Files folder on your desktop to open the folder.

7   Change the finder to column view, if that isn't the current view setting.

8   Select the SomethingAboutYou-vocals file to open it in the preview column, and then click the Play button to preview (listen to) the file.

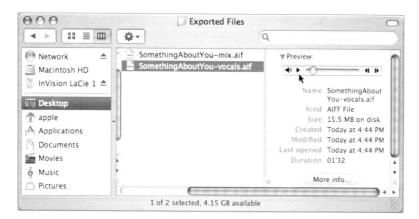

There you have it, a karaoke-friendly version and a full mix of the project.

9   Press and hold Cmd-Tab to see all open applications, and then repeatedly press the Tab key while holding Cmd until you select Soundtrack Pro.

You can also click the Soundtrack Pro icon in the Dock to show the application.

10 Unmute the LEAD VOCAL track, and then close the **9-5 Final FX** project.

TIP ▶ It's a good idea to save the project with a different name for each type of mix, so that you will always be able to go back to a specific mix when needed.

Exporting a Selected Track

The middle option in the Export menu changes depending upon the selected tracks, busses, or outputs in the project. If nothing is selected, the export option is Export All Mixer Objects. If you select a track, the export option changes to Export Selected Track. This option is flexible enough to let you export an individual track, bus, or output, or multiple tracks, busses, and outputs to a stereo

AIFF file with the same name as the Timeline track being exported. You can also export a track to dual mono files, one left (L) and one right (R). You would export the files this way if the final music score were going to be mixed or mastered at a professional studio using an application such as Logic or Pro Tools.

When you export a track, Soundtrack Pro combines all of the files in that track into one file that begins at the start of the Timeline, and ends after the last clip from the exported track.

You can export all of the multitrack project's tracks this way, or just select the tracks you want to export. Muted tracks will not be exported.

To demonstrate this option, you'll open the **2-2 Jazz Final** project from the 01-02_Projects&Media folder.

1 Open the **2-2 Jazz Final** project.

2 Play the project once for nostalgia's sake.

You've learned a lot since you worked on this piece for Lesson 2 "Creating and Arranging a Multitrack Project."

3 Select the Jazz Guitar Single Note Riff 13 track.

Keep in mind that the exported track will have the same name as the selected track. The track automatically took the name of the first clip that was added to it. That was fine when you were just learning the interface, but with all of your new Soundtrack Pro knowledge, you might consider renaming it something more refined like Jazz Guitar 1, and the track below Jazz Guitar 2. Come to think of it, that's a fine idea. In fact, take a moment to rename all of the instrument tracks.

4   Rename the Jazz Guitar Single Note Riff 13 track *Jazz Guitar 1.*

5   Rename the Jazz Guitar Single Note Riff 15 track *Jazz Guitar 2.*

6   Rename the Upright Jazz Bass 38 track *Bass.*

7   Rename the Swinging Hi Hat Loop 09 track *Hi Hat.*

The new names are better for exporting the tracks and for mixing, should you ever decide to remix the project.

8   Save the project uncollected to the My Soundtrack Pro projects folder.

9   Select the Jazz Guitar 1 track, if it is not already selected.

10   Choose File > Export > Export Selected Track.

11   An Export window opens so that you can choose the location of the exported track.

12   Choose the Exported Files folder on the desktop, and then click the Export button.

Done. The exported track, Jazz Guitar 1.aif, should now be in the Exported Files folder.

Project Practice

Before you move on to the next section, let's take a moment to create a new track and import the Jazz Guitar track to see what it looks like.

Press Cmd-T to create a new track at the bottom of the Timeline. Click the Browser tab in the Utility window. Navigate to the Exported Files folder on the Desktop. Drag the **Jazz Guitar 1.aif** file from the Browser to the beginning of the empty track in the Timeline.

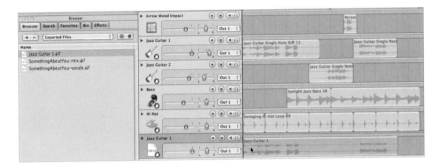

Notice that the **Jazz Guitar 1** file ends when the last clip in the exported track ends. Nice work. When you're finished with the new track, press Shift-Cmd-T to delete it. The track was merely for educational purposes, and you won't want it there for the next exercise.

Exporting All Tracks

Now you'll try exporting all of the project's tracks. To perform this export option, you can either select all of the tracks or simply deselect everything.

1   Click the video track header to deselect all of the Audio tracks.

2   Choose File > Export > Export All Mixer Objects.

3 Choose the Exported Files folder on the desktop if it is not already selected, then press Return.

An alert appears to warn you that one of the files (Jazz Guitar 1) is already in that location.

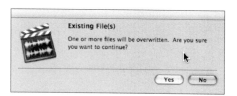

4 Click the Yes button to continue and overwrite the original Jazz Guitar 1 file with the new one you're about to export.

5 Hide Soundtrack Pro and open the Exported Files folder on the desktop.

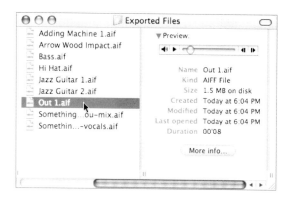

Interesting. Notice that not only did you export all of the individual tracks, but also the output (Out 1). If this was a cooking show, all of the individual tracks would be the measured ingredients, and the Out 1 file would be the finished baked dish. Since all of the tracks were assigned to the output Out 1 file, it was exported essentially as a mix of all the tracks and will sound the same as if you had exported a mix. The difference is that it will be named after the output, rather than a saved file name. If you're exporting a project to send to another professional sound designer or engineer, this is an ideal method because you'll supply all of the individual tracks as well as a mix (Out 1).

6   Select Out 1 and play it in the Preview column.

7   Press Cmd-Tab and show Soundtrack Pro again.

Exporting with Compressor

If you'd like to export audio combined with the project's video clip, you can choose the export with Compressor option. You can also export with Compressor if you'd like to export an audio file as a different format, such as MP3.

Exporting with Compressor will create a copy of the original QuickTime movie file with your Soundtrack audio mixed into the movie's audio track.

QuickTime movies can be self-contained, or they can reference media in another program like Final Cut Pro. All QuickTime movies exported from Soundtrack Pro are *self-contained*, which means they can be copied or moved to another computer without needing to reference other media.

Compressor also allows you to export in the original video format, or compress the file into another file, such as MPEG2 for DVD Studio Pro.

The final movie will be the same length as the original video clip, or the end of the last clip in the Timeline, whichever is longer. If the audio files are longer than the video clip in the Timeline, the finished video will be extended with a black screen (slug) at the end.

1   Choose File > Export > With Compressor.

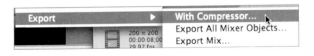

The Save As window opens with Compressor controls in the lower half of the window. This handy feature allows you to utilize the power of Apple's Compressor application, without the need to work directly in the Compressor interface.

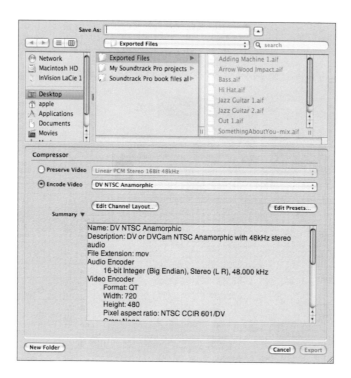

2 Select the Preserve Video radio button to export the audio and video without changing the video settings, such as frame size or file type.

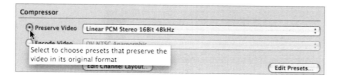

3 In the Save As field, type *Clapboard Final.*

4 Make sure that the Exported Files folder is the selected location for the exported file.

5 Click the Export button, or press Return.

6 When the file finishes exporting with Compressor, close the **2-2 Jazz Final** project.

7   Look for the exported movie in the Exported Files folder on the desktop.

8   Play the exported movie in the Preview column of the Finder.

9   Double-click the **Clapboard Final.mov** file to open it in the QuickTime player and see a full-size version.

10   Play the file in the QuickTime player, then press Cmd-Q to quit.

> **NOTE ▸** If you'd like to view the file information to see that the file settings have been preserved, you can go to the Show Movie Info (Cmd-I) in QuickTime Player.

Project Practice

You've successfully exported projects using all three different Soundtrack Pro methods. Now it's your turn to export another project with Compressor. If you recall, the ADA PSA that you worked with in Lesson 6, "Modifying and Repairing Dialog in the Waveform Editor," was an HDV project. Your goal in this practice exercise is to open the **6-5 ADA PSA Final** project and export it with Compressor to the Exported Files folder. You'll name the exported movie *ADA PSA Final* and preserve the video format as you export it. When you're finished exporting, close the project, go to the desktop, and double-click the movie to open it. Since the file is widescreen HDV, it may not fit completely on your computer screen. If not, press Cmd-F to view it full screen in the QuickTime application. Have fun.

Distributing Media Files with a Project

When you add files to a Soundtrack Pro project, you don't actually add the file; you simply add a reference to it. The original file remains in its original location on the computer before you added it from the Browser or Search tabs. As long as you save a project uncollected (without selecting the Collect Audio Files checkbox in the Save As window), the project will continue to reference the original files in their original locations.

An uncollected project is dependent upon the original media files until you export it as a mix, as tracks, or with Compressor. Until that point, your project references the media files wherever you originally found them in the Media and Effects manager. An exported mix can be played with other applications; it is self-contained and not dependent upon any other files to play.

If you save a project collected with all of its media files, the project and a copy of every file included in the project will be saved together. You should only save a project collected if the project is finished and you'd like to save it with all the media in one convenient folder so that you can move it to a different computer, or save it to another storage medium that doesn't require the full Soundtrack Pro loops library.

For this to make sense, let's walk through the process together.

1   Open the **1-2 Final** project, located in the 01-02_Projects&Media folder.

    Notice that the project opened perfectly with all of the media, including the QuickTime video, intact.

2   Play the project once, and reminisce about your first Soundtrack Pro project from this book.

3   Currently the project and all of its media files are located in the 01-02_Projects&Media folder.

    Your goal in this exercise is to save it collected to a new folder on the desktop.

4   Press Shift-Cmd-S, or choose File > Save As.

Notice that the normal Save feature shows (Collected) in parenthesis because the project was saved collected to the 01_02_Projects&Media folder.

5   In the Save As field, change the name to *Clapboard Rock final*.

6   Click the Desktop in the Sidebar, and then click the New Folder button to create a new folder on the desktop.

> **TIP** ▶ It's important to save collected multitrack projects to a designated folder. Otherwise, the project and ALL of its files will populate whatever location you saved them to. Sure, that's not a big deal with this little project that only includes 6 audio files and 1 video clip. Imagine a project with 200 or more audio files.

7   Name the new folder *Clapboard Rock* and click the Create button.

8   Make sure that both the Collect Audio Files and Collect Video File checkboxes are selected.

NOTE ▶ Soundtrack Pro projects can be up to four hours in length, and video files can be quite large and take up a lot of hard drive space. Determine whether you need the video file and have the space before you include it with the project.

9 Close the project.

10 Locate the Clapboard Rock folder on the desktop, and open the folder.

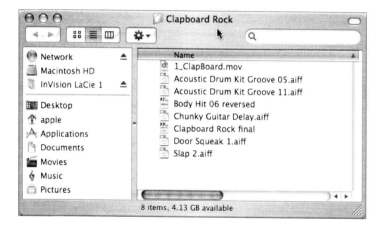

NOTE ▶ Don't worry if the icons in your project look slightly different than the ones in these figures. The icons may vary depending on whether they were saved with file extensions showing and which applications are installed on your computer. Chances are, your audio files are tagged to open in QuickTime, instead of the Apple Loops Utility.

The Clapboard Rock folder includes the Clapboard Rock final project, as well as five audio files, one audio file project (Body Hit 06 reversed), and one video clip (1_ClapBoard.mov). You could move this folder to your laptop computer or another computer without needing to reference any other files.

11 Double-click the Clapboard Rock final project to open it in Soundtrack Pro.

12 Select any of the Audio files in the project, then press Cmd-I to view the file's details in the Details tab.

13 On the Details tab, click the File button to view the file details, including the file's Path.

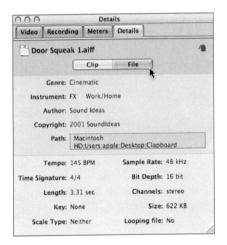

Your project opens perfectly and is no longer referencing the files in the 01-02_Projects&Media folder.

Why does it work? Because all the files it needs have been neatly packaged with it in the same folder. As you can see, this folder is all you need to take with you to open this project anywhere, anytime, on any computer (as long as the computer has Soundtrack Pro). I often find myself finishing projects on my laptop computer in airports, hotels, wherever. Saving files collected makes them very travel-friendly. In fact, the Projects&Media folders used for this book contain the collected files of all the projects for each lesson. However, so far in this book, when you've resaved the projects at the beginning of each lesson, you've been saving them uncollected by deselecting the collect audio files checkbox. The projects in the My Soundtrack Pro projects folder should all be uncollected projects that reference the media in the Projects&Media folders.

14 Press Cmd-1 to return the Utility window to the Video tab.

15 Save and Close the project.

> **NOTE ▶** Once you've saved a file collected, that becomes the default setting and you should continue to save it collected to ensure that all of its media will be contained in the same folder.

Reconnecting Project Files

What happens if you move a collected project to a location that doesn't include the media? The 10-1 Reconnect project was originally saved collected into the 10 Media folder in the 10_Projects&Media folder. Then, for the purposes of this demonstration, I moved the file out of the folder. So, what do you anticipate will happen when you try to open the project? I could tell you, but it will be more fun to show you.

1 Open the **10-1 Reconnect** project, located in the 10_Projects&Media folder.

An Alert window opens.

This alert gives you three choices: Skip File, Cancel, and Find File.

If you skip a file, the filename will still show up in the project, but the name will be in red, indicating that the file is offline—disconnected from the project.

Let's use the Find File option.

2   Click the Find File button.

A new window of your file directory opens so you can direct the software to the correct file.

3   Navigate to 10_Projects&Media > 10 media.

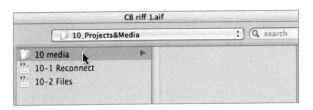

The file you're looking for is displayed in the window's title bar (**CB riff 1.aif**) and also at the bottom of the window in the Reconnecting path. The last part of the path is the name of the file you are looking for.

4   Select the **CB riff 1.aif** file in the 10 media folder.

NOTE ▶ The length of the file path will vary depending upon where your project files are on the computer. Any time one part of the path changes, the project can lose the files, and they will need to be reconnected.

5   Select the Use selected path to reconnect other missing files checkbox in the lower-left corner of the window, if it's not already selected.

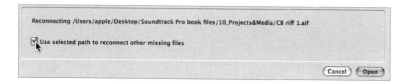

When you select this checkbox, the program will look for all of the other missing files in the same location. Otherwise, you will have to reconnect each file individually.

6   Click the Open button in the lower-right corner to reconnect the media file.

Done. The project opens containing two unrelated files. The first is a simple guitar riff recorded by a friend, Camillo Brena. The second file is the customized CrashHitScream file that was created in Lesson 5, "Designing Sound in the Waveform Editor."

In the next exercise you'll export both files—one as a file, the other as a loop. First, close the file without saving it so that it will need to be reconnected again next time you open it. If you save it after reconnecting, it will no longer need reconnecting.

7   Press Cmd-W to close the project.

A dialog window opens, asking if you want to save the changes.

8   Click the Don't Save button to close the file without saving.

Exporting Looping and Non-Looping Files

You can export recordings and other files as either looping or non-looping files. Once you've exported the files, you can tag them in the Apple Loops Utility and index them as part of your audio library.

You'll work with the Apple Loops Utility soon; first you'll need to export the files.

In this exercise you'll export part of the guitar riff as a loop, then you'll export the CrashHitScream file as a non-looping file. To export a file as a loop, you create a playback region that defines the loop and then export the file.

1   Open the **10-2 Files** project.

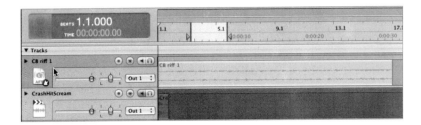

The project opens with a playback region already created. The guitar recording is on the first track, and the CrashHitScream is on the second.

2   Press Shift-Cmd-S and save the file uncollected in the My Soundtrack Pro projects folder.

3   Press End to move the playhead to the End of the playback region.

4   Press the spacebar to play the playback region.

> **TIP** ▶ If you're exporting part of a recording as a loop, it's a good idea to listen to the loop to make sure that it sounds good repeated over and over. Also, you'll want to make sure that the playback region starts and ends on a beat.

5   Select the CB riff 1 track, if it's not already selected.

6   Pause playback, then choose File > Export > Export Selected Track.

The Export window opens.

To make it easier to locate and index your exported files, let's make another folder on the desktop.

7   Click the Desktop icon in the window sidebar to choose the desktop.

8   Click the New Folder button, and name the new folder *Files to Index*.

9   Click the Create button to create the folder on the desktop.

10   Click the Export button to export the **CB riff 1** track.

Before you look at your newly exported loop, go ahead and export the sound effect first.

11   Clear the playback region.

12   Select and unmute the CrashHitScream track.

13   Choose File > Export > Export Selected Track.

14   Choose the Files to Index folder on the desktop, then click the Export button.

Project Practice

Take a moment to add the looped and non-looped files to the project to see how they turned out. Sure, there's nothing that special about importing files, except that these files were freshly exported from the previous exercise.

In the Browser, navigate to your Files to Index folder on the desktop. Drag the CB riff 1 file to Track 3 in the Timeline. Does it look like a loop? Drag the right edge to see if it extends like a loop. If so, extend it until it repeats three or four times. Next, add the CrashHitScream file to Track 4. Is it a looping or non-looping file?

Files that are exported with a playback region present are exported automatically as looping files. If you accidentally export a file as looping, you can always change it back to non-looping in the Details tab.

When you're finished, save your project.

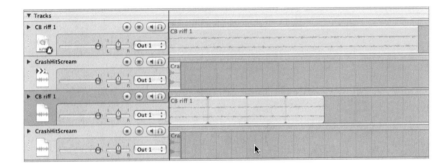

Knowing how to distribute files and how the files and projects relate to one another is incredibly important, especially when you start using Soundtrack Pro for real projects. Another important factor in managing your files is being able to find and use them again easily, a topic covered in the next section.

Working with the Apple Loops Utility

Have you ever wondered how Soundtrack Pro is able to match audio files from the Search tab or Browser to a specific project? Or how Soundtrack Pro's search feature identifies audio files by keyword, refines searches, and performs matches? Or how Soundtrack Pro is able to change the clip speed or project tempo without changing pitch? The secret to Soundtrack Pro's ability to perform these feats of audio magic can be found in the Apple Loops Utility.

The Apple Loops Utility is the companion software that comes with Soundtrack Pro, and it is used to tag audio files with information. You can add and change tags for up to 2000 files at a time.

You know how to build projects, and how to export projects as a mix or as individual tracks. In the next series of exercises, you'll learn how to tag audio files with information so they can be indexed in Soundtrack Pro's search database.

Opening Files in the Apple Loops Utility

You can open files in the Apple Loops Utility from the hard drive, from within a Soundtrack Pro project, or directly in the Apple Loops Utility. Let's start from within a Soundtrack Pro project.

1   In the 10-2 Files project, Ctrl-click the CB riff 1 loop on the third track from the top in the Timeline and choose Open in Apple Loops Utility from the shortcut menu.

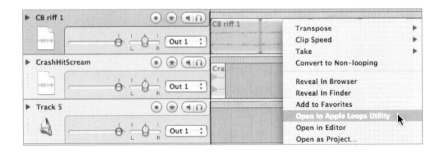

The Apple Loops Utility opens.

Don't let all of the menus and radio buttons scare you. The Apple Loops Utility is really quite easy to use.

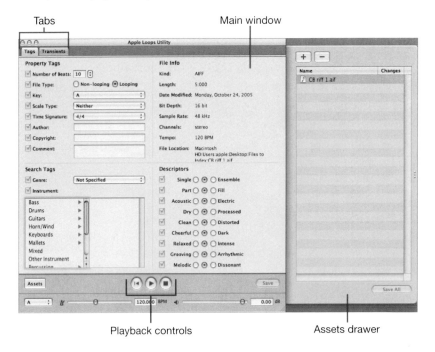

Tabs   Main window

Playback controls   Assets drawer

The Apple Loops Utility has one main window with two tabs and an Assets drawer.

The first tab in the main Apple Loops Utility window opens the Tags pane.

Tags are pieces of additional information (metadata) that you add to an audio file. A tag won't change the way a file sounds, so if you recorded something out of tune, you can't fix it in the Apple Loops Utility.

The second tab is the Transients Tab. *Transients* correspond to the peaks, or most pronounced changes in a sound's waveform. The Transients tab contains a large waveform display and markers to indicate the position of transients. Transients are used when transposing or changing tempo of a loop.

MORE INFO ▶ You can learn more about Transients in the *Soundtrack Pro Manual* available through the Help menu.

Adding a File to the Assets Drawer

The Assets drawer shows the files that are open in the Apple Loops Utility. You can have up to 2000 files open at a time. Let's add another file to the Assets drawer.

1   Locate the Assets drawer to the right of the main window.

Your **CB riff 1.aif** file is the only name in the list.

2   Click the Add File button (+) located in the top-left corner of the Assets drawer.

A window opens for you to locate the file that you want to add.

3   Navigate to the Files to Index folder on your Desktop and select the **CrashHitScream.aif** file.

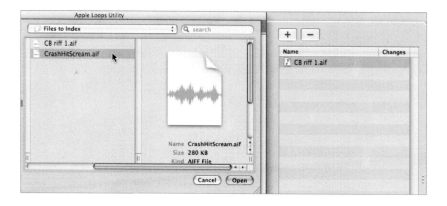

4   Click the Open button to open the file in the Assets drawer.

The **CrashHitScream.aif** file appears in the file list.

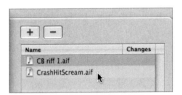

Setting Property Tags

The Tags pane is divided into four quadrants: Property Tags, File Info, Search Tags, and Descriptor Tags.

Property tags identify the different properties of an audio file.

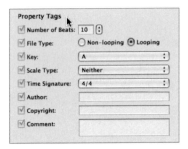

▶ *Number of Beats field:* This field displays the number of beats in the audio file.

▶ *File Type buttons:* These buttons set the audio file type, which is either Non-looping or Looping.

▶ *Key pop-up menu:* This menu sets the key of the audio file. The default is A.

▶ *Scale Type pop-up menu:* This menu sets the file's scale type. The choices are Major, Minor, Good for Both, and Neither. These tags are unique to Soundtrack Pro and are very useful for working with guitar loops and with other instruments that use the major or minor scales. The default setting is Neither.

▶ *Time Signature pop-up menu:* This menu sets the audio file's time signature. The choices include: 3/4, 4/4, 5/4, 6/8, and 7/8. The default setting is 4/4.

▶ *Author field:* This field displays the name of the audio file's author. To enter a new name, type it in the field.

▶ *Copyright field:* This field displays copyright data for the audio file. To enter new data, type it in the field.

▶ *Comment field:* This field displays comments about the audio file. To enter new data, type it in the field.

Let's set the relevant Property tags for the **CB riff 1.aif** file. Remember, this file was recorded by Camillo Brena, so give him proper credit in the Author and Copyright fields.

1 Type *Camillo Brena* in the Author field.

When you finish this lesson, you can try exporting one of your own files as a looping file and be sure to take credit for your effort.

2 Type the date *2005* in the Copyright field.

NOTE ▶ If you have submitted your files for official copyright, type the full copyright information here. If not, the year will suffice.

Reading File Info

The File Info portion of the Tags pane includes information about the file. This information was determined when the file was recorded, and it can't be altered in the Apple Loops Utility. If the file is exported as a track, it will use the multitrack project's properties as the file info.

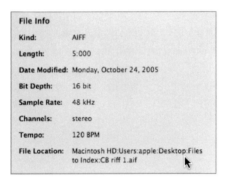

Setting Search Tags

Search tags are used to find files within the massive Soundtrack Pro search database. How would you search for the **CB riff 1.aif** file if you were looking for it in the Soundtrack Pro Search pane? Let's set the Search tags so that you—or anyone else—can find the **CB riff 1.aif** file in Soundtrack Pro.

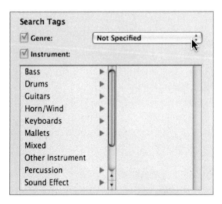

1 Select the Genre checkbox, and then select Rock/Blues in the pop-up menu.

2 Scroll down through the Instrument list and select Guitars, and then click the Acoustic Guitar subcategory.

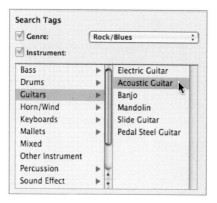

Setting Descriptor Tags

Descriptor tags are exactly what they sound like: tags that describe a particular file in greater detail. If the descriptors look familiar, they should. You have used them along with the Search tags almost every time you have searched for files in Soundtrack Pro. The Soundtrack Pro search database uses the Descriptor tags;

you simply click the buttons or columns with the descriptors to guide the search. The Descriptor tags are used to refine the search beyond instruments or genre.

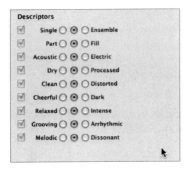

You can assign each descriptor one of three choices by selecting a circle. The left circle is for the choice on the left; the right circle is for the choice on the right; and the center circle, neither choice, means the descriptor is not included with the file. You may choose only one option for each descriptor.

Let's select the descriptors for the **CB riff 1.aif** file.

1   Press the spacebar to play the file in the Apple Loops Utility, as a reminder of what it sounds like. Pause playback once your memory has been refreshed.

2   Click the radio button next to Single to indicate a single instrument.

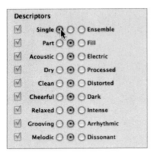

Clearly this was recorded by a single instrument (guitar). Ensemble usually means more than one different type of instrument.

3   Select the Acoustic, Clean, and Grooving radio buttons.

Clean refers to a recording without added effects.

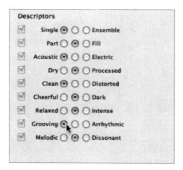

These are the only descriptors that apply to this file.

Saving Changes to a File

Once you have tagged your file, you will need to save the changes. Before you save the changes, let's look at the Changes column in the Assets drawer.

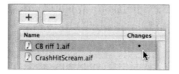

Notice the bullet in the Changes column of the **CB riff 1.aif** file. This indicates that you have made changes to the file and that they have not yet been saved.

Let's save the changes to the file.

1   With the **CB riff 1.aif** file still selected in the Assets drawer, click the Save button at the bottom-right corner of the main window.

The tags you have selected are processed and saved to your file.

2   Look at the Change column next to the **CB riff 1.aif** file again.

The bullet is no longer present.

Project Practice

Now it's your turn to tag the **CrashHitScream** file. Use your best judgment to assign appropriate tags. Remember, **CrashHitScream** was created by combining three different sound effects that come with Soundtrack Pro. Start by selecting the **CrashHitScream** file in the Assets drawer. Leave the Author and Copyright fields blank. Select the search tags that fit the sound effect, then save the changes to the file and quit the Apple Loops Utility.

MORE INFO ▶ If you'd like to learn more about working with the Apple Loops Utility, you can read the *Apple Loops Utility Manual* accessible through the Apple Loops Utility Help menu.

Adding Your New Files to the Soundtrack Pro Search Database

Now that you have tagged both of the files in the Files to Index folder, you can add them to the Soundtrack Pro search database.

1   Click the Search tab in the Media and Effects manager of Soundtrack Pro.

NOTE ▶ If the **10-2 Files** project is not still open in Soundtrack Pro, go to the My Soundtrack Pro projects folder on your desktop and open the **10-2 Files** project before continuing.

Since the **CB riff 1** and **CrashHitScream** files are both in the Files to Index folder, you will index the entire folder.

2   Click the Setup button in the upper-right corner of the Media and Effects
Manager to see the Directories list.

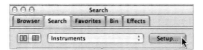

3   Click the Add Directory button (+) to add a new directory.

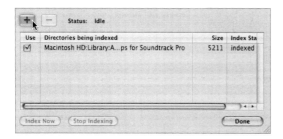

An Open window appears.

4   In the Open window, locate the Files to Index folder on your hard drive,
and select it; then click the Open button to add the folder.

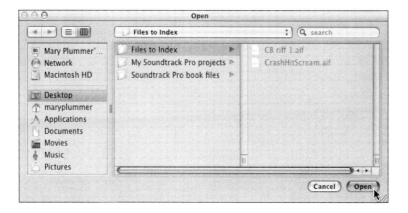

The folder is added to the Directories list, but you can see that it's not indexed, so let's do that next.

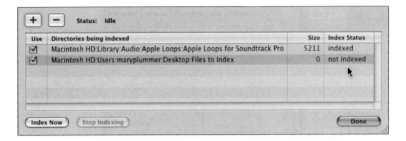

5   Making sure that the Files to Index folder is selected, click the Index Now button to start indexing the files within the folder.

The Directories list indicates that the two files have been indexed.

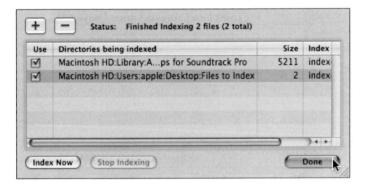

6   Click the Done button to close the Directories list.

Now let's find your files in the database.

7   Change the Search tab to button view, if it is not already showing keyword buttons.

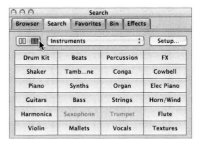

8   Change the Keyword Category pop-up menu to Best Mix.

9   Click the Guitars Keyword button in the Search pane.

There are over 500 Guitar files to choose from. Let's narrow the search.

To choose more than one Keyword button, hold the Command key before clicking the additional buttons.

10 Cmd-click the Acoustic, Clean, Single, and Rock/Blues buttons to narrow the search.

There are now just over 100 choices.

NOTE ▶ If you've indexed additional loops libraries, you may have more files in the search results. The numbers above are based upon the files that come with Soundtrack Pro. If you work with GarageBand, you can index the files in the Jam packs to use in Soundtrack Pro. The Jam Pack files will all be indexed as real instrument loops. There are also many loop libraries available through third-party companies. Soundtrack Pro will recognize WAV and ACID files. If you have a third-party loop library that you want to add to your Soundtrack Pro files, just add the directory to the search database using the search setup in the Media and Effects Manager.

11 Type *riff* in the Refine Search field to find only files with the word *riff* in the name.

12 Scroll down through the search results list until you find the **CB riff 1.aif** file.

> **NOTE** ▶ If you don't see the files right away in the Search tab, you may need to quit Soundtrack Pro, then reopen the **10-2 Files** project and try the search again.

That's all it takes. You can use these tagging techniques for all of your recorded files.

> **TIP** ▶ Once you have recorded and tagged files, it's a good idea to save them all to a designated folder that you can index in the directory.

Project Practice

Your final challenge in this lesson is to locate the **CrashHitScream** file in the Search database. You can use either button or column view to locate the file. Just remember which descriptors you used. Happy hunting! When you're finished, close the project.

Guess what? You made it through the distributing and managing Soundtrack Pro files lesson! Chances are you had a little fun along the way.

Lesson Review

1. Which exporting method combines the sound of all the tracks, busses, and outputs into one exported file?

2. What can you do to exclude a track or tracks from being exported?

3. If you export all Mixer objects, how many files will be exported?

4. When exporting Mixer objects or selected objects, what determines the names and duration of the exported files?

5. If a project cannot find the associated media files, what process is necessary to point the project to the files again?

6. How can you export a clip from the Timeline as a looping file?

7. What application can be used to tag files so they can be used in the Search database?

Answers

1. Exporting a project as a mix combines the sound of all the tracks, busses, and outputs into one exported file.

2. Muting tracks before exporting will exclude them from an exported file or files.

3. Exporting all Mixer objects includes one file for each unmuted track, bus, and output.

4. Exporting Mixer objects creates files that are named after the track, bus, or output that is exported. These exported files are the length of the track, bus, or output, from the beginning of the Timeline to the end of the last file within that track, bus or output.

5. You can reconnect a file to its media by clicking the Find File button in the Alert window when you are first notified that the project can't find some of the media files. This process is called reconnecting media to a project.

6. Creating a playback region in the Timeline before exporting will export looping files the same duration as the playback region.

7. You can tag files in the Apple Loops Utility to be used in the Soundtrack Pro Search database.

11

Lesson Files   Soundtrack Pro book files > 11_Projects&Media > 11-1 Scoring Marker, 11-3 Bloodlust Tempo, 11-5 PSA Transpose, 11-7 Files and Loops, 11-8 Timeslice, 11-10 WCS_Intro

Time   This lesson takes approximately 60 minutes to complete.

Goals   Automate a Project Key

Automate a Project tempo

Score a marker to the playhead

Work with timeslices

Change the Offset of an audio clip

Replace the Source Audio in a clip

Work with multiple outputs

Learn to set up Control Surfaces

Lesson **11**

Advanced Editing, Mixing, and Sound Design Techniques

At this point, if you've been following along with all of the lessons, you know how to work with the interface; arrange and edit multitrack projects; plan and build soundtracks; work in the Waveform Editor; repair, enhance, and modify dialog; add effects; mix tracks; and output the finished project as a mix, selected tracks, or with Compressor. So what's left? Now that you understand the basic Soundtrack Pro features and techniques, there are some advanced features that may be useful as you create more complex soundtracks.

The goal in this lesson is to cover a lot of different advanced Soundtrack Pro features, functions, tips, and techniques. Rather than start each project from scratch, you'll work on just the parts necessary to learn the new techniques. Along the way, you'll also be reminded of many of the shortcuts and features that you've already learned. So be prepared to proceed into uncharted territories. And by all means, do try these techniques at home.

Preparing the Project

You'll begin this lesson by opening the first project, **11-1 Scoring Marker**, located in the 11_Projects&Media folder.

1   Quit all open applications, except for Soundtrack Pro.

2   Close any open Soundtrack Pro projects.

3   Open the **11-1 Scoring Marker** multitrack project, if it's not already open.

   This project is a *temporary score* for *The Tangerine Dream* trailer.

4   Save the project uncollected to the My Soundtrack Pro projects folder on your desktop.

5   Press Cmd-1 to show the Video tab, if it's not already showing.

6   Play the project once to see the video with the music.

   NOTE ▶ The music in this project is a temporary score that was created in Soundtrack Pro, then exported as a mix to Final Cut Pro for the video edit. Once the video editing was finished, a QuickTime movie was exported with scoring markers from Final Cut Pro and imported into this project. This process is also referred to as a round trip.

7   Move the playhead to the spill over marker located at 39;27 in the Time ruler.

   Remember that you can use Shift-M to move forward to the next marker, or Option-M to move to the previous marker.

8   Press the up arrow key to zoom in to the playhead/marker until you can clearly see both the elk horns and spill over markers.

9 Create a playback region between the elk horns marker and about one gridline to the right of the spill over marker.

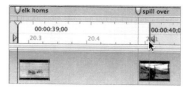

10 Press the spacebar to listen to the playback region and watch the video clip.

Toward the end of the playback region, there's a shot of a guy spilling over on his snowmobile (hence the spill over marker). A shot like that deserves a little acoustic attention. As luck would have it, there is a perfect drum hit right before he spills over that would work much better if it was synched to the actual event. But how do you do that without actually moving the drum loop in the Timeline? Remember, moving music loops to match video can throw them out of musical time. Is it possible to sync music that is beats-based to video that is timecode-based?

Scoring a Marker to the Playhead

You are about to try one of the coolest, most amazing features in the entire Soundtrack Pro program. As you know, scoring markers can be added to a project in Final Cut Pro, then exported with the video file and imported into Soundtrack Pro. In fact, if you look at the Timeline, you will see all of the orange scoring markers that you worked with in Lesson 5, "Designing Sound in the Waveform Editor."

So what's the big deal with scoring markers? They are useful for several things. First, they create a new thumbnail in the video track—all markers do that. Second, you can score the marker to the playhead!

In other words, you can click and drag the scoring marker to the playhead to sync the audio to the picture. This is the exact feature we need to pull off our snowmobile-spill-drum-hit-timing thing.

Let's take a closer look at the drum hit located in the Drummers of Motown 09 track (4th track from the top).

1   Press Cmd-9, or Ctrl–up arrow several times to change the track height.

   The track height is now the largest size, giving you a front-row seat—and a much better view—for this awesome Soundtrack Pro stunt.

2   Scroll downward in the Timeline until the Drummers of Motown 09 track is just below the playback region in the Time ruler.

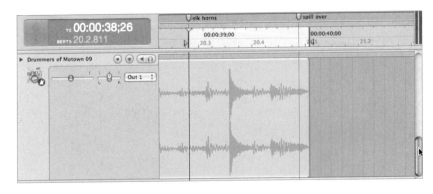

Now you need to identify the waveform of the drum hit. It's actually a large hit followed by several short hits. You'll focus on the large hit. It's easy to see, as it's the largest part of the waveform, near the middle of the playback region.

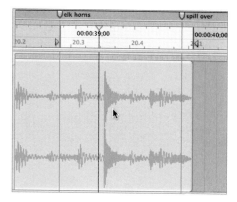

3 Turn off snapping, if it is on, then drag the playhead to the start of the large drum hit waveform (39;07).

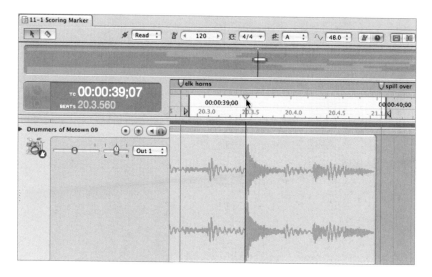

There is a gap between the playhead and the spill over marker.

When we sync the playhead to the marker, we will close that gap.

Before you make the move, take a look at the Project tempo in the Tempo Value slider above the Global Timeline view.

4   Press Cmd-S to save your project before proceeding.

5   Click the head of the spill over scoring marker to select the marker.

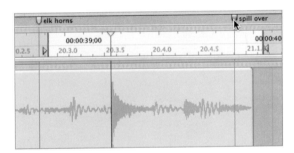

6   Choose Mark > Score Marker To Playhead.

That's it. Operation completed.

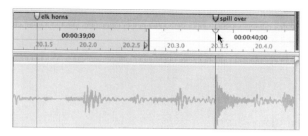

The gap is gone, and the snowmobile spill and large drum hit should now be in perfect sync.

NOTE ▸ You can also score a marker to the playhead by Option-dragging a scoring marker to the playhead.

7   Press Cmd-7 to change the track height back to small.

8   Clear the playback region, and play the project from the elk horns marker through the snowmobile spill and watch the action in the Video tab.

Amazing. So how did it work? Did the video track change speed? Did the audio track change speed? Did the laws of physics cease to exist on your Timeline? Listen to the playback region before continuing to see if you can figure it out.

9   Move the playhead to the elk horns marker, and look at the Project tempo.

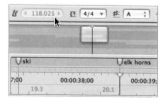

The Tempo Value slider is grayed out, and shows a value of approximately 118.025 BPM.

NOTE ▸ Your tempo (BPM) may be slightly different depending upon where your playhead was when you synced the marker to it.

10 Press Shift-M to move the playhead to the spill over marker, and look at the tempo.

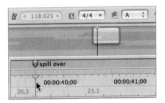

The tempo is 118.025 BPM here too.

11 Press Shift-M to move to the next marker (race car) and check the tempo.

The race car marker has a tempo of 120 BPM.

12 Press the Home key to move the playhead to the beginning of the Timeline. Look at the Project tempo.

The opening tempo has changed to 118.025 BPM.

13 Press the End key to move the playhead to the end of the Timeline. Look at the Project tempo (120 BPM).

You can sync a scoring marker to the playhead to change the Project tempo on all beats-based (musical) tracks. This allows you to sync music to a specific frame of timecode.

When you synced the scoring marker to the playhead, the tempo changed to accomplish your goal. In other words, you slowed down the tempo slightly so that it would to take longer to get to the large drum hit, allowing it to sync up with the spill in the video clip. The best part is that the tempo changes only between the beginning of the Timeline and the scoring marker—or between other tempo changes if you've already made changes within the Timeline.

14 Unsolo the Drummers of Motown 09 track and press Shift-Z to fit the project to the Timeline window.

15 Scroll to the bottom of the Timeline to see the Tempo envelope, located in the Master Envelopes.

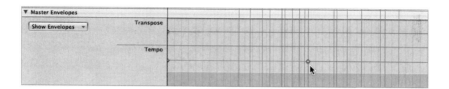

NOTE ▶ If the Master Envelopes aren't showing, click the Master Envelopes disclosure triangle to show the envelopes in the Timeline.

Notice the envelope point at the spill over marker on the Tempo envelope. The Project tempo to the left of the envelope point is around 118.025 BPM and the envelope line is red to show it has been changed. The tempo to the right of the envelope point is 120 BPM.

The tempo changes created by scoring a marker to the playhead are abrupt. You can also create more subtle tempo changes with envelope points. You'll try that in the next exercise. To prepare, let's listen to the project once more to hear it from start to finish with the newly synched drum hit spill effect in context.

16 Play the project once more, then save and close the project.

The project still looks great with the temporary score. The next step would be to add more music loops to complete the score.

NOTE ▶ You can score a marker to the playhead at any step along the way in building a soundtrack. It's important to make sure that you are working with the finished video edit before you try syncing beats-based tracks to the picture. You can also wait until the entire score is completed to tweak the tempo using this method.

Understanding the Round Trip Workflow

Music is a vital component in motion-picture editing. Whether you are creating a promo, a movie trailer, an action sequence, or a commercial, it's the music that drives the pacing and emotion of the piece. So, when do you create the music?

The previous project was an example of one of Soundtrack Pro's most valuable scoring techniques—creating a temporary score. An editor needs music as a foundation to edit the picture; meanwhile, the composer needs the edited project to create the right music. The solution to this age-old dilemma is a temporary score. Editors use temporary music to edit a scene, knowing that eventually the music will be replaced with a real score. Soundtrack Pro not only makes it easy to create a temp score before the picture edit, but also makes it possible to use that temp score as a foundation for the final score.

Once you've created a temp score, usually consisting of rhythm tracks, you can export it as a mix. Then the video editor can use the mix in Final Cut Pro to edit the picture and add scoring markers. Once the picture edit is finished, the video editor can export a QuickTime movie with scoring markers. You can then bring the finished QuickTime back into the Temp Score project in Soundtrack Pro and finish editing the music and sound. That workflow is also referred to as a "round trip" because the project starts in Soundtrack Pro, goes to Final Cut Pro, then comes back to Soundtrack Pro for finishing.

Feel free to work on the music after this lesson. For now, you should keep moving forward to learn more advanced tricks and techniques.

Automating the Master Envelopes

Automating a project's tempo and key can create either subtle or dramatic changes within the project's beats-based tracks. Scoring a marker to the playhead was one example of automating a project's tempo. In the next series of exercises, you will use the Master Envelopes to automate the tempo of one project to change the tempo over time, and then automate the key of another to transpose the entire song. Many self-taught Soundtrack Pro explorers never venture into the Master Envelopes, but you should appreciate their value as advanced scoring tools.

1   Open the **11-3 Bloodlust Tempo** project.

This is a slightly modified version of the project that you built from scratch in Lessons 3 and 4.

2   Press Shift-Cmd-S, and save the project uncollected to the My Soundtrack Pro projects folder.

3   Scroll to the bottom of the Timeline to see the Master Envelopes.

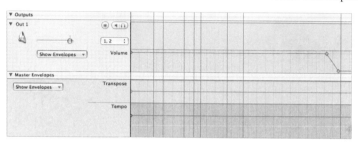

Notice that the Volume envelope on the Out 1 track has been automated to fade out the volume at the end of the project.

Automating Project Tempo

Automating tempo is a composer's trick to change the feel of a score gradually or suddenly to enhance the scene. To automate Project tempo, double-click the Tempo envelope line to create envelope points, then adjust them as needed. Remember that the Tempo envelope only changes the beats-based tracks, which include the Designer Synth music tracks in this project. Your goal is to gradually slow down the music, and the character's heartbeat, at the end of the project. The current Project tempo is 120 BPM. You'll slowly lower it starting when she is outside, so that by the time she turns around to face the vampire, the tempo and her heartbeat will be 72 BPM. The effect should be quite haunting and really work well with this scene.

1   Scroll up to the Exposition/Character track (which contains the Heartbeat clip).

2 Ctrl-click the drag handle (the line of vertical dots on the left edge of the Exposition/Character track header) and choose Make Beats-Based from the shortcut menu.

The metronome icon appears, showing that the track is now beats-based.

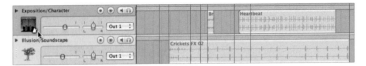

3 Scroll back down to the bottom of the Timeline to see the Master Envelopes.

4 Play the project once to hear the sound design and remember all of your hard work.

5 Turn off the Snap feature if it is turned on.

6 Move the playhead to 35;20 and double-click the Tempo envelope line to create an envelope point at that position with a value of 120 BPM.

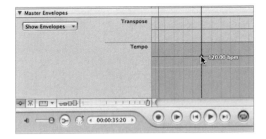

The entire project before this envelope point will remain at 120 BPM.

7 Move the playhead to 40;20 and set another envelope point on the Tempo envelope line.

To lower the tempo, you could drag the envelope point downward, you could press Option–down arrow, or you could Ctrl-click the envelope point and set the value. Since you've never tried the third option, let's try it now.

8   Ctrl-click the tempo envelope point at the playhead position and choose
Set Value from the shortcut menu.

A dialog opens.

9   Type *72* in the Enter the envelope point value field.

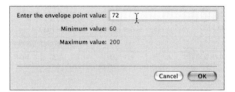

10   Click OK to close the dialog and set the envelope point's value.

11   Click the selected envelope point to see its new value.

12   Play the second half of the project and listen carefully for the change in
tempo.

> **NOTE** ▸ You may need to raise the volume level of the Exposition/
> Character track to hear the effect of the slowed heartbeat. Or you can
> solo the track to hear it by itself.

13   Save and close the project.

Nice work. Did you notice that the music slowed but the pitch never changed?
That's because Soundtrack Pro allows you to modify tempo without changing
pitch (key). In the next exercise you'll change a project's key in the middle of
a song.

Automating Project Key

In this exercise you'll work with the music project for the ADA Tour de Cure PSA and use the Transpose envelope to change the project's key in the middle of the song. Your goal is to change the second half of the song from the current Project key (A) to the native key of the Classic Rock Standup loops (C). First, you'll need to open and save the project.

1 Open the **11-5 PSA Transpose** project, and save it uncollected to the My Soundtrack Pro projects folder.

2 Play the project once to see and hear how the song was arranged in the Timeline.

> **NOTE ▶** You can build music, dialog, and sound effects tracks together in the same Timeline. However for larger projects, it works well to build the music in a separate project and simply export it as a mix to use in your main project. That way you won't tax your computer with excessive tracks.

3 Select one of the Classic Rock Standup Piano loops on the Digital Piano Loop 28 track (2nd track from the top).

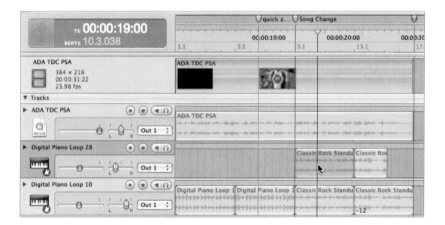

4 Press Cmd-I (for info) to see the selected clip's info in the Details tab.

5   Click the File button on the Details tab and locate the clip's Key in the lower-left corner of the window.

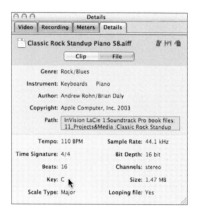

The Project key is A, and the clip's original key is C, which is three semi-tones higher. If you transpose the project three semitones, the Project key will become C. Let's try it. Of course, you don't have to transpose a project to match the native key of the music loops, but generally, music loops sound better when they are played within a few semitones of their native key.

6   Scroll down to the bottom of the Timeline to see the Master Envelopes. If they aren't showing, click the Master Envelopes automation disclosure triangle.

A purple Song Change beat marker has been added to indicate the position where the piano parts change, which is where you'll transpose the song.

7   Double-click the Transpose envelope line at the purple song change marker.

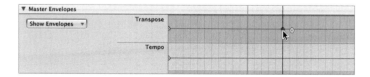

A Transpose envelope point appears with a value of 0 (zero change to the Project key).

You'll change the value of the envelope to 3 (3 semitones higher), but first listen to the incremental changes along the way.

8 Mute the ADA TDC PSA track so you can focus on the music tracks without hearing the dialog.

9 Select the Transpose envelope point, if it isn't already selected.

10 Press Option–up arrow key once to transpose the keyframe by one semitone higher and play tempo change to hear how it sounds.

11 Press Option–up arrow key again to transpose another semitone higher, then listen to the change in key.

You still need to raise the value to 3 full semitones higher. You can do this in four ways: Use the Value slider in the Details tab; Ctrl-click the envelope point, choose Set Value, then change the value in the dialog; drag the Transpose envelope point upward to a value of 3 semitones higher; or press Option–up arrow three times.

12 Drag the envelope point upward until you see the value of 3 next to the pointer to indicate a total change of 3 semitones higher.

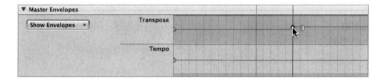

13 Press Cmd-1 to show the Video tab in the Utility window.

14 Press Shift-Return to start playback from the beginning of the Timeline, and listen to the key change in the middle of the song.

Sounds great. The music changes key just as the piano part changes.

NOTE ▶ If the envelope point isn't exactly on the purple song change marker, the song won't change key smoothly. The trick to making a quick key change is to do it on a beat between parts. You can always nudge the envelope point left or right by holding the Option key and pressing the left or right arrow keys.

Project Practice

Before you move on, try experimenting with the transpose envelope point. Try moving it a few measures earlier to hear the change within the earlier piano part. Try making it higher or lower to hear the changes to the song.

You can shift the selected envelope one gridline at a time left or right by pressing Shift-Option–left or right arrow key. To nudge it, simply press Option–left or right arrow key.

When you're finished, move it back to the purple song change marker, and feel free to transpose it as much or as little as you like. Then save and close the project.

Replacing Audio Files in the Timeline

Soundtrack Pro includes a handy replace feature that lets you replace any selected clip or clips in the Timeline with another file. This project is a simple example containing only four different loops, but you'll be able to apply what you learn to any of your own projects.

1   Open the **11-7 Files and Loops** project and save it to the My Soundtrack Pro projects folder.

2   Play the project once.

It's not much, but it will work for the next series of exercises. If you played the project, you may have noticed that the **Acoustic Drum Kit Groove 01** loop doesn't fit well with the **R&B Horn Section 58** loop or the **Basic High Hat Pattern.** There's nothing particularly wrong with the loop—it will be perfect for some project, just not this one. Luckily, if you come across a file in your project that you'd like to change, all you need to do is select it and find a replacement file in the Media and Effects Manager.

3   Select the **Acoustic Drum Kit Groove 01** clip in the top track of the Timeline.

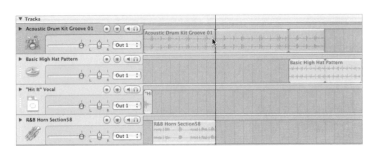

4   Click the Search tab in the Media and Effects manager, click Button view, and choose Best Mix from the category pulldown menu.

5   Click the Drums button on the Search tab.

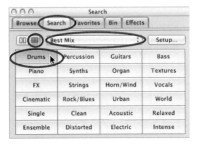

NOTE ▶ To select multiple buttons you can Cmd-click the additional Keyword buttons. To deselect all but one Keyword button, simply click a different unselected button.

6   Select the **Acoustic Drum Kit Groove 05.aiff** loop from the results list to preview the loop.

This drum loop is more upbeat and will work better with the other loops in the project.

7 Ctrl-click the **Acoustic Drum Kit Groove 05.aiff** file in the results list and choose Replace Selected Clips with Acoustic Drum Kit Groove 05 from the shortcut menu.

8 The selected loop in the Timeline is replaced with the loop from the Search tab.

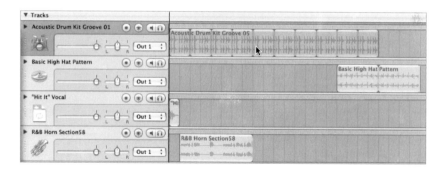

It really is that easy.

9 Play the project to hear it with the new drum loop.

NOTE ▶ You can use this technique to replace any selected audio file in the Timeline, including voiceover or sound effects files.

10 Press Cmd-S to save your progress.

Changing Clip Speed

You learned how to transpose a clip in Lesson 4, "Building Suspense with Editing Techniques." You can also change the speed of a clip to play it faster or slower. This feature works for looping files. In this exercise you'll duplicate the Basic High Hat Pattern clip to double it. Then you'll halve the clip speed of the duplicate to create an interesting drum pattern.

1 Turn on snapping, if it isn't already on.

2 Option-drag the Basic High Hat Pattern clip on the 2nd track to the 3rd track to create a duplicate on the 3rd track.

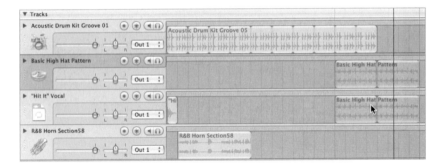

3 Ctrl-click the Basic High Hat Pattern loop on the 3rd track and choose Clip Speed > Half Speed from the shortcut menu.

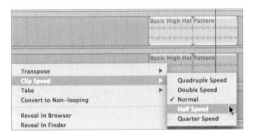

The speed of the Basic High Hat Pattern slows to half-speed and you can see that where there were two loops, there is now only one. Let's modify the drum arrangement so that you can hear the half-speed version, then bring in the full-speed version of the clip. You'll start by making the Acoustic Drum Kit Groove 05 clip half its current length.

4   Drag the right edge of the clip on the 1st track to the left until it is only 5 looped segments in length and ends at 10.00 in the Timeline.

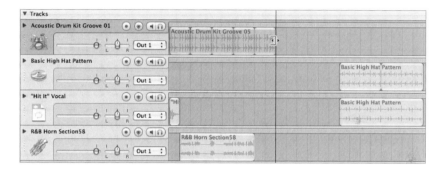

5   Drag the Basic High Hat Pattern clip on the 3rd track to the left so that it starts at 8.00 in the Timeline.

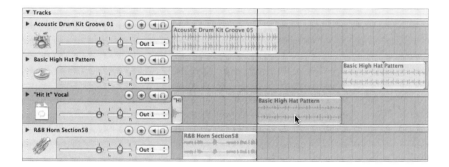

6   Drag the Basic High Hat Pattern clip on the 2nd track to the left so that the first loop segment overlaps the High hat clip on the 3rd track (12.00).

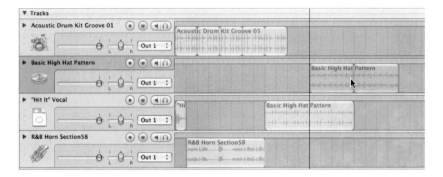

7   Play the project and listen to the combined High Hat parts.

8   Save the project.

As you've just demonstrated, changing a clip's speed can be an effective way of creating interesting drum patterns. Changing the speed of a musical part does not alter the pitch, only the speed at which the part plays. This technique is also handy with synth patterns and other musical parts that may be too fast or too slow and you'd like to change their speed to better fit your project.

Changing the Offset of an Audio Clip

Changing the offset of an audio clip allows you to change where a clip's wave-form begins or ends without changing its length. This feature is similar to the Slip feature in Final Cut Pro. In this exercise you'll change the offset of the R&B Horn Section58 loop to reveal a solo horn blare at the beginning of the clip. The solo horn blare is normally at the beginning of this loop, but was trimmed off. The media is still available; it just needs to be slipped to the right to reveal what is no longer showing in the Timeline.

To change the offset of an audio file, press and hold the Option and Cmd keys while dragging the waveform within the clip either left or right.

1   Locate the R&B Horn loop in the 4th track of the Timeline.

Notice that the right edge of the loop is curved to show the end of a full loop segment, but the left edge is straight to indicate that it has been trimmed.

2   Option-Cmd–drag the waveform in the horn clip on the 4th track to the right as far as you can until you see the curved edge at the front of the loop and the solo horn blare waveform at the beginning of the clip.

You successfully changed the clip's offset so that it now starts with the beginning of the loop.

3   Play the project to hear the change in the clip's offset.

4   Save, and then close the finished project.

Sure, this is a song in progress, but you've just learned three very powerful tools that you can use when building your projects to replace, change the speed, or change the offset of clips in the Timeline.

Project Practice

Take a moment to try all three of your new skills. First, replace one of the clips in the project with another loop in the Search tab. Then change the speed of one of the clips. Finally, trim one of the loops and change the offset. Feel free to add more than one new loop to flesh out the piece and make it your own. Although you may not use these tricks every day, knowing how to apply these techniques when you need them brings you closer to mastering Soundtrack Pro.

Working with Timeslices

In Lesson 4 you created a master timeslice to select all tracks at once and delete the excess media at the end of the project.

You can also select timeslices within a track or tracks for editing within the Timeline. You can cut, copy, paste, and delete timeslices the same as you would clips or envelope points. The difference is that timeslices let you select the contents of a track or multiple tracks, and the track's envelopes for a specific section of time. In this exercise you'll create timeslices for the guitar and percussion parts in the song "Something About You."

To create a timeslice, drag the selection bar at the top of the track in the Timeline. Let's start with the Guitar FX track.

1   Open the **11-8 Timeslice project** and save it uncollected to the My Soundtrack Pro projects folder.

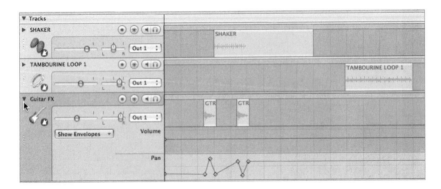

NOTE ▶ Click the Guitar FX automation disclosure triangle to show the track's envelopes if they are not already showing.

2   Select both of the GTR FX clips on the Guitar FX track and press Option-Z to zoom in and fit the selected clips in the Timeline window.

There should be gridlines at the beginning and end of the selected clips.

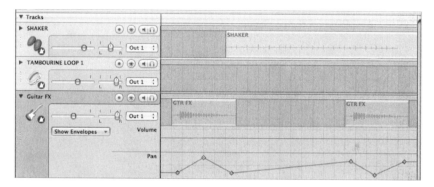

NOTE ▶ If you're making timeslices of beats-based tracks, it's a good idea to work with snapping turned on. Snapping will help you make selections that start and end on a beat.

3   Turn on snapping, if it is not already on.

4   Locate the selection bar directly above the track. It looks like a belt of thin vertical lines.

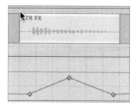

5   Click-drag the selection bar from the beginning of the first GTR FX clip to the end of the second GTR FX clip.

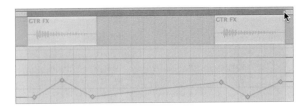

You have just created a timeslice. The timeslice selection area is highlighted in blue, including the envelopes and envelope points.

NOTE ▶ You can also extend a timeslice by dragging the Selection Length value slider at the lower-right corner of the Project window, located at the right of the transport controls.

6   Press Cmd-C to copy the timeslice.

7   Press Shift-Z to fit the clips in the Timeline window.

8   Select the Guitar FX track, if it is not already selected.

9   Move the playhead to 17.1.000 in the Timeline, and press Cmd-V to paste the timeslice at the playhead position on the selected track.

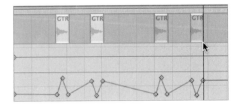

Both clips plus their envelope points are pasted into the track.

This technique can be very handy for copying and pasting timeslices of repeating parts within songs. The timeslice will include all envelopes, even those with automation.

Selecting Timeslices in Multiple Tracks

For this exercise you'll create a timeslice in the SHAKER track from the beginning of the SHAKER clip to the end of the TAMBOURINE LOOP 1 clip. Then you'll select the same timeslice on the TAMBOURINE LOOP 1 track. Once both tracks are highlighted, you can copy and paste the information from both tracks simultaneously.

1   Zoom in until there are gridlines at the beginning and end of the SHAKER and TAMBOURINE LOOP 1 clips.

2   Create a timeslice on the SHAKER track that is the length of the clips in both tracks.

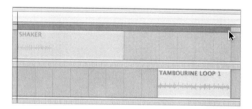

3   Cmd-click the selection bar on the TAMBOURINE LOOP 1 track to add the same timeslice selection to that track.

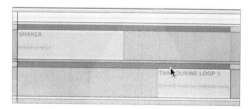

NOTE ▶ You can select contiguous tracks by creating a timeslice on one track, then Shift-clicking the selection bar of the last track that you'd like to include in the multiple track selection. Also, Cmd-clicking a track's selection bar will either include it in the selection, or deselect the track.

4   Press Cmd-C to copy the selections, or choose Edit > Copy.

5   Move the playhead to 33.1.000 in the Timeline.

6   Select the Shaker track, if it is not already selected, then press Cmd-V to paste the clips.

The Shaker and Tambourine timeslices are pasted into their respective tracks at the playhead position (33.1.000).

Pasted timeslices always start at the playhead position, on the selected track and paste downward. If you select a lower track in the Timeline and don't have enough tracks to paste the timeslice, more tracks will be created at the bottom of the Timeline.

7   Save and Close the project.

NOTE ▶ Timeslices can be inserted into tracks at the playhead position by choosing Edit > Paste Special > Insert. You can also ripple delete a timeslice, which removes that entire section of the track or tracks and moves the remainder of the track or tracks to the left to the position of the deleted timeslice.

The next time you need to cut, copy, paste, delete, or insert clips, tracks, or parts of the entire song, you can use timeslices to save time, maintain musical time, and make sure that the clips and the envelopes are included in the editing operations.

Project Practice

Your mission is twofold. First, you'll trim the silence off of the right edge of the Shaker clip (both instances) in the Timeline. Then you'll create a new timeslice that includes all of the clips in the Shaker track, with the newly trimmed shaker clips, and the same timeslice in the Tambourine track. Copy and paste the timeslice after the last clip in the Timeline. Make sure that you select the Shaker track before pasting, and move the playhead to the beginning of a measure. Viola! If you need your score to go on another measure or you need to add another verse or chorus, you can use timeslices to copy and paste as much as you need from any or all tracks!

Working with Multiple Outputs

All Soundtrack Pro multitrack projects include one output (Out 1). You can have up to a total of 128 tracks, busses, and outputs in a multitrack project. All of the projects you've worked with so far in this book have had only one output. In this exercise, you'll work with three outputs that are common in professional film and video projects. Your goal will be to record automation in the output envelopes for the Dialog, Effects, and Music outputs. Why separate the dialog from the music and effects? Because if you ever need to dub the project in a different language, it's important that the dialog is mixed separately from the music and effects so that it can be replaced without needing to rebuild and remix all of the other tracks. The combined Music and Effects outputs are often referred to as the M&E mix.

1   Open the **11-10 WCS_Intro** project and save it uncollected to the My Soundtrack Pro projects folder.

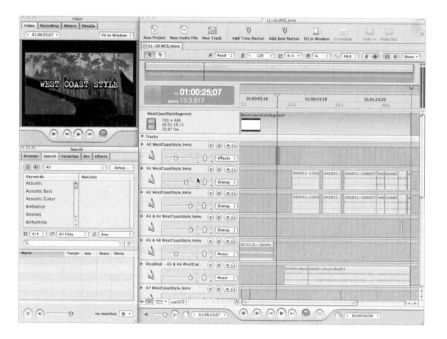

2 Play the project once to see and hear it for the first time.

This project is part of the intro for an instructional DVD that was edited in Final Cut Pro, and the DVD was then authored in DVD Studio Pro. The current project was exported from Final Cut Pro and includes a combination of Dialog, Music, and Sound Effects tracks. Each track has already been balanced for volume levels, and now it's time to create the overall mix.

3 Scroll down to the bottom of the Timeline to see the three different outputs.

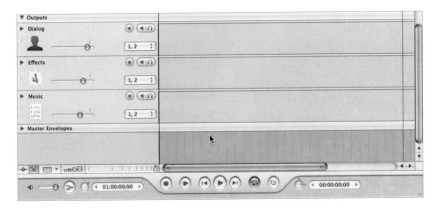

Each track has been assigned to one of the three outputs. For example, the various FX tracks are assigned to the Effects output.

NOTE ▶ By default you are capable of exporting two channels of audio (1, 2). If you have approved audio hardware, you may be able to export up to 24 channels of audio. You can choose which channel the output will be assigned to when you create the output. All of the outputs in this project are set to channels 1, 2 so they will work on every computer setup without additional hardware.

4   Click the Output pop-up menu on the FX Mix 2 track (lowest track in
Timeline) to see the three different outputs.

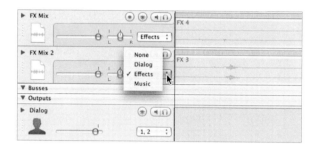

Make sure that you leave the menu selected to the Effects output.

Each output includes a Volume envelope that you can automate with envelope points, just as you would a track or bus envelope.

NOTE ▶ To add a new output, choose Multitrack > Add Output, or press
Option-Cmd-T.

5   Click the automation disclosure triangles for each of the outputs to see the
envelopes in the Timeline.

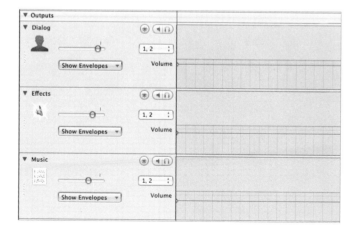

As you can see, the output envelopes have not been automated—yet. You'll record automation to them using the Mixer in the next section.

6   Press Cmd-2 to open the Mixer.

7   Scroll to the far right of the Mixer to see the three Output faders.

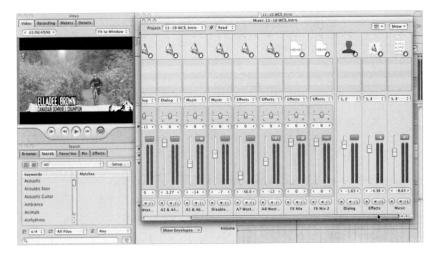

8   Press Shift-Return to start playback from the beginning of the Timeline.

9   Adjust the Dialog, Effects, and Music levels using the corresponding outputs in the Mixer.

You can solo or mute outputs as it plays. You'll notice that there is no dialog at the beginning of the project, and very few effects toward the end. The Music changes once the dialog starts. Your goal is to adjust the levels so that the dialog can always be at a clear level, and the music level doesn't compete with the dialog. At the beginning, where there is no dialog, you can keep the music levels louder. The effects can be mixed to taste. Also, you'll want to make sure that the output levels don't exceed 0 dB and cause clipping.

10 Practice adjusting the levels for one full pass of the project.

It's much easier to balance the levels of three outputs than to balance a lot of separate tracks in the Mixer. Another advantage of using multiple outputs is that you can create multiple mixes easily and save each with a different name. For example, you could create a mix that is heavier on the effects and another with no effects, or one mix with only music and effects and another with only dialog.

Recording Output Automation

Now that you've practiced mixing the different output levels, you'll record the automation for the final mix. First, you'll check the Automation Recording Sensitivity in the Soundtrack Pro General Preferences.

1 Press Cmd-, (comma) or choose Soundtrack Pro > Preferences to open the Preferences window.

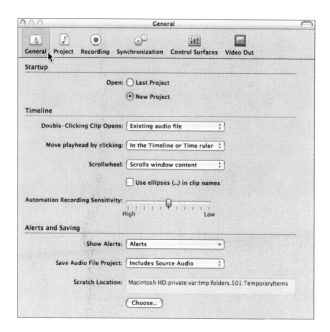

In the middle of the window you'll see the Automation Recording Sensitivity slider.

The default sensitivity level is in the middle. The lower the sensitivity, the fewer envelope points will be recorded; the higher the sensitivity, the more envelope points will be recorded. Leave the slider in the middle for now. If later you decide you'd like to record more or fewer envelope points, you know where to adjust the sensitivity.

2   Set the Automation Recording Sensitivity slider to the middle setting, if it is not already in that position.

3   Close the General Preferences window.

4   In the top-left region of the Mixer, change the automation pop-up menu to Latch mode.

5   Turn off the Cycle button in the transport controls so the project will automatically stop playing when you reach the end of the project.

TIP ▶ If you deselect the Cycle button in the transport controls, the project will automatically stop playing when you reach the end of the project. This is useful when mixing so that it doesn't start repeating the song and cause you to record over your previous automation.

6   Press Shift-Return to begin playback, and adjust the different output faders as needed until you reach the end of the project.

7   Mix the different output levels and pause playback when the project finishes.

8   Once you finish recording your mix, close the Mixer window and look at the automation that you recorded in the Timeline outputs.

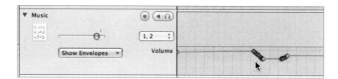

9   If you'd like to try again, you can undo the previous automation recording and record again, or you can just modify the envelope points by selecting them and moving them in the Timeline.

10   When you're finished mixing the tracks, set the automation mode pop-up menu back to the Read mode.

11   Save and close the project.

Once you've completed mixing and recording the output automation, you can select the outputs and export them as selected outputs for Final Cut Pro.

Setting Up Control Surfaces

You can use external mixing hardware (control surfaces) to automate recording, mixing, and other tasks in Soundtrack Pro.

Control surfaces provide a set of hardware controls that let you edit and mix your projects with greater flexibility and precision than using a mouse to move onscreen controls. You can also modify multiple parameters at once using a control surface.

Most control surfaces include faders, knobs, and buttons, including channel strip controls for volume, pan, mute, solo, and track selection. There are a variety of control surfaces available for use with video and audio production applications. When you use a control surface with Soundtrack Pro, some controls are premapped to common functions. You can also map other controls to Soundtrack Pro commands and functions in the Control Surfaces Preferences pane.

To use a control surface, you first need to connect it to your computer, then add it to Soundtrack Pro. Once the control surface has been added to Soundtrack Pro, you can record control surface automation data in your project.

Connecting Control Surfaces

Soundtrack Pro supports control surfaces that use the Mackie Control and Logic Control protocols to communicate with your computer. To use a control surface, you first need to connect the control surface to a MIDI interface, and connect the MIDI interface to your computer, unless the control surface allows direct connection to the computer.

> **NOTE** ▶ Make sure your computer supports the MIDI interface you plan to use before connecting the MIDI interface. Read the installation instructions included with the MIDI interface, and install the latest version of any appropriate firmware or driver software if needed.

Adding and Deleting Control Surfaces

Once the MIDI interface and control surface is connected to your computer, you can add the control surface in Soundtrack Pro Control Surface Preferences. If you don't have a control surface, you can follow along for future reference.

1   Choose Soundtrack Pro > Preferences, then click the Control Surfaces button.

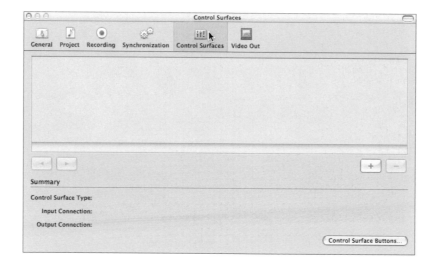

2   Click the Add (+) button to add the control surface.

3 Select the Control Surface Type, Input Connection, and Output Connection from the three pop-up menus.

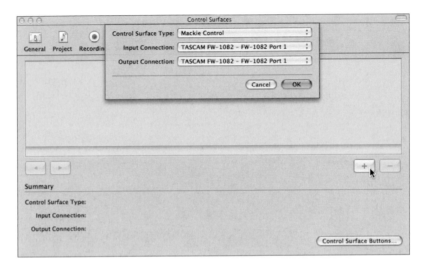

In this example I'm using the TASCAM FW-1082 Port 1, with the Mackie Control as the Control Surface Type.

4 Click OK.

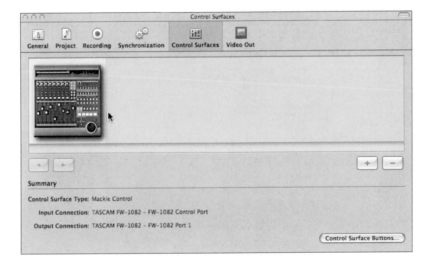

A visual representation of the control surface appears in the panel in the upper part of the window.

If you want to map controls to Soundtrack Pro commands and functions, click Control Surface Buttons.

5   Close the Preferences window.

Once you have connected the control surface, you can use it to adjust the faders in the Mixer and other track controls.

> **MORE INFO ▶** For more specific information on your mixing hardware, check the documentation that comes with your hardware. You can also find more information about working with control surfaces in the Soundtrack Pro Manual available through the Help menu.

Congratulations! You've finished the lesson and learned many new techniques and tricks that you can apply to your own projects.

Lesson Review

1. Which envelopes are included in the Master Envelopes?
2. Does automating the project's tempo automatically change the pitch (transpose) as well?
3. What feature allows you to sync beats-based tracks to the timecode of a scoring marker?
4. How do you create a timeslice selection within a track?
5. What modifier key allows you to extend a timeslice selection to an additional track?
6. How do you change the offset of a clip in the Timeline?
7. How do you replace the source audio in a clip?
8. What are the three common ouputs that may be used in mixing and exporting professional film and video projects?

Answers

1. The Master Envelopes include the Tempo and Transpose envelopes.

2. Automating the project's tempo only changes the tempo without changing the pitch.

3. Scoring the playhead to a marker allows you to sync beats-based tracks to the timecode of a scoring marker.

4. You can create a timeslice in a track by dragging the selection bar above the track.

5. Cmd-clicking a track's drag handle allows you to include it in the timeslice selection. Shift-clicking includes all contiguous tracks in the timeslice selection.

6. You can change the offset of a clip by Option-Cmd–dragging the waveform within the clip.

7. You can replace a clip's source audio by selecting the clip, Ctrl-clicking the file you'd like to replace it with in the Media and Effects Manager, and then choosing Replace Selected Clip(s) from the shortcut menu.

8. The three most common outputs in mixing and exporting professional film and video projects are Dialog, Music, and Effects.

Keyboard Shortcuts

Timeline

Option-Cmd–drag   changes a clip's offset

Option-drag   copies a clip

Option-Cmd-T   adds a new output

Option-Z   fits the selected clip(s) to the Timeline

Scoring Markers

Option-drag   scores the playhead to the marker

12

Lesson Files Soundtrack Pro book files > 12_Projects&Media > 12 FCP, 12 Motion, 12 DVD Studio Pro

Time This lesson takes approximately 45 minutes to complete.

Goals Open an Audio File Project in Final Cut Pro

Save Waveform Editor actions as an AppleScript

Send a Final Cut Pro sequence to a multitrack project

Work with an Audio File Project in Motion

Open DVD Studio Pro audio in the Editor

Using Soundtrack Pro with Other Apple Pro Applications

Soundtrack Pro is one application in Apple's Final Cut Studio. This is a brief lesson in integration that shows how easy it is to use exported Soundtrack Pro files with the rest of the Studio: Final Cut Pro, Motion, and DVD Studio Pro. You'll also explore how to send audio from all three applications to Soundtrack Pro so that you can edit them destructively as audio files, or non-destructively as Audio File Projects in the Waveform Editor. If you have all of these applications, there are projects that you can open as examples of each form of integration. If you don't have the other applications, you can still read along so you'll be ready when you do get your hands on the other Final Cut Studio Applications.

Using Soundtrack Pro with Final Cut Pro

There are three ways to move between Soundtrack Pro and Final Cut Pro (version 5 and higher). You can send an individual audio file from Final Cut Pro's browser or Timeline to Soundtrack Pro to edit in the Waveform Editor. In this case, you can edit the file either non-destructively as an Audio File Project (.stap) or destructively by editing and saving the actual audio file (.aif).

If you particularly like a combination of adjustments in an Audio File Project, you can save it in the Waveform Editor as a Soundtrack Pro Script and then apply that script to multiple audio files in Final Cut Pro. You can also send an entire Final Cut Pro sequence to Soundtrack Pro as an Audio File Project for mixing.

If you have Final Cut Pro (version 5 or higher) you can open the project and follow along. If you don't have the application, you can just follow the book.

1   Quit Soundtrack Pro and all other applications.

2   Go to the 12_Projects&Media folder in the Soundtrack Pro book files folder and double-click the **12 FCP** project to open it in Final Cut Pro.

3   Choose File > Save Project As and save it to the My Soundtrack Pro projects folder.

4 Press the Home key and then the spacebar to play the project in the Timeline from the beginning.

> **NOTE ▶** The Home key and spacebar work the same in Final Cut Pro as they do in Soundtrack Pro.

The project is part of a short film called *Same Conversation.* The dialog includes an excessive amount of ambient sound. I intentionally used sound that needed a lot of work for this exercise, rather than using the clean microphone sound that was recorded during the taping of the scene. Chances are you'll encounter noisy dialog sometime in your sound editing career, so now is a good time to learn a few tricks for dealing with it.

In this case, you'll send the first clip to the Soundtrack Pro Waveform Editor, then adjust the amplitude and reduce the noise. To send an audio clip to Soundtrack Pro, you simply Ctrl-click the file and choose Send To > Soundtrack Pro Audio File Project. Let's try it.

5   Ctrl-click the first clip in the Timeline and choose Send To > Soundtrack
Pro Audio File Project.

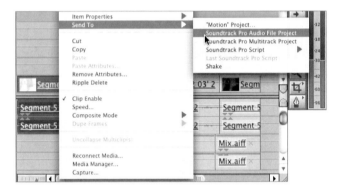

6   Save the Audio File Project to the My Soundtrack Pro Projects folder on
your computer.

The Audio File Project opens in the Soundtrack Pro Waveform Editor.

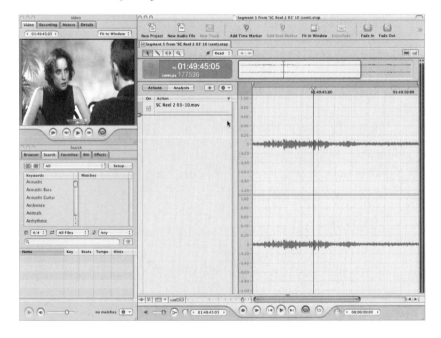

7   Choose Process > Adjust Amplitude and raise the volume level by 6 DB.

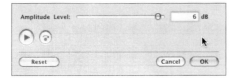

The overall waveform gets louder, including the noise and the dialog.

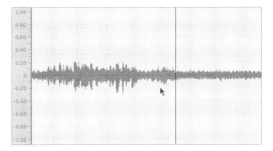

8   Select a section of the noise in the waveform that doesn't contain any dialog and choose Process > Set Noise Print.

9   Clear the selection and choose Process > Reduce Noise.

10   Make adjustments to the Reduce Noise dialog to clean up some of the noise.

> **NOTE ▶** This file is very noisy, so you won't be able to clear it all up without compromising the dialog. Clear it up the best you can.

If you're not sure which settings to use, try those in the following figure.

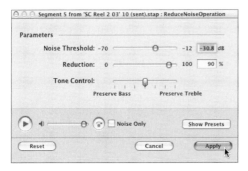

It still needs some audio tweaking, but let's assume it's good enough for now since this lesson is about integration and not tweaking.

Let's pretend you want to apply these actions to the other clips in the scene back in the Final Cut Pro project. Any changes you make and save to an Audio File Project will automatically be updated in the Final Cut Pro project.

11   Press Cmd-S to save the changes to the Audio File Project.

Any changes you make and save to an audio file project will automatically be updated in the Final Cut Pro project.

Project Practice

If you'd like to take a crack at cleaning up the audio further, feel free to modify, add to, or delete and start fresh with the actions already applied to the audio file project. You can also try adding some real time effects by choosing Processs > Effects and selecting an effect from the submenus. Once you're satisfied with the sound, move on to the next exercise to save it as an AppleScript. If you don't want to make changes to the current actions, move on to the next exercise. If you do modify the audio file project, be sure to save the changes before continuing with the next exercise.

Saving a File as AppleScript

Let's say you've found the magic combination of filters, processes, and effects to perfectly clean up or enhance an audio file. If other files in your Final Cut Pro project have the same issues, and were recorded at the same time, you could create an AppleScript that will automatically apply all of the same changes to any file that you send to the AppleScript. In this exercise you'll create an AppleScript, and then see how to apply it to files in FCP.

1   In Soundtrack Pro, choose File > Save As AppleScript, or press Option-Cmd-S.

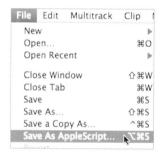

The Save As window opens with the Soundtrack Pro Scripts folder selected. It is very important that you do not change the location of the saved script. If you don't save it to the Soundtrack Pro Scripts folder, you won't be able to access the AppleScript in Final Cut Pro.

2 Type *Same Conversation* in the Save As field to name the script after the short file it will be applied to, then press Return.

That's all there is to it. You've saved an AppleScript. You can now access the AppleScript in Soundtrack Pro's AppleScript menu at the top of the interface between the Window and Help menus.

TIP ▶ This AppleScript is very specific for the short film *Same Conversation*. However, if you work with music and have favorite combinations of actions or effects that you like to apply to particular instrument tracks or vocals, you can save those as AppleScript and name them for the sound or instrument.

3 Click the AppleScript menu to see the two options, Open Scripts Folder and the saved Same Conversation AppleScript.

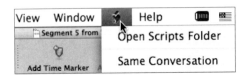

4 Choose Open Scripts Folder from the AppleScripts pop-up menu.

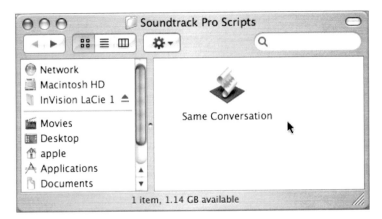

The Same Conversation AppleScript appears as a droplet in the folder. You can drag audio files to this droplet to automatically open them in the Waveform Editor and apply all of the actions to them.

NOTE ▶ Applying AppleScripts to audio files in Final Cut Pro is destructive editing because the actions are applied and saved to the actual audio file. Destructive editing isn't a bad thing. If the files need work, and you're confident that the AppleScript will help, go for it. If you don't like the idea of permanently changing the audio files, make a copy of them before applying the AppleScript.

5   Close the Soundtrack Pro Scripts folder,

6   Press Cmd-S to save the Audio File Project, then Press Cmd-Tab to switch from Soundtrack Pro to Final Cut Pro.

Cmd-Tab allows you to toggle between open applications on your computer. You can apply the AppleScript to a clip in Final Cut Pro's Timeline or Browser by Ctrl-clicking the clip and choosing Send To > Soundtrack Pro Script > Same Conversation from the shortcut menu.

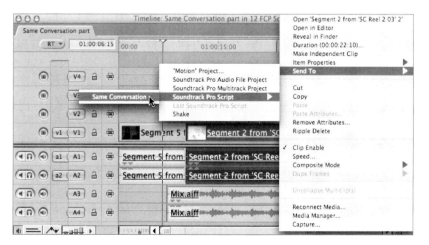

You don't need to apply the AppleScript at this time. I just wanted to make sure you know how to create and apply AppleScripts in the future.

Sending a Sequence to Soundtrack Pro

You've already seen that you can send an audio file to the Waveform Editor. You can also send an entire sequence to Soundtrack Pro as a multitrack project. This is often the last step in finishing a project, and is a one-way trip. Once you send a sequence to Soundtrack Pro, it won't automatically update in Final Cut Pro. Instead, you can export the finished mix, or selected tracks or outputs, from Soundtrack Pro and import them into Final Cut Pro once they are finished. Of course, you don't *have* to go back to Final Cut Pro when you finish the audio mixing in Soundtrack Pro. Instead, you can just export from Soundtrack Pro with Compressor, which will include the video and audio files together.

Let's take a quick look at how easy it is to send a Final Cut Pro sequence to Soundtrack Pro.

1   Select the Same Conversation part sequence in the Browser and Choose File > Send To > Soundtrack Pro Multitrack Project. These options are also available from the shortcut menu if you Ctrl-click the sequence.

A Save As window opens.

2   Save the project to the My Soundtrack Pro projects folder. Make sure the Open in Soundtrack Pro Multitrack Editor and Include Background Video checkboxes are selected.

Those checkboxes ensure that the project opens as a Soundtrack Pro Multitrack Project, and that the video is included with the project.

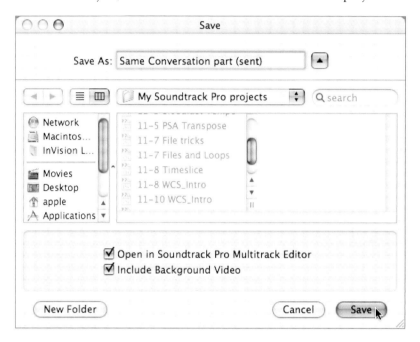

A multitrack project opens with two audio tracks that include the audio clips from the project saved as stereo files, and one video clip.

NOTE ▶ When sending a Final Cut Pro sequence to a Soundtrack Pro Multitrack project, it may take a few minutes to create a single QuickTime video file to use as a reference. Remember, Soundtrack Pro can only include one video clip. If the sequence consists of multiple clips, then they will be exported automatically as one clip for Soundtrack Pro. Also take into account if the project is unrendered, it will take time for the Final Cut Pro project to render before it can open in Soundtrack Pro.

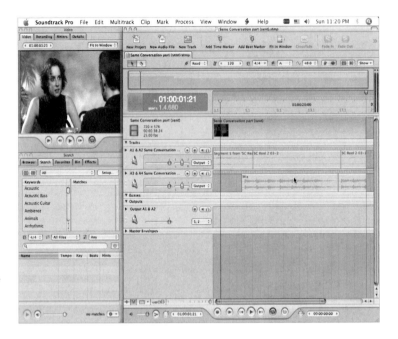

3   Click the automation disclosure triangle on the A1 & A2 Same Conversation track to see the track's envelopes.

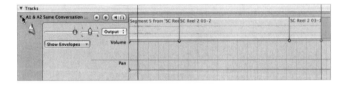

Soundtrack Pro includes an envelope point at the beginning and end of each audio clip sent from Final Cut Pro to make it easier to adjust the levels on the envelope.

If the Final Cut Pro tracks included *keyframes* (FCP term for envelope points) for audio volume level or panning, they would be included automatically in the multitrack project.

TIP ▶ If you wish to clear all of the envelope points that were automatically added from Final Cut Pro, select one envelope point, press Cmd-A (select all) to select all of them, and then press Delete.

Once you've sent a Final Cut Pro sequence to a Soundtrack Pro multitrack project, you can apply all of your new Soundtrack Pro skills to add and arrange additional audio files and effects, edit, mix, and output the final project.

4   Press Cmd-Q to quit Soundtrack Pro.

5   Press Cmd-Q to quit Final Cut Pro.

Now that you know how to integrate Final Cut Pro with Soundtrack Pro, let's take a look at integration with Motion.

Using Soundtrack Pro with Motion

If you export a Motion project as a QuickTime file, you can import it into a Soundtrack Pro multitrack project. The animated clapboard that you worked with in Lessons 1, 2, and 10 was exported from Motion.

If a Motion project includes audio files, you can send them from Motion to the Soundtrack Pro Waveform Editor to edit either destructively or non-destructively. Once you save the modified file in Soundtrack Pro, it will automatically update in the Motion project.

If you have Motion (version 2 or higher), you can open the project and follow along. If you don't have the application, you can just follow the book.

1   Quit all open applications.

2 Go to the 12_Projects&Media folder in the Soundtrack Pro book files folder, and double-click the **12 Motion** project to open it in Motion.

3 Choose File > Save Project As and save it to the My Soundtrack Pro projects folder.

4 Press the spacebar to play the project.

The audio should sound familiar; you created it in Lesson 1, "Working with the Interface." The video was just modified in Motion using the Replicator feature.

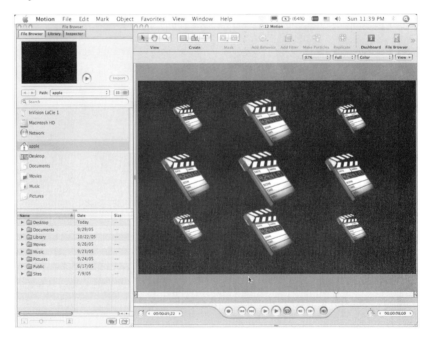

5   Press Cmd-6 to open the Audio tab in the Project pane.

6   Select the Clapboard Music audio file on the Audio tab.

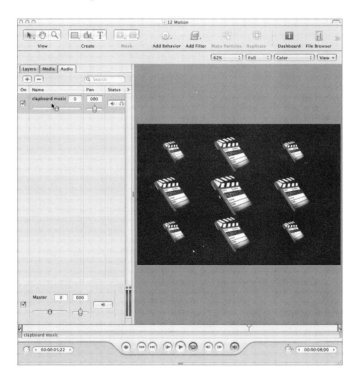

7   Choose Edit > Send Audio to Soundtrack Pro.

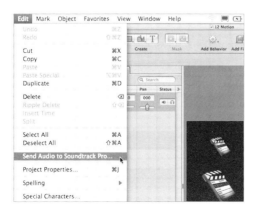

8 The Save As window opens. Save the file to the My Soundtrack Pro projects folder.

9 Click the Save as Soundtrack Pro Audio button.

Soundtrack Pro launches, and the **clapboard music.aif** (audio file) opens in the Waveform Editor as an Audio File Project (.stap).

Any changes that you make and save to the Audio File Project will automatically update in the Motion project without reimporting the audio clip. The key to this integration is saving. If you don't save the changes in the Audio File Project, it won't update in Motion.

10 Quit Soundtrack Pro and Motion without saving the changes to the projects.

Using Soundtrack Pro with DVD Studio Pro

DVD Studio Pro is integrated with Soundtrack Pro in a way very similar to the integration with Motion. From DVD Studio Pro (version 4 or higher), you can open an audio file in Editor, which will automatically open it in the Waveform Editor. Let's try it.

If you have DVD Studio Pro (version 4 or higher) with all of the templates installed to the default location, you can open the project and follow along. If you don't have the application, you can just follow the book.

1 Quit all open applications.

2 Go to the 12_Projects&Media folder in the Soundtrack Pro book files folder, and double-click the **12 DVD Studio Pro** project to open it in DVD Studio Pro.

3 Choose File > Save Project As and save it to the My Soundtrack Pro projects folder.

4   Press F2 to change the layout to the Extended configuration.

5   Click the Simulate button in the upper-right corner of the toolbar to simulate (preview) the DVD project.

Once again you'll see the animated clapboard in action, and hear the familiar tune that you arranged in Lesson 1.

6   Press Cmd-W to close the Simulator.

7 Locate the **clapboard music.aif** file in the Assets tab in the upper-left corner of the interface.

8 Ctrl-click the **clapboard music.aif** file and choose Open In Editor from the shortcut menu.

Either the file opens in Soundtrack Pro or you may see a dialog box with two options for opening the file: you can choose Open Audio File, which allows you to open the audio file in the Waveform Editor and edit destructively, or you can choose Open Project to open the actual multi-track project that created the file.

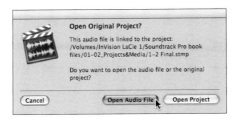

9   If you see the dialog, click the Open Audio File button to open the audio file in the Waveform Editor.

Once again, you can make changes to the file—just remember that these are destructive changes to the actual audio file. Once you save the changes, they will automatically update in DVD Studio Pro.

10   Press Cmd-Q to quit Soundtrack Pro.

Seeing is believing! You've now witnessed the integration between Soundtrack Pro and all of the Final Cut Studio Applications. Not only that, you've completed the last lesson in this book. Now it's your turn to apply your new skills to your own projects to make them sound professional and acoustically interesting. You should also have all the tools to exercise your creativity in sound design, music arrangement, audio editing, and mixing. Just remember, if it sounds good, you know it. If you're not sure, keep working on it. Also, save often (uncollected), and save collected when you're finished with a project if you want to move it. And most important of all—have fun!

Lesson Review

1.   Can you send an audio file in Final Cut Pro to the Soundtrack Pro Waveform Editor or a multitrack project?

2.   How do you send an audio file in Final Cut Pro to the Soundtrack Pro Waveform Editor?

3.   How can you save all of the actions in the Waveform Editor so that you can easily apply them to other audio files on the computer, or in Final Cut Pro?

4.   How do you send an audio file from Motion to the Soundtrack Pro Waveform Editor?

5.   What step is essential when you modify an Audio File Project in the Waveform Editor that is integrated with one of the Final Cut Studio applications?

Answers

1. You can send an audio file from Final Cut Pro to the Soundtrack Pro Waveform Editor. You can also send an audio file or a sequence from Final Cut Pro to a multitrack project.

2. You can send an audio file in Final Cut Pro to the Soundtrack Pro Waveform Editor by selecting the file and choosing File > Send To > Soundtrack Pro Audio File Project, or you can Ctrl-click the file and choose Send To > Soundtrack Pro Waveform Editor, or Soundtrack Pro Audio File Project.

3. You can save all of the actions in the Waveform Editor as an AppleScript so that you can easily apply the AppleScript to other audio files on the computer or in Final Cut Pro.

4. You can send an audio file from Motion to the Soundtrack Pro Waveform Editor by selecting the audio file and choosing Edit > Send Audio to Soundtrack Pro.

5. It is essential to always save an integrated Audio File Project once you've modified it so that the project will automatically update in the Final Cut Studio applications that references it. If you need to modify an integrated audio file project, be sure to open it from from the application with which it is integated and resave the changes to the Audio File Project.

Final Cut Studio Workflows

Apple's professional audio and video applications are designed to work together seamlessly, even in the most demanding postproduction workflows. The Final Cut Studio product line—a comprehensive and integrated postproduction package—comprises Final Cut Pro 5, Soundtrack Pro, Motion 2, DVD Studio Pro 4, Compressor 2, LiveType 2, Cinema Tools 3, Shake 4, and Logic Pro.

The appendix on the DVD accompanying this book details the roles of each application in the Final Cut Pro movie production process. You will also find a sample Final Cut Studio workflow and information on "roundtripping," the ability to embed and open project files while working in another application. See Soundtrack Pro book files > **Appendix-Final Cut Studio Workflows.pdf.**

Index

M

M key, setting time marker with, 116, 133

Mackie Control surface type, using, 464

Mark menu, using, 102

markers
    adding to Timeline, 102–104
    including with snapping, 108
    keyboard shortcuts for, 116
    moving between, 106
    moving to, 166
    moving to beginning of projects, 107
    naming, 104–105
    navigating, 428
    navigating with, 171–174
    scoring playheads to, 467
    scoring to playhead, 430–435
    setting in Waveform Editor, 211

Master Envelopes
    automating, 436–442
    displaying, 435
    hiding, 372

master timeslices, creating, 155–158

Master Volume slider, impact of, 383

MatrixReverb effect
    turning off, 350
    viewing parameters of, 351

Mech/Tech category, using with multitrack projects, 62–63

Media and Effects Manager
    adding files to Favorites tab in, 18–19
    Browser tab in, 13–15
    displaying Directories list in, 421
    features of, 12
    indexing files in, 422
    keyboard shortcuts for, 79
    location of, 4
    Search tab in, 21–25
    using files in Bin tab of, 19–21

media files, distributing with projects, 401–405

melody, listening to, 308–309

meters
    displaying, 380
    observing, 381

Meters tab in Utility window
    options on, 304
    reviewing output levels in, 315

microphones
    selecting preferences for, 280
    tips for use of, 291

MIDI interfaces, using with control surfaces, 462–463

mistakes, fixing with undo and redo, 127

Mix fader, manipulating, 362

Mix levels, raising, 369

Mixer
    features of, 318
    keyboard shortcuts for, 344
    modifying volume levels in, 316–319
    opening, 35–36, 317, 325, 338, 359, 365, 379, 458
    recording envelope points in, 337–343
    using effects with, 359–366

Mixer layout, displaying, 117

mixes
    adding tracks to, 313–314
    exporting, 388–391, 391–393
    listening to with headphones, 314
    pasting in Waveform Editor, 219–221

mixing
    overview of, 310
    with volume levels, 320

Monitor pop-up menu, options on, 281

mono files, recording, 283

mono mixes, listening to, 383

mono to stereo, converting waveforms from, 237–240

moods, setting for scenes, 101

Motion, using Soundtrack Pro with, 481–485

mouse pointer, modifying crossfades in Timeline with, 152

moving
    files, 29
    tabs, 86–88

multiple outputs, working with, 455–461

multiple takes. See also single takes; takes
    extending, 297
    recording, 285–290, 294–295

selecting timeslices in, 453–454

tips for recording of, 292

Multitake VO script, reviewing, 290

multitrack projects. See also projects
    adding tracks in Timeline for, 58–59
    versus audio file projects, 167
    changing playback mode of clips in, 65–69
    changing time base of tracks in, 57
    choosing sound effects for, 61–63
    counting empty tracks in, 44
    creating, 76
    keyboard shortcuts for, 385
    maintaining musical time in, 69–71
    moving clips in manually, 63–64
    moving tabs in Project window of, 54
    moving tracks in Timeline for, 59–60
    opening, 42, 53
    opening from Soundtrack Pro, 45–46
    Project controls for, 43
    properties of, 42
    removing tracks from, 65
    resizing tracks in, 63–64
    saving, 58, 65, 69
    saving to folders, 402
    setting preferences for, 75–77
    setting track formats in, 56–58
    using Key control with, 52–53
    using project format controls with, 53–54
    using Tempo control with, 49–52
    using Time Signature control with, 47–49

music
    crafting suspense with, 139–148
    recording versus arranging, 69

music loops
    auditioning, 140–141
    beat-based aspect of, 69–70
    tips for recording of, 291, 292
    trimming, 71–74

The Apple Pro Training Series

The best way to learn Apple's professional digital video and audio software!

The Apple Pro Training Series is the official training curriculum for Apple Pro applications. Upon completing the course material in these books you can become a certified Apple Pro by taking the certification exam at an Apple Authorized Training Center.

To find an Authorized Training Center near you, visit:

www.apple.com/software/pro/training

Final Cut Pro 5
0-321-33481-7 • $49.99

Advanced Editing Techniques in Final Cut Pro 5
0-321-33549-X • $49.99

Getting Started with Motion
0-321-30533-7 • $34.99

Final Cut Express 2
0-321-25615-8 • $44.99

Optimizing Your Final Cut Pro System
0-321-26871-7 • $44.99

Logic Pro 7 and Logic Express 7
0-321-25614-X • $44.99

Shake 4
0-321-25609-3 • $44.99

DVD Studio Pro 4
0-321-33482-5 • $49.99

Advanced Logic Pro 7
0-321-25607-7 • $49.99

Motion
0-321-27826-7 • $49.99

Xsan Quick-Reference Guide
0-321-36900-9 • $19.99

The Apple Training Series

The best way to learn Apple's hardware, Mac OS X, and iLife applications.

iLife '05
0-321-33020-X • $29.99

GarageBand 2
0-321-33019-6 • $34.99

Mac OS X Support Essentials
0-321-33547-3 • $49.99

Desktop and Portable Systems, Second Edition
0-321-33546-5 • $54.99

Mac OS X Server Essentials
0-321-35758-2

Security Best Practice for Mac OS X v 10.4
0-321-36988-2

Mac OS X System Administration Reference
0-321-36984-X

To order books or find out about the Apple Pro Training Series, visit: **www.peachpit.com/appleprotraining**